GREAT ITALIAN FILMS

GREAT
ITALIAN FILMS

Jerry Vermilye

A CITADEL PRESS BOOK

Published by Carol Publishing Group

For my Italian-American friends—Paul Caputo, Tony Carobine, Patty Cucco, Tomie de Paola, Roch-Josef di Lisio, Angela Fabbri, Joe Fallacaro, Aida Langella Gorman, Mary and Angelo Marcotrigiano, Judy Mastroianni, Vicky Parente, Jeannie Piro, Joe Pirolli, Amelia Romano, Thomas Luce Summa, Thom Toney, Romano Tozzi, Lou Valentino, and the late Mark Ricci and his well-remembered Memory Shop.

ACKNOWLEDGMENTS

The author wishes to express his gratitude to the following individuals and organizations for helping locate rare stills and videocassettes and/or for giving so generously of their time in offering editorial assistance and advice: Laurie Britton, Judith Crist, Bob Finn, Harry Forbes, Global Imports, Bill Grayson of Stone/Hallinan Associates, Don Hauptman, Alvin H. Marill, the late Mark Ricci and The Memory Shop, Jerry Ohlinger's Movie Material Store, Michael Scheinfeld, Thom Toney, Romano Tozzi, Allan Turner, George Zeno, and Citadel Press editor Allan Wilson for his continued interest, support, and patience.

And a salute to all of the anonymous still and portrait photographers whose aristry illustrates these pages as well as to the companies—many long defunct—that distributed these films: Allied Artists; American International; Analysis Film Releasing; Angelika Films; Astor Pictures; Audio-Brandon Films; Brandon Films, Inc.; The Cannon Group, Inc.; Castle Hill Productions; Cinema V/Cinema 5; Columbia Pictures; Continental Distributing; Distinguished Films, Inc.; Distributors Corp. of America; Edward Harrison; Ellis Films; Embassy Pictures; Esperia Film Distributing Corp.; Euro International; Films Around the World, Inc.; Films International of America; Fleetwood Films of Mount Vernon; Italian Films Export; Janus Films; Joseph Burstyn; Lionex Films; Lopert Films; Lux Films; Mayer-Burstyn, Inc.; Metro-Goldwyn-Mayer; Miramax Films; New World Pictures; New Yorker Films; Paramount Pictures; Pathe-Contemporary; Premiere Films; Quartet Films; Rizzoli Films; Superfilm Distributing Corp.; Times Film Corp.; Trans-Lux Films; 20th Century-Fox; United Artists; United Artists Classics; United Motion Picture Organization; Warner Bros.; and World-Northal Corp.

A Citadel Press Book
Published by Carol Publishing Group
Citadel Press is a registered trademark of Carol Communications, Inc.
Editorial Offices: 600 Madison Avenue, New York, N.Y. 10022
Sales and Distribution Offices: 120 Enterprise Avenue, Secaucus, N.J. 07094
In Canada: Canadian Manda Group, P.O. Box 920, Station U, Toronto, Ontario M8Z 5P9
Queries regarding rights and permissions should be addressed to Carol Publishing Group, 600 Madison Avenue, New York, N.Y. 10022

Carol Publishing Group books are available at special discounts for bulk purchases, sales promotions, fund-raising, or educational purposes. Special editions can be created to specifications. For details, contact Special Sales Department, Carol Publishing Group, 120 Enterprise Avenue, Secaucus, N.J. 07094

Designed by A. Christopher Simon

Manufactured in the United States of America
10 9 8 7 6 5 4 3 2 1

LIBRARY OF CONGRESS CATALOGING-IN-PUBLICATION DATA

Vermilye, Jerry.
    Great Italian films / by Jerry Vermilye.
        p.   cm.
    "A Citadel Press book."
    ISBN 0-8065-1480-9 (pbk.) :
    1. Motion pictures—Italy—History.
    2. Motion pictures—Italy—Catalogs. I. Title.
PN1993.5.I88V47   1994
791.43′75′0945—dc20   93-45771
                                                       CIP

Contents

Vittorio De Sica directing Sophia Loren and Marcello Mastroianni in *MARRIAGE ITALIAN STYLE* (1964).

Sophia Loren on Director Vittorio De Sica

"It was a wonderful marriage, if I can say that, for twenty or more years. I couldn't have found a better man for me, to be beside me, in the beginning of my career.

"The thing that I always remember now, when I go to the movies and see what the other actors do, is De Sica saying: 'When the camera comes close up, *do* something so you won't be frightened by the camera.'

So many actors I see *are* frightened by the camera.

"Acting is so personal—to be able to portray what's inside—and nobody can give you the treasure that's inside. But with De Sica I learned how to bring out what's inside.

"He was my school, my teacher, my mentor, my everything. I really owe it all to him."

Anita Ekberg dances in Fellini's *La Dolce Vita*.

The Italian Film Abroad

Bartolomeo Pagano as Maciste in *Cabiria*.

From the inception of its feature-film industry in 1905 with, prophetically, the historical spectacle *La Presa di Roma/The Sack of Rome*, directed by Filoteo Alberini, Italy established her place among the more important moviemaking countries of Europe. In those early silent years of the Italian screen, there followed such eye-filling epics as *The Last Days of Pompeii* (1908), *Quo Vadis?* (1912), and—the granddaddy of all spectacles—*Cabiria*, directed in 1914 by Giovanni Pastrone under the curious pseudonym of Piero Fosco. Shot in Turin (then the center of Italian movie production), *Cabiria* cost over a record-setting million dollars and was in production for almost two years, with exteriors filmed on location in Sicily, Tunisia, and the Italian Alps. Pastrone's advanced camera techniques put this production on a higher artistic plane than its ambitious predecessors, and when successfully shown in the United States, *Cabiria* proved highly influential in the future works of D. W. Griffith and Cecil B. DeMille.

The international success of Italian films in that first decade of the cinema also brought with it the beginnings of the star system, including among the men *Cabiria*'s Bartolomeo Pagano (better known as "Maciste," the muscular role he played in that classic) and Emilio Ghione. Their distaff counterparts were the dramatic and glamorous Francesca Bertini, Lyda Borelli, Lina Cavalieri, Maria Jacobini, the single-named Hesperia, and the compensating Italia Almirante Manzini. In 1916, Eleanora Duse, Italy's fabled fifty-seven-year-old stage diva, made a rare film appearance in Febo Mari's *Cenere/Ashes*.

The Italian film industry's prosperity continued on through the years of World War I but suffered a decline in the early twenties due to increasing competition from the wave of imports coming from Germany and North America. There followed a virtual exodus of Italian actors, directors, and technicians to France, Germany, and the United States and then a temporary surge of industry when American companies sought out Italian locations to authenticate such productions as *The White Sister* (1923), *Romola* (1924), and, in 1925, *Ben-Hur* (before a succession of misfortunes sent that company back to Hollywood and the controlled advantages of Metro's soundstages).

However, just before the advent of talking pictures, Italy enjoyed a mild cinematic resurgence with Mario Camerini's *Kiffi Tebbi* (1927) and *Rotaie/Rails* (1929) and Alessandro Blasetti's *Sole/Sun* (1929), a realistic provincial drama that was embraced by the Fascists as exemplifying the Italian nationalist spirit.

Sound didn't make its mark on Italy's screens until 1930, when Gennaro Righelli's *La Canzone* dell'Amore/Love Song, starring Dria Paola, Elio Steiner, Camillo Pilotto, and Isa Pola, made its inexpert bow. The only directors to master the early Italian sound screen were, not surprisingly, silent masters Camerini and Blasetti. Early successes of the era included the former's *Gli Uomini che Mascalzoni/What Rascals Men Are!* (1932), with Vittorio De Sica and Lia Franca, and *1860*, with Otello Toso and Maria Denis, directed by Blasetti in 1933. But the decade was best characterized by that notorious brand of glossy, glamorous comedies and dramas that imitated Hollywood and were referred to by the disparaging term "white telephone" films, produced to satisfy the public's need for escape in a time of encroaching fascism. In 1933, as *their* home film industry became ever more problematic, German directors made a fleeting mark on Italian filmmaking: Walter Ruttmann with the working-class drama *Acciaio/Steel* (1933) and Max Ophüls with *La Signora di Tutti/Everybody's Woman* (1934), the picture that made a star of strikingly beautiful Isa Miranda. Vittorio De Sica established himself as a popular star of light comedy in such Mario Camerini comedies as *Daro un Milione/I'd Give a Million* (1935) and *Il Signor Max/Mr. Max* (1937). Along with Isa Miranda, Assia Noris and Maria Denis were among the most popular of distaff glamour stars. The talented but not attractive Anna Magnani, who had appeared since 1934 in supporting movie roles, was then considered, even by her director-husband Goffredo Alessandrini, especially "unsuited to the cinema."

In the mid-thirties, Mussolini's dictatorship fostered an expansion of the Italian film industry to better serve the state. And in 1935 the renowned motion-picture school Centro Sperimentale di Cinematografica was established, followed two years later, in 1937, by the opening of Cinecittà studios near Rome. That facility boasted sixteen soundstages with state-of-the-art production facilities, arguably Il Duce's greatest achievement. Propaganda films of the period were topped by Carmine Gallone's grandiose Roman spectacle *Scipione L'Africano* (1937), after which he returned to directing such opera-oriented dramas as *Giuseppe Verdi* (1938) and *Il Sogno di Butterfly/The Dream of Butterfly* (1939) with the beloved soprano Maria Cebotari. Augusto Genina followed his popular colonialist desert epic *Lo Squadrone Bianco/White Squadron* (1936) with *L'Assedio dell'Alcazar/The Siege of the Alcazar* (1940), a Fascist propaganda piece, coproduced with the Spanish government.

The advent of World War II found the Italian screen awash with mediocrity. And yet new talent began to emerge among the filmmakers, with Mario Soldati's much-praised *Piccolo Mondo Antico/Old-Fashioned World* (1941) and *Malombra* (1942) adding to the wealth of costume pictures from his well-established colleagues, among them Blasetti's *La Corona di Ferro/The Iron Crown* and *La Cena della Beffe/The Jester's Supper* (both 1941) as well as Castellani's *Un Colpo di Pistola/A Pistol Shot* (1942). But more realistic matters began to color the wartime Italian screen with the branching out of Vittorio De Sica from actor to director with *Rose Scarlatte* (1940), in which he also appeared, and especially his 1943 drama *I Bambini ci Guardano/The Children Are Watching Us*. Roberto Rossellini began his directing career with short subjects, collaborations, and other Fascist-commissioned works before turning out his first solo feature *La Nava Bianca/The White Ship* (1941), a docudrama about a hospital vessel. He would then shift gears toward a neorealist style with the prostitute drama *Desiderio/Woman*. That film was abandoned in 1943, in mid-production, only to be completed in 1946 by another director, Marcello Pagliero. (Rossellini later repudiated the film.)

But it was Luchino Visconti who most conspicuously advanced into the naturalistic film style with his debut feature *Ossessione/Obsession* (1942), an unauthorized appropriation of James M. Cain's novel *The Postman Always Rings Twice*. (Its illegal status would keep it from U.S. screens until decades after the war's end.) The cessation of World War II hostilities brought with it a fascinating wave of gritty, realistic motion pictures that profoundly influenced American critics and audiences in the relatively few urban venues in which they were shown—most notably, Rossellini's *Open City* (1945) and De Sica's prizewinners *Shoeshine* (1946) and *The Bicycle Thief* (1948).

It has been reported that when the American film critic James Agee first witnessed *Open City* in early 1946, he wrote, "You will seldom see as pure freshness and vitality in a film, or as little unreality and affectation among the players." In New York City, the movie ran for many months at the small World Theatre, enjoying a similar critical reception as it moved to other American cities, with word of mouth and published acclaim attracting the more adventuresome moviegoers. (U.S. audiences were later surprised to learn that *their* enthusiasm over these no-frills Italian dramas was, in fact, often stronger than that of *Italian* moviegoers.) Americans also became fascinated by the Italian stars of these exotic neorealist films, encouraging the more enterprising of distributors to seek out the earlier and lesser works of Anna Magnani, Rossano Brazzi, and Gino Cervi for importation.

With the increasing wave of foreign imports, there

Clara Calamai and Massimo Girotti in Visconti's *Ossessione*.

"Unsuited to the cinema?" Early Anna Magnani.

Rinaldo Smordoni and Franco Interlenghi in De Sica's *Shoeshine*.

was the inevitable incursion of *sex* of a frankness that American films could not then countenance. Of the more visible successes, the forerunner may well have been Giuseppe De Santis's socioerotic *Bitter Rice* (1949), the sensational picture that introduced Silvana Mangano, Italy's first postwar female star to make a genuine mark, with her blend of sexy, voluptuous glamour and acting ability. A big hit, *Bitter Rice* was followed in 1951 by the equally popular *Anna*, directed by Alberto Lattuada and reuniting Mangano with her *Bitter Rice* teammates Vittorio Gassman and Raf Vallone, both of whom would become increasingly popular with American art-house audiences. Following in the wake of Mangano came Gina Lollobrigida, best seen to her early advantage in Luigi Comencini's *Bread, Love and Dreams* (1953), and the talented Sophia Loren in *Aida* (1953), destined to become the most enduring of all the Italian screen beauties. And Marcello Mastroianni, an actor first seen in the United States in the steamy melodrama *Sensualitá* (1952) opposite Eleonora Rossi-Drago, a sexy star of less staying power.

But Italian films were also becoming equally well known for their *directors*. Names like Michelangelo Antonioni and Federico Fellini were added to the ranks of the most important, with acclaimed works like Fellini's amusing *The White Sheik* (1952), *l Vitelloni/*

11

Raf Vallone and Silvana Mangano in De Santis's *Bitter Rice*.

Maria Michi loses control in Rossellini's *Open City*.

Gina Lollobrigida in Comencini's *Bread, Love and Dreams*.

The Young and the Passionate (1953), and—most celebrated of all—*La Strada* (1954). The teaming of American actors Anthony Quinn and Richard Basehart with one of Italy's finest dramatic actresses, the then-little-known Giulietta Masina—who was also Fellini's wife—helped that film find an international audience. Antonioni's enigmatic filmmaking style, seen first in *Il Grido/The Outcry* (1957) and *L'Avventura* (1960), appealed more to the intelligentsia, who apparently found deeper meanings in his elliptical style of filmmaking.

With the sixties, Italian films found their greatest worldwide popularity, with ambitious productions like Fellini's *La Dolce Vita* (1960), *8½* (1963), and *Juliet of the Spirits* (1965), while Antonioni turned out *La Notte/The Night* (1961), *Eclipse* (1962), and *Red Desert* (1964). Vittorio De Sica, returning from a directorial slump following the grim *Umberto D.* (1952), made a thrilling impact—and helped bring Sophia Loren her Oscar—with *Two Women* (1960). A

Giulietta Masina in Fellini's *La Strada*.

Antonioni directing *L'Avventura*.

decade later, he made yet another comeback with the moving *The Garden of the Finzi-Continis* (1971).

By now the Italian screen as often as not featured actors from France (Dominique Sanda, Yves Montand, Jean-Louis Trintignant, Jean-Paul Belmondo, Alain Delon, Annie Girardot, and Marina Vlady), Germany (Horst Buchholz, Romy Schneider, and Helmut Berger), Belgium (Catherine Spaak), and the United States (Burt Lancaster, Bette Davis, Steve Cochran, and Arthur Kennedy), as well as new Italian stars (Claudia Cardinale, Giancarlo Giannini, Stefania San-drelli, Ugo Tognazzi, and Renato Salvatori). In the United States, pictures like *La Dolce Vita* and *Two Women* were felt to be sufficiently popular to warrant the expense of making an English-dubbed version, to alternate with the original-language, subtitled print released in the larger cities. For this, credit the growing popular appeal of Sophia Loren (whose English was good enough to engage her for American productions) and Marcello Mastroianni (whose linguistic limitations still confined him to Europe). Of course, large-scale international-cast movies like Visconti's *The Leopard* (1963) were at least *partially* dubbed *everywhere*, necessitated by its hybrid cast of American Burt Lancaster, Italian Claudia Cardinale, and French Alain Delon in the leading roles. But then, dubbing was a long-established custom in Italy, where even stars like the husky-toned Cardinale began their film careers mouthing the words of actors whose voices fell more pleasingly on the public ear.

Fabio Tesi and Dominique Sanda in De Sica's *The Garden of the Finzi-Continis*.

13

Steve Reeves in Francisci's *Hercules*.

Burt Lancaster and Claudia Cardinale in Visconti's *The Leopard*.

The sixties also brought a wave of cheaply turned out, pseudohistorical adventure melodramas, commonly referred to as "sword-and-sandal flicks," since they were quickly made pictures with unimportant casts (albeit occasionally starring a Hollywood name-on-the-wane) and often featured muscle-bound Italian actors who assumed American-sounding names (or the genuine article, like Steve Reeves, Ed Fury, and Gordon Scott). That chapter had all begun with the importation of *Hercules* (1959) by Joseph E. Levine, the American showman who put Reeves's muscles on the world movie map and fostered the actor's subsequent career in colorful adventure pictures. Soon U.S. screens would be flooded with these low-budget epics; harder to locate were prestige films for the "art" circuit.

Fellini, Antonioni, Visconti, De Sica, and company continued to make pictures for their special audiences, but not all were successful. In the mid-sixties, De Sica enjoyed international acclaim with the Loren-Mastroianni vehicles *Yesterday, Today and Tomorrow* and *Marriage Italian Style*. But there were also his less well remembered *Woman Times Seven* and *Sunflower*. After a fallow period, Fellini came back to win awards with *Amarcord* (1974), while Visconti, after the failure

Marcello Mastroianni and Sophia Loren in De Sica's *Yesterday, Today and Tomorrow*.

of *Ludwig* (1973) and *Conversation Piece* (1975), won new respect for his final work, *The Innocent* (1976). With Visconti's passing, a grand style of filmmaking also left the Italian screen, to be replaced by a grittier, more "personal" cadre of directors: Pier Paolo Pasolini won a certain following for a time, first through his street dramas *Accatone* (1961) and *Mamma Roma* (1962), then with a rare excursion into religious subject matter with *The Gospel According to St. Matthew* (1964) and the pretentious *Teorema* (1968), before finally descending to salacious retellings of *The Decameron* (1970) and *The Canterbury Tales* (1974). He peaked with the much-banned shocker *Salo—The 120 Days of Sodom* (1975). Sergio Leone, the king of showy, operatic-style "spaghetti westerns," not only put American TV-cowboy Clint Eastwood in the major-star league but also left us with such cult western epics as *The Good, the Bad, and the Ugly* (1966) and *Once Upon a Time in the West* (1968) before turning out the ultimate gangster saga *Once Upon a Time in America* (1984). Another interesting new element in Italian filmmaking was the emergence of that rarity, a noteworthy *woman* director, namely, Lina Wertmuller, whose most significant contributions have included *The Seduction of Mimi* (1972), the marathon-

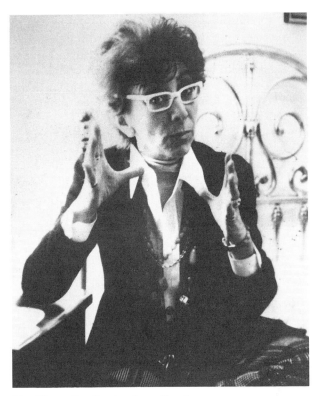

Lina Wertmuller directing *Seven Beauties.*

Pasolini's censor-beset *Salo—The 120 Days of Sodom.*

15

titled *Swept Away . . . by an Unusual Destiny in the Blue Sea of August* (1974), and—most acclaimed of all—*Seven Beauties* (1976). Wertmuller's closest female competition was Liliana Cavani, who caused a momentary furor in 1974 with her sexy, violent *The Night Porter.* Franco Brusati won acclaim that same year with his satirical *Bread and Chocolate,* followed by the frank, morbid drama *To Forget Venice.* And the Taviani brothers, Paolo and Vittorio, drew accolades for avoiding star actors to tell the engaging stories of *Padre Padrone* (1977) and *The Night of the Shooting Stars* (1982). The equally single-minded Ermanno Olmi also drew praise for his artful direction of amateur performers in *Il Posto/The Sound of Trumpets* (1961) and *The Tree of Wooden Clogs* (1979). But the most important Italian filmmaker to emerge from this period was without doubt Bernardo Bertolucci, who first won major attention with his second feature, *Before the Revolution* (1964), followed by the increasingly more ambitious *oeuvre* that includes *The Conformist* (1970), *Last Tango in Paris* (1972), *1900* (1976), and *The Last Emperor* (1987).

In the eighties, profound changes in the Italian film industry failed to create any important new international stars of lasting duration. Loren, Cardinale, and Mastroianni—among the veteran Italian luminaries—continued to work, if less frequently than in their prime. But few of their films were brought to the United States. More recent Italian imports that have enjoyed varying degrees of success include the operatic films of Franco Zeffirelli, *La Traviata* (1982) and *Otello* (1986); Francesco Rosi's *Three Brothers* (1981); Maurizio Nichetti's *The Icicle Thief* (1989); Gianni Amelio's *Open Doors* (1989) and *Il Ladro di Bambini/Stolen Children* (1992); Pupi Avati's *The Story of Boys and Girls* (1989); Giuseppe Tornatore's popular, Oscar-winning *Cinema Paradiso* (1988) and its less acclaimed successor *Everybody's Fine;* director/comedian Roberto Benigni's *Johnny Stecchino* (1991); and Gabriele Salvatores's Academy Award winner *Mediterraneo* (1991). Significantly, the great Fellini's 1987 *Intervista* didn't find an American theatrical release until 1992, and then only through the joint auspices of Martin Scorsese and Julian Schlossberg. Thus, in the nineties, the importation of foreign-language films has shrunk to a select few in a field dominated by the French. Star names apparently mean little today; as this book is being completed in the summer of 1993, a 1990 Lina Wertmuller film *(Saturday, Sunday and Monday)* starring Sophia Loren has yet to interest any U.S. distributor. Sadly, it is a fate shared by Fellini's 1990 *Voices of the Moon.* The current state of the Italian film industry seems to reflect a general slump in all of the arts that has reached international proportions. Perhaps a reexamination of the cinematic past may lead to a resurgence in the future.

Philippe Noiret and Salvatore Cascio in Tornatore's *Cinema Paradiso.*

16

THE FILMS

LA SIGNORA DI TUTTI   Isa Miranda.

LA SIGNORA DI TUTTI   Isa Miranda and Memo Benassi.

18

La Signora di Tutti

(EVERYBODY'S WOMAN)

A Novella Films Production/1934

(U.S. release: 1936)

CREDITS

Director: Max Ophüls; *Producer:* Emilio Rizzoli; *Associate Producer:* Tomaso Monicelli; *Screenwriters:* Max Ophüls, Hans Wilhelm, and Curt Alexander; *Based on the novel by* Salvator Gotta; *Cinematographer:* Ubaldo Arata; *Editor:* Ferdinando M. Poggioli; *Art Director:* Giuseppe Capponi; *Costumes:* Sandro Radice; *Music:* Daniele Amfitheatrof; *Song* "La Signora di Tutti" *by* Daniel Dax, *performed by* Nelly Nelson; *Running time:* 89 minutes.

CAST

Isa Miranda *(Gabriella Murge/"Gaby Doriot")*; Memo Benassi *(Leonardo Nanni)*; Tatiana Pavlova *(Alma Nanni)*; Federico Benfer *(Roberto Nanni)*; Nelly Corradi *(Anna)*.

THE FILM

German-born Max Ophüls began his theatrical career in his teens as a stage actor before turning to the direction of plays in Germany and Austria. By 1930, when he was twenty-eight, Ophüls had made the transition to motion pictures, initially as dialogue director for Anatole Litvak at UFA and later as a full-fledged director himself, with 1933's noteworthy *Liebelei.* That same year, the rising tide of Nazism drove Ophüls to move his family and career base to France, whence he was engaged by the influential publisher Angelo Rizzoli to come to Italy to direct an adaptation of Salvator Gotta's novel *La Signora di Tutti.* Ophüls also collaborated on the screenplay.

In flashback form, the film recounts the story of Franco-Italian movie star Gaby Doriot (Isa Miranda, in her first important lead), who has attempted suicide even as her studio grinds out publicity posters for her latest vehicle, *La Signora di Tutti.* Rushed to the hospital, Gaby undergoes surgery in an effort to save her life. As the ether cone descends, she recalls the ill-starred events of her life, from the schoolgirl scandal of an involvement with a married teacher through her association with a wealthy young man, Roberto Nanni (Federico Benfer), whose father Leonardo (Memo Benassi) is smitten by Gaby. Tragedy follows when, during the elder Nanni's garden rendezvous with Gaby, his invalid wife Alma (Tatiana Pavlova), suffers a fatal fall. For a few months Gaby becomes Leonardo's mistress, and they travel about Europe. Later on, back home in Italy, Gaby's conscience bothers her, and she leaves Leonardo (who is now accused by his firm of embezzlement), relocating to Paris, where she eventually finds fame as a film star. But the past returns to burden Gaby when she learns that Leonardo, released from prison a broken man, has been killed in a street accident. A reunion with Roberto reveals that he has always loved her. But it is already too late for him and Gaby; Roberto is now married to her younger sister Anna (Nelly Corradi). As the story concludes, Gaby succumbs in the operating room, and the printing presses producing her posters are stilled.

With her high-cheekboned face and ash-blond hair, the Milanese Isa Miranda bears a superficial resemblance to Marlene Dietrich that immediately puts her in the "femme fatale" category. But Miranda's is a warmer, softer beauty than Dietrich's, and her Gaby Doriot is more the acquiescent convenience of the opposite sex than the coolly calculating man killer of Dietrich.

La Signora di Tutti made a star of the stunning Miranda, whose burgeoning thirties career in French and Italian films brought her briefly to Hollywood for a pair of little-remembered Paramount pictures, *Hotel Imperial* (1939) and *Adventure in Diamonds* (1940). In 1950, Miranda was again seen to advantage in another Max Ophüls film, the French-made *La Ronde.* She was also Katherine Hepburn's worldly landlady in 1955's *Summertime.*

At the second Venice Biennale, *La Signora di Tutti* was awarded the Coppa del Ministero della Corporazione as 1934's "technically best Italian film."

Lo Squadrone Bianco

(THE WHITE SQUADRON)

A Rome Film Production/1936

(U.S. release by Esperia Film Distributing Corp.: 1939)

CREDITS

Director: Augusto Genina; *Screenwriters:* Augusto Genina and Joseph Peyre; *Based on the novel* L'Escadron Blanc *by* Joseph Peyre; *Music:* Antonio Veretti; *Running Time:* 90 minutes.

CAST

Antonio Centa; Fosco Giachetti; Fulvia Lanzi; Olinto Cristina.

THE FILM

Very much a product of its Fascist era, *The White Squadron*, which propagandizes about Italy's place in the African sun, is a cinematic celebration of Italian colonialism played out in the form of a traditional romantic adventure story. The film's director, Augusto Genina, had entered motion pictures in 1913, turning out a succession of silent melodramas. From the late twenties to the mid-fifties, he also worked occasionally in Germany, Austria, and France, where he is best known for having directed Louise Brooks in her only French picture, *Prix de Beauté* (1930). But, of his thirties films, *The White Squadron* is deservedly the best remembered.

Filmed mostly on location in Libya, *The White*

LO SQUADRONE BIANCO   Antonio Centa.

20

LO SQUADRONE BIANCO Fosco Giachetti and Antonio Centa.

Squadron (the title reflects the dress code of its uniformed troops) celebrates Italy's invasion of Africa and the "heroism" of its fighting in that land, where the battlefield becomes the means by which a soldier comes to terms with his manhood and his duty. Realistically told, the story is structured around a punitive expedition of troops sent out to quell a native rebellion. Central to the narrative is a young cavalry lieutenant (portrayed by Antonio Centa) who has managed to be transferred to Libya to help him forget his infatuation with a heartless society beauty (Fulvia Lanzi, making an uncertain movie debut in a career that ultimately went nowhere).

Fosco Giachetti, now a long-forgotten actor (except perhaps to older Italian audiences), was then among the busiest leading men of the Fascist screen. In *The White Squadron*, he shares leading-man honors with Centa (an actor practically unknown outside his own country) as the older commanding officer, a disciplinarian who nevertheless commands the respect of his men. The plot focuses on the unhappy young officer's evolution into a good soldier, transformed by his own exemplary behavior in battle. In a rather facile finale, the young man's improvement is so marked that he eventually regains the attention of his former lady friend, who is suitably taken with the man he has now become.

The movie's propaganda value so impressed the judges that it was named Best Italian Film at the 1936 Venice Film Festival. Moreover, it is an excellent adventure drama on its own, with a fine performance by Giachetti as the captain, and exemplary handling of the desert sequences by director Genina.

Scipione L'Africano

(SCIPIO AFRICANUS / THE DEFEAT OF HANNIBAL)

A Consorzio Scipio L'Africano Production / 1937

(U.S. release by Esperia Film Distributing Corp.: 1939)

CREDITS

Director: Carmine Gallone; *Executive Producer:* Vittorio Mussolini [uncredited]; *Producer:* Federico Curiosi; *Screenwriters:* Camillo Mariani dell' Anguillara, S. A. Luciani, Carmine Gallone, and Silvio Maurano; *Cinematographers:* Ubaldo Arata and Anchise Brizzi; *Art Director:* Carmine Gallone; *Music:* Ildebrando Pizzetti; *Running Time:* 109 minutes.

CAST

Annibale Ninchi *(Scipio)*; Camillo Pilotto *(Hannibal)*; Isa Miranda *(Velia)*; Memo Benassi *(Cato)*; Fosco Giachetti *(Massinissa)*; Francesca Braggiotti *(Sofonisba)*; Marcello Giorda *(Siface)*; Lamberto Picasso *(Asdrubale)*; Franco Coop *(Mezio)*; Piero Carnabuci *(Reduce Romano)*; Guglielmo Barnabo *(Furio)*; Carlo Lombardi *(Lucio)*; Carlo Ninchi *(Lelio)*; Clara Padoa *(Sofonisba's Slave)*; Marcello Spada *(Arunte)*; Raimondo Van Riel *(Maharbale)*; Gino Viotti *(Mercante Fenicio)*.

THE FILM

At least partially inspired by *The Sign of the Cross,* that grandiose portrait of Rome brought to the American screen by Cecil B. DeMille in 1932, Carmine Gallone's noisy, eye-filling spectacle *Scipione L'Africano* was filmed under the auspices of Benito Mussolini on the soundstages of his Roman superstudio Cinecittá. In many ways, it was a throwback to the early days of

21

Italian cinema, when movies like *Quo Vadis?*, *Cabiria*, and *Messalina* led the world in depicting giant spectacles set in ancient times. Filmed in 1936, *Scipione L'Africano's* account of Italy's vanquishing of Carthage and Hannibal not only underscored that country's right to dominate the world but also bore obvious parallels to mid-thirties North Africa, with its "civilizing" power of Roman rule.

With its visual operatics and its cast of the proverbial "thousands," *Scipione L'Africano* has been aptly assessed as "like a Verdi variation of a Wagnerian theme." Its most striking episode is the burning of Carthage, with its choral underscoring of the chiaroscuro images of desperate figures silhouetted against the flames.

At fifty, Carmine Gallone was then a film veteran of some twenty-three years, having begun directing in the heyday of Italy's silent spectacles of the early teens. Pro-Fascist in his political sympathies, he also harbored an affinity for grand opera, as illustrated by such thirties Gallone film titles as *Casta Diva*, *Giuseppe Verdi*, and *Il Sogno di Butterfly/The Dream of Butterfly*. All of these attributes are present in his spectacular, if occasionally dull, *Scipione L'Africano*.

Its plot concerns the youthful exploits of Scipio (portrayed by Annibale Ninchi), who persuades the

SCIPIONE L'AFRICANO   Isa Miranda.

SCIPIONE L'AFRICANO.

Roman Senate to sanction his invasion of Africa in 202 B.C. With his troops, Scipio achieves a notable victory over the Carthaginians, returning home a great hero. Although women aren't given much importance in this story, Francesca Braggiotti and Isa Miranda both have their moments.

Mussolini, who put his inexperienced young son Vittorio in charge of production, planned the film as a source of inspiration to his North African veterans, who, it was realized, might soon be called upon to fight elsewhere in the world. Apparently, money was no object to Il Duce, for *Scipione L'Africano* is reputed to

SCIPIONE L'AFRICANO.

have cost twenty times the average mid-thirties Italian production. But size alone couldn't sell this film, which enjoyed equally brief engagements in both Rome and New York.

In 1971, the Italians coproduced a sequel entitled *Scipione, Detto Anche "L'Africano"/Scipio, Also Called "The African,"* which made little impact on the film industry and was never exported to the U.S. despite the presence of Marcello Mastroianni, Vittorio Gassman, and Silvana Mangano as its stars.

But the 1937 *Scipione* lives on in its eye-filling grandiosity as Italy's costliest monument to the Fascist film era.

L'Assedio dell' Alcazar

(THE SIEGE OF THE ALCAZAR)

A Bassoli Ulargui Production / 1940

(No U.S. release)

CREDITS

Director: Augusto Genina; *Producer:* Carlo Bassoli; *Screenwriters:* Alessandro Stefani and Carlo Bassoli; *Cinematographer:* Vincenzo Seratrice; *Music:* Antonio Verelli; *Running Time:* 105 minutes.

CAST

Fosco Giachetti; Mireille Balin; Maria Denis; Rafael Calvo; Nino Crisman; Guido Notari; Carlo Tamberlani; Carlos Muñoz.

THE FILM

Filmed in Spain not long after Franco's 1939 victory in the civil war, this striking Italian-Spanish production never reached U.S. cinemas. A late-1940 release in World War II Italy, the movie's subject matter—centering on the seventy-day defense of the Alcazar at Toledo by the Nationalist forces under General Moscardo—was hardly suitable for American distribution when the war's end gradually brought a trickle of Italian films to our shores. Unfortunately, we thus lost the opportunity to witness works such as this fine docudrama from director Augusto Genina, whose intended market was primarily the Spanish audience.

Screenwriters Alessandro Stefani and Carlo Bassoli (the latter also the film's producer) stick closely to the facts, keeping their story narrative both simple and restrained. The movie relates how a group of officers and soldiers of the Toledo garrison, after learning of the Nationalist outbreak, rally to their leader, General Moscardo (played by Rafael Calvo), a steadfast rightist. Preparations are made for the defense of the city, followed by preliminary skirmishes that force the Nationalists to seek shelter in the fortresslike Alcazar. Subsequently, they are besieged by an unrelenting

23

L'ASSEDIO DELL' ALCAZAR Mireille Balin, unknown actress and
Maria Denis.

wave of air and land attacks. None of this would seem to leave time for romance. But since this is an entertainment film and not a documentary, we have a love story played out against this explosive backdrop involving a tough but patriotic officer (Fosco Giachetti) and a spoiled rich girl (Mireille Balin).

Giachetti and Calvo give strong performances, but this isn't really an actors' film. Instead, *The Siege of the Alcazar* remains very much an impressive production and a credit to the logistic talents of director Genina. In 1940, a year in which the Venice Film Festival, curiously enough, awarded only two prizes, this production was named Best Italian Film. When *L'Assedio dell' Alcazar* was retrospectively honored at Venice in 1959, the French director Yves Boisset was moved to write: "Convinced, passionate, and grandiose, the film assures a heroic style to extol the fierce resistance put up by a small group of Falangists who take refuge with their wives and children in Alcazar at Toledo. The appalling suffering of the besieged families is communicated with moving restraint."

La Corona di Ferro

(THE IRON CROWN)

A Minerva Films Production / 1941

(U.S. release by Superfilm Distributing Corp.: 1949)

CREDITS

Director: Alessandro Blasetti; *Screenwriters:* Alessandro Blasetti, Corrado Pavolini, Guglielmo Zorzi, Giuseppe Zucca, and Renato Castellani; *Based on a story by* Alessandro Blasetti and Renato Castellani; *Cinematographers:* Vaclav Vich and Mario Craveri; *Editor:* Mario Serandrei; *Art Director:* Virgilio Marchi; *Artistic Consultant:* Corrado Pavolini; *Costumes:* Gino Sensani; *Music:* Alessandro Cicognini; *Assistant Directors:* Renato Castellani, Mario Chiari, and Lionello De Felice; *Running Time:* 104 minutes.

CAST

Gino Cervi *(King Sedemondo)*; Elisa Cegani *(Elsa/Elsa's Mother)*; Massimo Girotti *(Arminio)*; Luisa Ferida *(Tundra/Tundra's Mother)*; Osvaldo Valenti *(Eriberto)*; Rina Morelli *(Old Prophetess)*; Paolo Stoppa *(Trifilli)*; Primo Carnera *(Klasa)*.

THE FILM

If Alessandro Blasetti's grandiose spectacle *The Iron Crown* seems an unlikely movie to have emerged from Mussolini's Fascist Italy, its romantic excesses were nonetheless consistent with then-current trends toward escapist historical projects in the Italian film industry. However, at a budget of 40 million lire, this was an ambitious production for 1941, made costly by its bizarre sets and costumes and a large cast of extras augmented by the use of seven thousand horses and a veritable zoo of wild animals. Its carefree blending of myths, styles, and eras has elicited such subsequent critical assessments as "historical baroque carried to the point of burlesque" and "as delirious a pseudohistorical fantasy as any of those dear to the hearts of Italian filmmakers in the days of D'Annunzio."

In his book *The Italian Cinema*, Pierre Leprohon conjectures that Alessandro Blasetti must have directed *The Iron Crown* with tongue in cheek, although the filmmaker once confirmed that the picture was meant to be a message of peace—undoubtedly inspired by Cecil B. DeMille's thirties spectacles *The Sign of the Cross* and *The Crusades*, along with echoes of such silent epics as *Ben-Hur*, *Quo Vadis?*, and even *The Thief of Bagdad*. Its handsome hero, embodied by the athletic young Massimo Girotti (although noticeably devoid of the pumped-up musculature of today's coun-

LA CORONA DI FERRO Massimo Girotti.

LA CORONA DI FERRO Paolo Stoppa and Gino Cervi.

terparts), carries on the mythological Maciste super-hero tradition of Italy's silent era, with liberal borrowings from the Tarzan stories of Edgar Rice Burroughs.

Without making much sense, the confused, multi-generational plot—set in a nebulous thirteenth-century milieu—hinges on a crown manufactured from Roman sword metal and a nail from the cross of Christ. Gino Cervi portrays the ruthless king whose greed causes most of the trouble, with serenely beautiful Elisa Cegani and swashbuckling Luisa Ferida as the women who vie for the agile Girotti, whose energetic participation in a savagely combative arena tournament provides the movie's longest and most compelling action sequence.

The Iron Crown amused, entertained, and distracted wartime Europeans, and it copped the Grand Prix at 1941's Venice Biennale, which, as Leprohon points out, "was not much more than the festival of the Rome-Berlin axis." Postwar U.S. moviegoers had the opportunity to enjoy this film's escapist delights eight years after its original Italian premiere, by which time its director, Alessandro Blasetti, had achieved an even greater success with *Fabiola* (1948).

LA CORONA DI FERRO Luisa Ferida and Massimo Girotti.

26

Noi Vivi

(WE THE LIVING)

A Scalera Films Production / 1942

(U.S. release by Angelika Films: 1988)

CREDITS

Director: Goffredo Alessandrini; *Producer:* Franco Magli; *Screenwriter:* Anton Giulio Majano; *Based on the novel* We the Living *by* Ayn Rand, *as adapted by* Corrado Alvaro and Orio Vergani; *Cinematographer:* Giuseppe Caracciolo; *Editor:* Eraldo Da Roma; *Art Directors:* Andrea Belobborodoff, Giorgio Abkhasi, and Amleto Bonetti; *Costumes:* Rosi Gori; *Music:* Renzo Rossellini; *Restoration:* Duncan Scott Productions in association with Henry Mark Holzer and Erika Holzer; *Running Time:* 174 minutes (*Original Two-Part Running Time:* approx. 270 minutes).

CAST

Fosco Giachetti *(Andrei Taganov)*; Alida Valli *(Kira Argounova)*; Rossano Brazzi *(Leo Kovalensky)*; Giovanni Grasso *(Tiskenko;* Emilio Cigoli *(Pavel Syerov)*; Cesarina Gheraldi *(Comrade Sonia)*; Mario Pisu *(Victor Dunaev)*; Guglielmo Sinaz *(Morozov)*; Gero Zambuto *(Alexei Argounov)*; Annibale Betrone *(Vassili Dunaev)*; Elvira Betrone *(Maria Petrovna Dunaev)*; Sylvia Manto *(Marisha)*; Claudia Marti *(Lydia Argounova)*; Evelina Paoli *(Galina Petrovna Argounova)*; Gina Sammarco *(Tonia)*; Lamberto Picasso *(GPU Captain)*.

THE FILM

Until its mid-eighties restoration by Erika and Henry Mark Holzer, lawyers in the 1960s for novelist Ayn Rand, *We the Living* was overlooked in the film-history books and thought to be lost, a casualty of World War II suppression. A costly and unauthorized adaptation of Rand's popular 1936 novel, its filming was the brainchild of director Goffredo Alessandrini. The result was a motion picture whose over-four-and-a-half-hour length mandated a two-part Italian release in 1942–the first half entitled *Noi Vivi* and the concluding part called *Addio Kira.* At the 1942 Venice Film Festival, *We the Living* won the Volpe Cup and enjoyed a huge popular success. This was enhanced by the

NOI VIVI Alida Valli and Rossano Brazzi.

NOI VIVI Alida Valli, Fosco Giachetti and Rossano Brazzi.

Leo's sanitarium costs. Later, with his illness cured, Leo returns to St. Petersburg a changed and cynical man, entering into a black-market business. Eventually, he discovers Kira's well-motivated deception, and the outcome is tragic for all three.

A half century after its initial release, *We the Living* has received much critical praise for its rediscovery, especially of the performance of Valli, whose free-thinking "modern" woman was unlike other Italian film heroines of 1942. Six years before her glamorous Hollywood debut in Hitchcock's *The Paradine Case,* the actress is breathtaking in her photogenic vitality and impassioned, emotional acting. Brazzi is at times almost unrecognizable in his callow, curly-haired youthfulness, and Giachetti bears the sober façade that masks the inner anguish of an idealist undermined by his faith.

teaming of Fosco Giachetti, then Italy's top box-office actor, with Alida Valli, at twenty-one an audience favorite in her twentieth film, and Rossano Brazzi, already a highly paid movie star.

The novels of Ayn Rand (1905–82), the best known of which remain *The Fountainhead* and the monumental *Atlas Shrugged,* espouse the philosophy of "objectivism," which made her a cult figure in the 1960s and 1970s. Originally named Alice Rosenbaum, the Russian-born writer immigrated to the United States in 1924, eventually settling in Hollywood, where she worked as a movie extra and secretary, including employment in the RKO wardrobe department. She also wrote film scripts before completing her first novel, *We the Living.* Although her permission was not sought for its Italian production, Rand later saw and admired its screen adaptation. And she eventually received compensation from Scalera Films, the producing studio.

Superficially an indictment of communism, *We the Living* is essentially a love story, centering on Kira Argounova (Alida Valli), an independent-minded young woman who is determined to become an engineer in postrevolutionary Russia. Rand's philosophy is inherent in the character of this romantic-minded St. Petersburg student, whose self-interested ambitions threaten her with social ostracism. Leo Kovalensky (Rossano Brazzi) is the tubercular, unemployed fugitive who becomes her lover; and then there is Kira's reluctant friendship with the policeman Andrei Taganov (Fosco Giachetti), an older man with whom she begins a heartless affair, using his money to pay for

Ossessione

(OBSESSION)

An Industrie Cinematografiche Italiane Production / 1942

(U.S. release by Audio-Brandon Films: 1977)

CREDITS

Director: Luchino Visconti; *Producer:* Libero Solaroli; *Screenwriters:* Mario Alicata, Antonio Pietrangeli, Gianni Puccini, Giuseppe de Santis, and Luchino Visconti; *Based on the novel* The Postman Always Rings Twice *by* James M. Cain; *Cinematographers:* Aldo Tonti and Domenico Scala; *Editor:* Mario Serandrei; *Art Director:* Gino Rosati; *Music:* Giuseppe Rosati; *Running Time:* 135 minutes.

CAST

Clara Calamai *(Giovanna)*; Massimo Girotti *(Gino)*; Juan de Landa *(Bragana)*; Elio Marcuzzo *(the "Spaniard")*; Dhia Cristani *(Anita)*; Vittorio Duse *(Truck Driver)*.

THE FILM

Adapted without permission from *The Postman Always Rings Twice,* James M. Cain's American crime

OSSESSIONE Massimo Girotti and Clara Calamai.

novel, *Ossessione* stands as a landmark in the evolution of the Italian film. Its debuting director was a Milanese nobleman in his mid-thirties named Luchino Visconti whose previous experience encompassed double duty as costume designer/assistant director to France's Jean Renoir on two 1936 pictures, *Une Partie de Compagne/A Day in the Country* and *Les Bas Fonds/ The Lower Depths*, and—completed by Visconti and Carl Koch, who received sole credit—*La Tosca* (1940). It has frequently been stated that with *Ossessione*'s raw-textured, naturalistic account of illicit rural passion, murder, and betrayal, Visconti initiated the so-called neorealist movement that would later be more fully explored by Roberto Rossellini and Vittorio De Sica. That most Americans consider Rossellini's *Roma, Città Aperta/Open City* the advent of neorealism can be blamed partly on World War II and the fact that the earlier *Ossessione*'s illegal adaptation—as compared with M-G-M's authorized *The Postman Always Rings Twice* (1946)—delayed its American release for an incredible thirty-five years!

Its Po Valley setting is markedly Italian, but *Ossessione*'s comparisons with Metro's mid-forties *Postman* are unavoidable. Massimo Girotti and Clara Calamai portray the handsome drifter and the truck-stop own-

OSSESSIONE   Massimo Girotti and Elio Marcuzzo.

OSSESSIONE Clara Calamai and Massimo Girotti.

er's neglected wife who become lovers before conspiring to kill her middle-aged husband (Juan de Landa). Their more glamorous Hollywood counterparts, John Garfield and Lana Turner, offer a glossier sort of eroticism—or as close to eroticism as the Code-restricted American studios could then suggest—as they become romantically involved under the roof of Turner's elderly husband Cecil Kellaway. Tay Garnett directed that now-classic M-G-M version. But aside from an essential similarity in basic plots, there is little in common between that movie and its Italian predecessor.

Ossessione's Clara Calamai was a less ethereal Luise Rainer look-alike who never had a better film role than this unhappy, straying wife. *Ossessione* proved more advantageous for Calamai's hunky costar, Massimo Girotti. Having recently impressed European audiences as the athletic hero of Blasetti's *The Iron Crown*, Girotti shifted gears under Visconti's direction. His display of moody machismo and erotic energy created such chemistry with Calamai that the film immediately realizes a sensual electricity that fairly rivets the viewer throughout a running time in excess of two hours. A sidebar to the main story throws Girotti into a passing acquaintance with a strange traveling salesman called "the Spaniard" (Elio Marcuzzo), who may or may not

harbor homosexual feelings for Girotti during one nervously innocent night in a necessarily shared bed.

Ossessione's conclusion is as melodramatically swift as it is unsentimental. Having killed Clara's husband and made it look like a truck accident, the lovers are divided by their constant quarreling, in addition to the drifter's drinking and infidelities with other women. Finally, they are reunited by the adulterous widow's pregnancy but are pursued by the suspicious police. When Girotti's truck runs off a road and crashes into a river, Calamai is killed. And now the authorities have him.

It has been noted that Visconti's direction reflects the influence of Renoir in its naturalism. And it remains a remarkable motion picture to have come out of wartime, Fascist Italy, paving the way for Visconti's future masterworks, from the naturalistic docudrama *La Terra Tema/The Earth Trembles* to that romantic epic of nineteenth-century Sicily, *Il Gattopardo/The Leopard*.

Quattro Passi fra le Nuvole

(FOUR STEPS IN THE CLOUDS)

A Cines Production / 1942

(U.S. release by Distinguished Films, Inc.: 1948)

CREDITS

Director: Alessandro Blasetti; *Producer:* Giuseppe Amato; *Screenwriters:* Aldo De Benedetti, Cesare Zavattini, Giuseppe Amato, and Alessandro Blasetti; *Cinematographer:* Vaclav Vich; *Editor:* Mario Serandrei; *Art Director:* Virgilio Marchi; *Set Decorator:* Ferdinando Ruffo; *Music:* Alessandro Cicognini; *Running Time:* 90 minutes.

CAST

Gino Cervi *(Paolo Bianchi)*; Adriana Benetti *(Maria)*; Enrico Viarisio *(Magnaghi)*; Carlo Romano *(Antonio)*; Giuditta Rissone *(Clara Bianchi)*; Lauro Gazzolo *(the Conductor)*; Umberto Sacripanti *(First Hurdy-Gurdy Man)*; Silvio Bagolini *(Second Hurdy-Gurdy Man)*; Aldo Silvani *(Father)*; Giacinto Molteni *(Grandfather)*; Armando Migliari *(Stationmaster)*; Arturo Bragaglia *(a Passenger)*; Pina Gallini *(Woman Passen-*

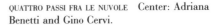
QUATTRO PASSI FRA LE NUVOLE   Center: Adriana Benetti and Gino Cervi.

ger); Oreste Bilancia *(Another Passenger).*

THE FILM

Screenwriter Cesare Zavattini, whom historian Pierre Leprohon credits as the man "responsible for introducing satire and feeling into the Italian cinema," brought momentary escape to World War II audiences in the form of this charming, bittersweet comedy. In its depiction of the foibles and failings of working-class Italians, *Four Steps in the Clouds* helped pave the way of neorealism with more humor than is usually associated with that naturalistic film movement.

Zavattini's frequent preoccupation as a writer was the depiction of a day in the life of an ordinary man—as he does here with the dullish candy salesman Paolo Bianchi (portrayed by Gino Cervi in what may have been the best role of his lengthy film career). In his middle thirties and married to a nagging wife (Giuditta Rissone), Paolo sets out on a working day that proves to be anything but ordinary. Traveling, in his job, on a rural bus that cannot help but recall Frank Capra's *It Happened One Night*, Paolo befriends a pregnant but unwed girl named Maria (Adriana Benetti), who desperately persuades him to pose as her "husband" on a night's stopover with her provincial family. With some doubt, he agrees to the deception, although he's ultimately unmasked as an imposter. But before leaving the family's farm, Paolo eloquently succeeds in convincing Maria's angry father (Aldo Silvani) of the virtues in forgiveness. And although it's

QUATTRO PASSI FRA LE NUVOLE   Gino Cervi and Adriana Benetti.

apparent that the brief but unusual friendship of Paolo and Maria could lead to a more serious, romantic alliance, no such relationship transpires. Instead, he returns to his loveless marriage and his children.

Unlike the casts of nonprofessionals who would so effectively populate some of the neorealist classics yet to come, *Four Steps in the Clouds* features one of Italy's then most popular stars at his zenith. That Gino Cervi was also the favorite actor of his director, Alessandro Blasetti, could not have hurt, for their obvious creative rapport made of this simple story a film of considerable wit and gentle charm that is enhanced by the poignant performance of Benetti as the anguished mother-to-be.

In the late forties, following the film's postwar international acclaim, producer Alexander Korda planned to star Ralph Richardson in a British remake. Instead, it became a French vehicle for Fernandel in 1957, retitled *Sous le Ciel de Provence/The Virtuous Bigamist.*

31

I BAMBINI CI GUARDANO   Luciano De Ambrosis.

I Bambini ci Guardano

(THE CHILDREN ARE WATCHING US)

A Scalera Film–Invicta Production / 1943
(U.S. release by Brandon Films, Inc.: 1958)

CREDITS

Director: Vittorio De Sica; *Producer:* Franco Magli;
Screenwriters: Cesare Giulio Viola, Margherita Maglione, Cesare Zavattini, Adolfo Franci, Gherardo Gherardi, and Vittorio De Sica; *Based on the novel* Prico *by* Cesare Giulio Viola; *Cinematographer:* Giuseppe Caracciolo; *Editor:* Mario Bonotto; *Art Director:* Amleto Bonetti; *Set Designer:* Vittorio Valentini; *Music:* Renzo Rossellini; *Running Time:* 85 minutes.

CAST

Emilio Cigoli *(Andrea, the Father)*; Luciano De Ambrosis *(Prico)*; Isa Pola *(Ines, the Mother)*; Adriano Rimoldi *(Ines's Lover)*; Giovanna Cigoli *(Agnese)*; Ione Frigerio *(the Grandmother)*; Maria Gardena *(Signora*

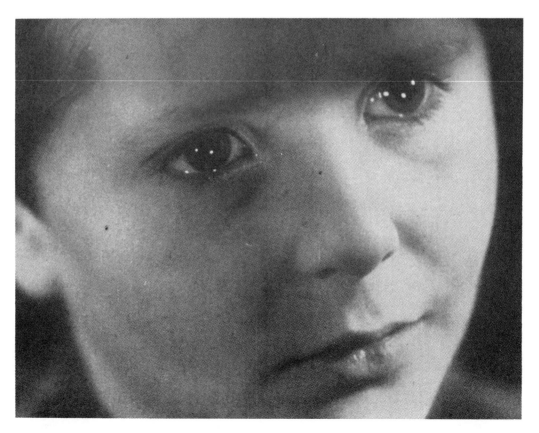

I BAMBINI CI GUARDANO   Luciano De Ambrosis.

Uberti); Dina Perbellini *(Aunt Berelli)*; Nicoletta Parodi *(Giuliana)*; Tecla Scarano *(Signora Resta)*; Ernesto Calindri *(Claudio)*; Olinto Cristina *(the Headmaster)*.

THE FILM

The least known of Vittorio De Sica's early, serious films as a director is this little gem, based on a novel that interested De Sica, Cesare Giulio Viola's *Prico. The Children Are Watching Us*, which depicts the disintegration of a marriage as painfully witnessed by the couple's little boy, marked De Sica's first association with Cesare Zavattini, a screenwriter who would prove to be the most important and longest enduring of his collaborators. Filmed in 1942, *The Children Are Watching Us* seems to belong to the thirties not only in its costuming but also in the attitudes of its characters.

Prico is the solemn-faced little son of a seemingly loveless union between a self-contained, middle-class businessman named Andrea (Emilio Cigoli) and his pretty wife Ines (Isa Pola), who has been carrying on in secret with a handsome young man (Adriano Rimoldi) she meets in the park. On one such outing, she takes Prico to watch an outdoor puppet show while she enjoys a lovers' rendezvous. Prico notes their intense, quiet conversation and refuses to greet his mother's "friend" at her bidding. The man persuades Ines to leave her family and come away with him, and after tucking the boy in for the night, she takes advantage of her husband's absence at a meeting and disappears. Unable to cope with sole responsibility for a child, Andrea tries unsuccessfully to foist Prico on his sister-in-law and the boy's grandmother. When it is decided that Prico will remain with his father and their housekeeper Agnese (Giovanna Cigoli), Ines suddenly reappears, asking Andrea to take her back. Although he does so, it is only because of the boy. The marriage becomes like a business transaction, improving only slightly when the family takes a seaside holiday. When Andrea must return home on business, he leaves Ines and Prico to enjoy themselves, ignorant of the fact that his wife's lover, with whom she had broken off, has traced her whereabouts. Ines proves too weak to resist when her friend insists he cannot live without her. Little Prico sees them together again and attempts to follow his father home.

Andrea now decides to place Prico in a boarding school, where their final meeting leaves the boy in tears as his father bids him *addio*; the humiliated Andrea is intent only on suicide. After his funeral, Ines and Agnese visit the school to inform Prico of his father's death and to console him. But the boy cannot feel anything for his mother; instead, he runs to the motherly Agnese. Ines stands looking on with a mixture of coolness and parental guilt. As the headmaster urges the boy to embrace his mother, Prico goes to her. But neither can reach out to the other, and the child retreats to the safer shelter of the school. The sweet innocence of childhood has been brought to a wrenching and premature end.

Despite Renzo Rossellini's too syrupy background music, this is quite a realistic picture of dysfunctional family life, bourgeois-Italian style. And at the center of its success is the wonderful performance De Sica elicits from four-and-a-half-year-old Luciano De Ambrosis, whose sensitive reactions to the varying antagonistic moods of his unhappy parents seem uncannily natural for one so small.

Roma, Città Aperta

(OPEN CITY)

An Excelsa Film Production / 1945

(U.S. release by Mayer-Burstyn, Inc.: 1946)

CREDITS

Producer-Director: Roberto Rossellini; *Screenwriters:* Sergio Amidei, Federico Fellini, and Roberto Rossellini; *Cinematographer:* Ubaldo Arata; *Editor:* Eraldo

ROMA, CITTÀ APERTA Francesco Grandjacquet and Anna Magnani.

ROMA, CITTA APERTA   Maria Michi and Giovanna Galletti.

Da Roma; *Music:* Renzo Rossellini; *Running Time:* 105 minutes.

CAST

Anna Magnani *(Pina)*; Aldo Fabrizi *(Don Pietro)*; Marcello Pagliero *(Manfredi)*; Vito Annicchiarico *(Marcello)*; Maria Michi *(Marina Mari)*; Harry Feist *(Captain Bergmann)*; Francesco Grandjacquet *(Francesco)*; Giovanna Galletti *(Ingrid)*; Nando Bruno *(Sexton)*; Carla Rovere *(Lauretta)*.

THE FILM

Emerging in 1946 from war-ravaged Italy, Roberto Rossellini's *Open City* was welcomed in American "art" cinemas with such widespread praise that many a moviegoer attended, for the first time, a foreign-language film with English subtitles. It was utterly unlike any other World War II movie U.S. audiences had ever seen. Its grainy, semidocumentary verisimil-

itude was far removed from such Hollywood-glossy, Italian-set pictures as *A Bell for Adano* or *A Walk in the Sun.* And much of *Open City* looked as if it were a succession of unscripted, real-life incidents that had been captured by cameras at the moment of occurrence. Because of the war, Italian films had not been imported, and so the impact of neorealism came as a belated revelation to American audiences.

Originally, this first Rossellini feature to gain worldwide attention was planned as a modest, short documentary about Don Morosini, an Italian priest and member of the Resistance who was shot by the Germans in 1944. But the Italian film industry, like the rest of the country, was in ruins. As Rossellini has said: "Almost all the producers had disappeared. The field was wide open for innovation." Along with his friends Sergio Amidei and Federico Fellini, Rossellini had developed a screenplay during the German occupation, and in 1944 he began shooting under the most difficult of conditions. The director had engaged veteran actors Aldo Fabrizi and Anna Magnani, both best

known until then for playing comedy. As the director proceeded, the scope of the project expanded, stretching to encompass interconnecting episodes based on Italy's Resistance to German occupation of Rome.

In Rossellini's words: "I shot this film on a tiny budget, scraped together as I went along. There was only just enough to pay for the raw film and no hope of getting it developed, since I didn't have enough to pay the laboratories. Sometime later, having acquired a little money, I edited the film and showed it to a few people in the cinema—critics and friends. It was a great disappointment to most of them."

Surprisingly, *Open City* was warmly received by the Italian public, becoming the country's greatest box-office success of the 1945–1946 season. In Paris and New York, *Open City*'s popularity only increased.

In essence, this is the episodic story of Manfredi (Marcello Pagliero), a Resistance leader hunted by the Gestapo. Pina (Anna Magnani), the pregnant fiancée of his friend Francesco (Francesco Grandjacquet), offers him temporary shelter. But when she is later shot

ROMA, CITTA APERTA Aldo Fabrizi.

down in the street, he finds refuge with his mistress Marina (Maria Michi), a cheap actress and dope addict. She betrays him to the Nazis, including the sadistic Captain Bergmann (Harry Feist) and his colleague, the lesbian Ingrid (Giovanna Galletti), who preys on Marina's weakness. Manfredi is mercilessly tortured by the enemy, but he refuses to talk and eventually dies. Following his death, the Gestapo executes Don Pietro (Aldo Fabrizi), an activist priest who has supported the Resistance. As the movie ends, Rossellini's camera follows a group of children who have witnessed the outdoor execution. Perhaps theirs will be a better world.

For lack of studio facilities, *Open City* was filmed on real streets and in existing interiors. Its documentary look evolved as the result of dealing with makeshift lighting and the absence of power units and having to make do with odds and ends of film stock. When Rossellini's initial $25,000 budget was depleted, he and Magnani sold their clothing.

In the United States, *Open City* received an Academy Award nomination for Best Screenplay and was named Best Foreign Language Film in 1946 by both the New York Film Critics and the National Board of Review, which also voted Anna Magnani that year's Best Actress.

Sciuscià

(SHOESHINE)

An Alfa Cinematografica Production / 1946
(U.S. release by Lopert Films: 1947)

CREDITS

Director: Vittorio De Sica; *Producer:* Paolo W. Tamburella; *Screenwriters:* Sergio Amidei, Adolfo Franci, Cesare Giulio Viola, Cesare Zavattini, and Vittorio De Sica; *Cinematographer:* Alessandro Cicognini; *Running Time:* 93 minutes.

CAST

Rinaldo Smordoni *(Giuseppe)*; Franco Interlenghi *(Pasquale)*; Aniello Mele *(Raffaele)*; Bruno Ortensi *(Arcangeli)*; Pacifico Astrologo *(Vittorio)*; Francesco De Nicola *(Ciriola)*; Antonio Carlino *(the Abruzzese)*;

SCIUSCIA   Franco Interlenghi.

SCIUSCIA   Maria Campi, Rinaldo Smordoni and Franco Interlenghi.

36

Enrico de Silva *(Giorgio)*; Antonio Lo Nigro *(Righetto)*; Angelo D'Amico *(the Sicilian)*; Emilio Cigoli *(Staff-era)*; Giuseppe Spadaro *(Bonavino, the Lawyer)*; Leo Caravaglia *(the Police Officer)*; Luigi Saltamerenda *(Panza)*; Maria Campi *(the Fortune-Teller)*; Irene Smordoni *(Giuseppe's Mother)*; Anna Pedoni *(Nannarella)*.

THE FILM

Vittorio De Sica and his screenwriting colleague Cesare Zavattini had dealt evocatively with the darker sides of childhood before, in 1943, in the minor classic *I Bambini ci Guardano/The Children Are Watching Us*, in which parents fail to live up to a little boy's illusions about them. But it was *Sciuscià*, his seventh film as a director, that not only solidly established De Sica's international reputation as a major European film-maker but placed him in the vanguard of neorealists. Like its immediate predecessor (Rossellini's *Open City*), *Shoeshine* offered a gritty look at war-ravaged, impoverished Romans, this time focusing on two delinquent adolescents caught up in the wave of wartime social problems.

Deriving its unusual title from the street urchins with their shoe-shine boxes who sought the patronage of G.I.s with their cries of "Shoosha, Joe," the movie focuses on the fourteen-year-old orphan Pasquale (Franco Interlenghi) and his rootless younger buddy Giuseppe (Rinaldo Smordoni). Obsessed with the notion of owning a horse, the two street pals abandon shining shoes for dealing in black-market blankets, a moneymaking move that gets them their animal, which they proudly ride in the streets. But they are not clever enough to avoid being caught for their criminal activities and are incarcerated in the grim Regina Coeli prison, where harsh conditions toughen them to the point where each loses whatever redeeming qualities he once possessed. Pasquale is tricked into informing on Giuseppe, who retaliates by betraying his friend. The latter escapes, but Pasquale takes the authorities to his hiding place. Finally, Giuseppe is killed when a fight breaks out and the older boy accidentally knocks him off a bridge. As Pasquale jumps down to weep for his old friend and surrender to the police, their horse gallops off.

Except for the final scene, which was shot in a studio, *Shoeshine* has, throughout, the look of absolute reality, the benefit of actual street and prison locations. Similarly, De Sica took the chance of casting his film with nonprofessionals who had never faced a movie camera before. Young Rinaldo Smordoni and Franco Interlenghi (who went on to pursue a successful film career as an adult) are absolute perfection as the two lads. Never for a moment does either one appear to be acting. As *New York Times* critic Thomas M. Pryor summed it up: "*Shoeshine* is not an entertainment; rather, it is a brilliantly executed social document."

The film offered no solutions to the problems it reflected, but it was instrumental in substantially reforming Italian laws dealing with delinquent juveniles. Amusing in retrospect is that *Variety*, giving *Shoeshine* only a capsule review from Rome, foresaw little box-office hope for it in the United States, reasoning that American pictures had already sufficiently handled such subject matter. Nine years before foreign films categorically competed for Oscars, this landmark of the Italian cinema was given a special Academy Award as "proof to the world that the creative spirit can triumph over adversity."

Vivere in Pace

(TO LIVE IN PEACE)

A Lux-Pao Film / 1946

(U.S. release by Times Film Corp.: 1947)

CREDITS

Director: Luigi Zampa; *Producer:* Carlo Ponti; *Screenwriters:* Suso Cecci D'Amico, Aldo Fabrizi, and Piero Tellini; *Running Time:* 105 minutes *(U.S. Running Time:* 90 minutes).

CAST

Aldo Fabrizi *(Uncle Tigna)*; Gar Moore *(Ronald)*; Mirella Monti *(Silvia)*; John Kitzmiller *(Joe)*; Heinrich Bode *(Hans)*; Ave Ninchi *(Corinna)*; Ernesto Almirante *(the Grandfather)*; Nando Bruno *(Political Secretary)*; Aldo Silvani *(the Doctor)*; Gino Cavalieri *(the Priest)*; Piero Palermini *(Franco)*; Franco Serpilli *(Citto)*.

THE FILM

Luigi Zampa (1905–91) studied engineering and architecture before settling on a theatrical career, first as an actor and then entering Rome's Centro Sperimentale film school to study writing and directing in 1935.

VIVERE IN PACE   Aldo Fabrizi.

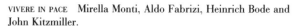

VIVERE IN PACE   Mirella Monti, Aldo Fabrizi, Heinrich Bode and John Kitzmiller.

VIVERE IN PACE   Gar Moore and Aldo Fabrizi.

In the Italian movie industry of the thirties, he initially wrote scripts and served as an assistant director. Zampa became a full-fledged director in 1941 with *L'Attore Scomparso/The Vanished Actor*, specializing in standard Fascist comedies of the "white telephone" variety. But his compassion for the ordinary man moved him artistically toward naturalism with *To Live in Peace*, a film that won the director international acclaim for his handling of social themes laced with a satiric, comic touch.

Although somewhat less remembered today in the annals of postwar Italian filmmaking, *To Live in Peace* easily stands alongside more celebrated neorealist classics like *Open City*, *Shoeshine*, and *The Bicycle Thief*. Its wartime setting is a small mountain village whose isolation had long kept it remote from the war—until the sudden appearance in town of two Americans, fugitives from their German captors. A middle-aged peasant farmer (Aldo Fabrizi) and his daughter (Mirella Monti) offer their barn as refuge to the pair: one, a white journalist (Gar Moore); the other, a black G.I. (John Kitzmiller). When the town's sole German soldier (Heinrich Bode) downs too much wine one night, he finds an unusual drinking buddy in a wine cellar—the black soldier. They stagger, arm in arm, through the village streets, loudly proclaiming the war's end. The townsfolk join them in their false revelry, at the same time raiding the Nazis' warehouse of its coveted flour and sugar. But the next day brings the truth, and the villagers flee to the hills—only to find relief in the arrival of the American army. This forces the Germans out of the area, but not before the Nazis kill the farmers in retaliation for their "vandalism."

Aldo Fabrizi, well remembered as the martyred Roman priest of Rossellini's *Open City*, demonstrates an endearing talent for character comedy (but a penchant for prosciutto in his death scene) in this screenplay he helped write with Suso Cecci D'Amico and Piero Tellini. American actors Gar Moore and John Kitzmiller bring Yank authenticity to roles they were each to echo in the subsequent postwar Italian movies *Paisan* and *Senza Pieta/Without Pity*.

Director Zampa thus entered into his most internationally productive period, following this comedy-drama with such highly praised working-class pictures as the Anna Magnani vehicle *L'Onorevole Angelina/Angelina* (1947) and *Anni Difficili/Difficult Years* (1948). His last film reflected a decidedly altered Italian cinema—the multipart, 1979 Ursula Andress-Laura Antonelli-Sylvia Kristel-Monica Vitti sex comedy *Letti Selvaggi* (U.S. title: *Tigers in Lipstick*).

To Live in Peace was voted Best Foreign Film (1947) by the New York Film Critics.

Il Bandito

(THE BANDIT)

A Lux Film Production/1946

(U.S. release by Times Film Corp.: 1949)

CREDITS

Director: Alberto Lattuada; *Producer:* Dino De Laurentiis; *Screenwriters:* Oreste Biancoli, Mino Caudana, and Ettore M. Margadonna; *From a Story by* Alberto Lattuada; *Cinematographer:* Aldo Tonti; *Editor:* Mario Bonotti; *Art Director:* Guglielmo Borzone; *Music:* Felice Lattuada; *Running Time:* 87 Minutes (*U.S. Running Time:* 77 minutes).

CAST

Amedeo Nazzari *(Ernesto)*; Anna Magnani *(Lydia)*; Carla Del Poggio *(Maria)*; Carlo Campanini *(Carlo)*;

IL BANDITO   Amedeo Nazzari and Carla Del Poggio.

Mino Doro *(Mirko)*; Eliana Banducci *(Rosetta)*; Folco Lulli *(Andrea)*.

THE FILM

Amedeo Nazzari—one of Italy's most popular stars over four decades, beginning in 1935—enjoyed his leading-man prime just before and during World War II and thus was never that well known in the United States. Among his better vehicles was this mid-forties underworld melodrama, filmed when the actor was thirty-nine and, as some have noted, an Italian Errol Flynn look-alike. For a time, Nazzari was his country's favorite movie actor, with his nearest competition coming from the somewhat older Fosco Giachetti and the younger Massimo Girotti.

It has been observed in its retrospective showings that *The Bandit* serves to combine the atmosphere of Hollywood film noir with the style and insights of neorealism. And yet the film avoids being pigeonholed in either category. For this, credit is due writer-director

IL BANDITO   Amedeo Nazzari and Anna Magnani.

the economy of screen acting. Nazzari is equally fine, whether exchanging lusty fireworks with the volatile Anna Magnani or taking charge of the gang in a style reminiscent of Bogart at his most effective. Unfortunately for American audiences, late-forties censorship sensibilities resulted in *The Bandit*'s losing ten of its eighty-seven minutes—and, with it, some of its frank, matter-of-fact continuity. In those days, sex on the U.S. screen, whether domestic or imported, consisted mostly of significant glances that could be termed "suggestive." Explicitness would have to wait for a more cynical, enlightened era.

Alberto Lattuada, with two features and a documentary to his name at thirty-two but unknown in the United States. His greatest popular success in America would come five years later with *Anna*, the sudsy but sexy Silvana Mangano vehicle.

Opening with a realistic picture of post–World War II Italy, the film follows a disillusioned returning soldier, Ernesto (Nazzari), who is appalled to discover the depths to which his native Turin has sunk during the occupation. Perhaps most shocking is the revelation that his own sister Maria (Carla Del Poggio) has become a prostitute. During Ernesto's fight with her pimp, Maria is accidentally shot and dies in his arms. Injured and pursued by the police, he falls in with bad company, soon becoming the head of a gang of kidnappers and the lover of Lydia (Anna Magnani), a flashy woman of the underworld. Eventually, Ernesto falls out of favor with the gang and is denounced and betrayed by his temperamental mistress. Choosing not to escape, he protectively walks home the little daughter (Eliana Banducci) of one of his former men. And when he fails to stop on the order of pursuing authorities, Ernesto is fatally shot down.

Lattuada's knack for atmosphere—with the help of Aldo Tonti's fine camera work of a postwar city's more sordid side—stands him in good stead here. And there's a fine supporting performance by director Lattuada's wife—and frequent future leading lady—Carla Del Poggio, who is seen briefly as the sister turned prostitute. The expression in her eyes when she first faces her returning brother speaks eloquently for

IL BANDITO   Amedeo Nazzari (left), Carlo Campanini, Mino Doro and Folco Lulli (seated).

Paisà

(PAISAN)

A Coproduction of Organization Films International, Foreign Film Productions, and Capitani Films / 1947

(U.S. release by Mayer-Burstyn, Inc.: 1948)

CREDITS

Director: Roberto Rossellini; *Producers:* Roberto Rossellini, Rod E. Geiger, and Mario Conti; *Screen-*

PAISA Dots M. Johnson and Alfonsino Pasca.

PAISA Gar Moore and Maria Michi.

writers: Federico Fellini, Roberto Rossellini, and Sergio Amidei; *Based on stories by* Victor Haines (*print credits* Alfred Hayes), Marcello Pagliero, Sergio Amidei, Federico Fellini, Roberto Rossellini, Klaus Mann, and Vasco Pratolini; *English Dialogue Scenes:* Annalena Limentani; *English Narrators:* Stuart Legg and Raymond Spottiswoode; *Cinematographer:* Otello Martelli; *Editor:* Eraldo Da Roma; *Music:* Renzo Rossellini; *Running Time:* 124 minutes.

CAST

SICILY: Carmela Sazio *(Carmela)*; Robert Van Loon *(Joe from Jersey)*; Carlo Piscane *(Peasant)*.
NAPLES: Dots M. Johnson *(MP)*; Alfonsino Pasca *(Boy)*.
ROME: Maria Michi *(Francesca)*; Gar Moore *(Fred)*.
FLORENCE: Harriet White *(Harriet)*; Renzo Avanzo *(Massimo)*; Gigi Gori *(Partisan)*.
ROMAGNA: Bill Tubbs *(Capt. Bill Martin)*.
PO DELTA: Dale Edmonds *(Dale)*; Cigolani *(Cigolani)*; Lorena Berg *(Maddalena)*.

PAISA.

41

THE FILM

Roberto Rossellini's follow-up to *Open City* has been called "the purist of all the neorealist films" and a movie "that must rank near the great foreign pictures of all time." It was made possible with the aid of Rod E. Geiger, an ex-G.I. who had, in 1945, formed a company to distribute in the United States the record-setting *Open City*, a print of which he had obtained during his Italian service. Later on, Geiger returned to Italy, supplying Rossellini with hard-to-get film stock and some American actors to supplement the Italian cast, most of whom were nonprofessionals. The film's title, *Paisà*, is a dialect word from southern Italy meaning "one who belongs to a village," its usage here encompassing the notion of community and comradeship.

Linked by narration and periodic glimpses of the Italian map, *Paisan* comprises six otherwise unconnected vignettes of wartime incidents. Each takes place during 1943–45 in a separate region of the country as we follow the Allied advance from Sicily to the Po Valley. A sympathetic young Sicilian woman (Carmela Sazio) is killed for warning the Americans about a nearby German patrol; a black MP (Dots M. Johnson) forgives a street urchin (Alfonsino Pasca) for stealing his boots when he observes the surrounding squalor of the child's Neapolitan home; a Roman prostitute (Maria Michi) shelters a drunken American soldier (Gar Moore) who fails to recognize that she was the innocent girl he fell in love with six months earlier; in Florence, a Resistance leader (Gigi Gori) is killed as his lover, an American nurse (Harriet White), frantically tries to locate him; in a monastery in the Romagna, Franciscan monks fast for the salvation of a Jew and a Protestant who are staying the night; in the marshlands of the Po delta, partisans are rounded up and massacred, including an American (Dale Edmonds) who protests the barbarity.

Essentially, Rossellini's probing cameras eloquently record the meshing of alien cultures, victor and vanquished, Italian and American, as well as the effect of war on individuals as they fight both tyranny and their own weaknesses. Again, lack of studio facilities forced Rossellini to use his country's scarred city streets, buildings, and countryside for his "sets." Understated in its acting and documentary looking in its gritty photography, *Paisan* suggests an extraordinary proximity to the incidents it relates.

As have so many noteworthy foreign films, *Paisan* received the token citation of an Academy Award nomination—but no Oscar.

CACCIA TRAGICA Andrea Checchi and Vivi Gioi.

Caccia Tragica

(TRAGIC HUNT)

A Titanus release of an ANPI Production / 1947

(U.S. release by Films International of America: 1948)

CREDITS

Director: Giuseppe De Santis; *Producer:* G. Giorgio Agliani; *Screenwriters:* Carlo Lizzani, Giuseppe De Santis, Cesare Zavattini, Michelangelo Antonioni, and Umberto Barbaro; *Cinematographer:* Otello Martelli; *Editor:* Mario Serandrei; *Music:* Giuseppe Rosati; *Running Time:* 86 minutes.

CAST

Vivi Gioi *(Daniela/"Lili Marlene")*; Andrea Checchi *(Alberto)*; Massimo Girotti *(Michele)*; Carla Del Poggio

(Giovanna); Vittorio Duse *(Giuseppe)*; Checcho Rissone *(Mimi)*; Umberto Sacripanti *("the Lame")*; Folco Lulli *(Driver)*; Guido Dalla Valle *(the German)*.

THE FILM

A decade before Giuseppe De Santis made an international name for himself guiding Silvana Mangano through her star-making performance in the sensational *Bitter Rice*, he began his film career as a *Cinema* magazine critic, then moved into screenwriting as a collaborator on the scripts of Luchino Visconti's *Ossessione*, Aldo Vergano's *Il Sole Sorge Ancora/Outcry*, and the Roberto Rossellini–Marcello Pagliero *Desiderio/Woman*. De Santis made an auspicious directorial debut at thirty with *Caccia Tragica/Tragic Hunt*, like his colleagues using subject matter reflecting the recent war and its aftermath. Fittingly, the movie was produced by the National Association of Italian Partisans, whose socialist ideology is clearly visible in this fact-based story of the peasants of a collective farm in the Romagna region uniting to track

CACCIA TRAGICA   Massimo Girotti, Andrea Checchi and Carla Del Poggio.

CACCIA TRAGICA   Vittorio Duse, Vivi Gioi, Andrea Checchi and Carla Del Poggio.

43

down the bandits who ambushed a van and stole their year's payroll.

Although accused by some critics of tending toward sentimentality, *Tragic Hunt* advances the movement of neorealism beyond the veristic scope of *Shoeshine* and *The Bicycle Thief* and into lusty melodrama. The bandit gang is led by Daniela, a complex and utterly calculating woman known as "Lili Marlene" because she had been a collaborator (a riveting delineation by Vivi Gioi in perhaps the best performance of her film career), who holds little concern for their hostage, a farmer's young bride (Carla Del Poggio). The bandit queen's lover and partner in crime Alberto (Andrea Checchi) is a partisan and a former concentration-camp inmate whose basic decency has been corrupted by fate and a fatal fascination with his ruthless mistress. Rounding out the central quartet is the kidnapped girl's husband Michele (Massimo Girotti), who recognizes one of the criminals as a fellow ex-prisoner of the Germans.

De Santis's incisive, visually striking direction won deserved praise for bringing urgency and naturalistic detail to a basically conventional plot. Otello Martelli's first-rate location photography helps immeasurably to create and sustain the appropriate atmosphere, as does the background score by Giuseppe Rosati. *Caccia Tragica* was named Best Italian Film at the 1947 Venice Film Festival.

L'Amore

PART ONE: ## Una Voce Umana
(THE HUMAN VOICE)

PART TWO: ## Il Miracolo
(THE MIRACLE)

A Tevere Film Production / 1948

(U.S. release of The Miracle by Joseph Burstyn: 1950)

CREDITS

Producer-Director: Roberto Rossellini; *Screenwriters: (Part One)* Roberto Rossellini, *based on the play* La Voix Humaine *by* Jean Cocteau. *(Part Two)* Tullio Pinelli and Roberto Rossellini, *from a story by* Federico Fellini; *Cinematographers: (Part One)* Robert Juilliard. *(Part Two)* Aldo Tonti; *Editor:* Eraldo Da Roma; *Art Director: (Part One)* Christian Berard; *Music:* Renzo Rossellini; *Running Time:* 79 minutes.

CAST

Part One: Anna Magnani *(The Woman)*.
Part Two: Anna Magnani *(Nannina)*; Federico Fellini *(the Stranger)*.

THE FILM

Roberto Rossellini's cinematic tribute "to the art of Anna Magnani" until recently has been relatively obscure and legendary, for various reasons. Once passionately involved with the volcanic star, who attained international fame with her impassioned performance in his *Open City*, Rossellini began this unintentional diptych in the form of a single feature. *The Human*

L'AMORE "Una Voce Umana" Anna Magnani.

L'AMORE "Il Miracolo" Anna Magnani and Federico Fellini.

Voice was shot in Paris, based on the Jean Cocteau monodrama in which a woman spends some thirty-five minutes on the telephone with her ex-lover, displaying a broad gamut of emotions on the eve of his marriage to her successor. In its various forms (Poulenc made of it an opera for solo soprano), it is a work that generally seems more gratifying as a tour de force for its performing artist than for its audience. Strong actress that she was, Magnani gives it all she's got, unintentionally tending to overwhelm the original one-act play and bring the emotions of Greek tragedy to one betrayed woman's self-absorbed desperation. But given the possibilities of the medium, Cocteau's static drama is perhaps best served on film, where a director like Rossellini can alternate close-ups with long shots and give the single setting a character of its own.

In strong contrast, *The Miracle* presents Magnani as a simple mountain peasant who innocently fancies that an attractive wandering stranger she encounters (portrayed in a rare acting performance by the then-writer Federico Fellini) is actually St. Joseph. Offered wine, she is easily seduced by the young man. Much later, while taking care of some village children, she faints and discovers that she's pregnant. She convinces herself that she'll give birth to a new Messiah and is made a figure of ridicule by her neighbors. Tormented and mocked, she finally climbs the mountain to give birth in a private sanctuary.

The Miracle owes its longtime notoriety to a censor-

ship case that went to the Supreme Court. Originally released separately in the United States in 1950 as part of the three-story *Ways of Love*, it was shown with Marcel Pagnol's *Jofroi* (1934) and Jean Renoir's *A Day in the Country* (1936). But what raised strong religious objections over forty years ago, both here and in Italy, now hardly seems worth the bother. What remains is the record of a bravura display of acting by one of the screen's great artists—Anna Magnani.

L'AMORE "Il Miracolo" Anna Magnani.

Fabiola

A Universalia de Salvo d'Angelo (Paris-Rome) Production / 1949

(U.S. release by United Artists: 1951)

CREDITS

Director: Alessandro Blasetti; *Producer:* Attilio Fattori; *Screenwriters:* Mario Chiari, Diego Fabbri, Cesare Zavattini, Alessandro Blasetti, Suso Cecchi

FABIOLA   Michele Morgan.

D'Amico, and Aldo Fabbri; *Based on the novel by* Nicholas Cardinal Wiseman; *Cinematographer:* Mario Craveri; *Art Director:* Arnaldo Foschini; *Editor:* Mario Sandrei; *Costumes:* Vittorio Colasanti: *Music:* Enzo Masetti; *Running Time:* 183 minutes.

CAST

Michele Morgan *(Fabiola)*; Michel Simon *(Fabio)*; Gino Cervi *(Quadrato)*; Elisa Cegani *(Sira)*; Henri Vidal *(Rhual)*; Massimo Girotti *(Sebastiano)*; Louis Salou *(Fulvio)*; Carlo Ninchi *(Galba)*; Paolo Stoppa *(Manlio Valerio)*; Sergio Tofano *(Luciano)*; Aldo Silvani *(Cassiano)*; Umberto Sacripante *(il Provocatore)*; Franco Interlenghi *(Corvino)*; Goliarda Sapienza *(Cevilia)*; Giovanni Hinrich *(the Judge)*; Silvana Jachino *(Lucilla)*; Virgilio Riento *(Pietro)*; Nerio Bernardi *(Imperial Messenger)*; Maurizio Di Nardo *(Tarcisio)*.

THE FILM

Italy's first postwar superspectacle, this French-Italian coproduction recalled, in its ambitious scope, the mid-teens heyday of such silent-screen epics as *Cabiria*, *Messalina*, *The Last Days of Pompeii* and *Fabiola*'s original 1917 incarnation. *Fabiola*'s 1949 director, Alessandro Blasetti, had handled crowd scenes and costume melodrama before in *1860* and *The Iron Crown*, but *Fabiola* was conceived on an even grander

FABIOLA   Louis Salou (second left), Michele Morgan and Paolo Stoppa (with beard).

46

scale, with a cast of over seven thousand and with millions of lire allotted to sets and costumes alone. This visually splendid black-and-white production was nearly a year in the making, at a reputed cost of a then-staggering 800 million lire. With its strikingly attractive French starring team of the Garboesque Michele Morgan and stalwart newcomer Henri Vidal (later to become husband and wife) and its Italian supporting cast, the three-hours-plus *Fabiola* correctly anticipated great popularity in those two countries. But in the United States, where it opened two years later, United Artists had little faith that it would hold the interest of Americans for so lengthy a "sit." Consequently, it was radically edited to an abridged ninety-six minutes and dubbed into English. To maintain a reasonably accessible narrative in the wake of all these excisions, Marc Connelly and Fred Pressburger were engaged to write an English adaptation, with dialogue by Forrest Izard, that would remain faithful to the ideas and atmosphere of the 183-minute version, which no less than six screenwriters had based loosely on the nineteenth-century novel by Nicholas Cardinal Wiseman.

The story is set in Ancient Rome, which the conquering emperor Constantine intends to convert en masse to Christianity. However, in his path, those Romans who remain faithful to their pagan gods increase their cruel persecution of the city's closeted Christians, with

FABIOLA   Henri Vidal and Michele Morgan.

47

the intent of decimating them before Constantine's arrival. The beautiful Fabiola (Michele Morgan) is the daughter of a Christian-sympathizing aristocrat, and she is torn between family loyalties and her love for the lithe young Roman gladiator Rhual (Henri Vidal), who is secretly an advance emissary for Constantine.

As adapted and dubbed into English, *Fabiola* made little sense, but Mario Craveri's stunning photography of Arnaldo Foschini's sets and Vittorio Colasanti's costumes gave the movie an aura of Hollywood-style glamour that was sufficient to divert and entertain postwar audiences, who had not been privy to such eye-filling screen images since the thirties epics of Carmine Gallone and Cecil B. DeMille.

In *Fabiola's* wake followed such now-forgotten spectacles as *The Queen of Sheba* and *Theodora, Slave Empress*, before the genre evolved into those cheaply made sixties sword-and-sandal adventures featuring the exploits of Maciste, Samson, and Hercules.

Ladri di Biciclette

(THE BICYCLE THIEF / BICYCLE THIEVES)

A Vittorio De Sica production for PDS (Stabilimenti Safa) / 1948

(U.S. release by Mayer-Burstyn, Inc.: 1949)

CREDITS

Director: Vittorio De Sica; *Producer:* Umberto Scarpelli; *Screenwriters:* Oreste Biancoli, Suso Cecchi D'Amico, Vittorio De Sica, Adolfo Franci, Gherardo Gherardi, Gerardo Guerrieri, and Cesare Zavattini; *Based on the novel by* Luigi Bartolini; *Cinematographer:* Carlo Montuori; *Editor:* Eraldo Da Roma; *Art Director:* Antonio Traverso; *Music:* Alessandro Cicognini; *Running Time:* 90 minutes.

CAST

Lamberto Maggiorani *(Antonio Ricci)*; Enzo Staiola *(Bruno Ricci)*; Lianella Carell *(Maria Ricci)*; Elena Altieri *(the Medium)*; Gino Satamerenda *(Baiocco)*; Vittorio Antonucci *(the Thief)*.

48

LADRI DI BICICLETTE Lianella Carell and Lamberto Maggiorani.

LADRI DI BICICLETTE Lamberto Maggiorani and Enzo Staiola.

LADRI DI BICICLETTE   Lamberto Maggiorani and Enzo Staiola.

THE FILM

It was Vittorio De Sica's screenwriter friend Cesare Zavattini who brought to the director's attention a minor novel by Luigi Bartolini called *Ladri di Biciclette* (Bicycle Thieves). Zavattini correctly guessed that the main story line would appeal to De Sica. The eventual adaptation—credited to no less than seven writers—was chiefly the collaboration of De Sica, Zavattini, and the Italian cinema's most important woman writer, Suso Cecchi D'Amico.

Financing the film, however, presented problems. Considering the high esteem U.S. critics and art-house audiences showered on both this film and De Sica's earlier *Shoeshine*, it may now seem difficult to comprehend that postwar Italian audiences couldn't (or wouldn't) support these uncomfortably realistic reflections of their lives, preferring more escapist local comedies and melodramas. American enthusiasm provided a bizarre turn when producer David O. Selznick offered to put up the money, but on the condition that Cary Grant play the leading role. Indeed, Italian eagerness to begin production nearly resulted in acceptance of Selznick's deal—until saner minds prevailed. Eventually, three Italian producers contributed sufficient lire to meet De Sica's customary bottom-line budget. Casting the "Cary Grant part" of Antonio Ricci, the unemployed Roman who finds a poster-hanging job that requires a bicycle to get around the city, was achieved through a fluke. Factory worker Lamberto Maggiorani had answered the casting call for a boy (to play the hero's young son) by bringing along his own offspring. The Maggiorani boy didn't get the role (played by the ideally chosen Enzo Staiola), but his *father's* lean and hungry look so impressed De Sica that he took a chance that paid off. Lamberto Maggiorani never made another important contribution to the screen, but his anguished performance in *The Bicycle Thief* (as the movie was called in the United States) remains one of the most haunting in Italian film history.

There is little in the way of plot. Antonio Ricci's new job depends on his bicycle, which is stolen soon after he begins posting bills in the streets of Rome. Accompanied by his little son Bruno, Ricci spends all of a Sunday searching through the city for the thief (played by the movie's sole professional, Vittorio Antonucci), whom he saw run off with his two-wheeler. Their quest takes them through a missionary soup kitchen, a brothel, and a secondhand bike market, occasionally glimpsing the stolen item and its thief before an eventual confrontation with the culprit. But the Riccis can't prove their case, and the desperate Antonio is

49

finally driven to steal a stranger's bicycle—but so clumsily that he is caught and publicly humiliated in front of his son.

De Sica never allows an essentially sad and tragic story to become maudlin. Instead, humor leavens the events from time to time, and the amateur cast is so well directed that emotions are carefully maintained on a fine line between laughter and tears.

But Italy's Christmas audiences had no interest in such neorealist entertainment and avoided *The Bicycle Thief* altogether. International acclaim ultimately inspired an Italian rerelease of the picture, whose belated Italian success helped De Sica pay back his creditors.

Sometimes referred to as "the keynote film of the Italian neorealist movement," *The Bicycle Thief* won a special 1949 Oscar for Best Foreign Film.

Cielo Sulla Palude

(HEAVEN OVER THE MARSHES)

A Bassoli-Arx Production / 1949

(No U.S. release)

CIELO SULLA PALUDE   Ines Orsini.

CREDITS

Director: Augusto Genina; *Producers:* Carlo and Renato Bassoli; *Screenwriters:* Augusto Genina, Suso Cecchi D'Amico, and Fausto Tozzi; *Cinematographer:* G. R. Aldo; *Editor:* Edmondo Lozzi; *Music:* Antonio Veretti; *Running Time:* 120 minutes.

CAST

Ines Orsini *(Maria Goretti)*; Mauro Matteuci *(Alessandro Serenelli)*; Giovanni Martella *(Maria's Father)*; Assunta Radico *(Maria's Mother)*; Francesco Tomolillo *(Luigi Serenelli)*.

THE FILM

Although he was the director of 150-odd films—ranging from romantic melodrama to Fascist propaganda—during a forty-year career, Augusto Genina (1892–1957) is little-remembered today outside of his native Italy. But foreigners studying the history of European cinema may note that he directed not only the only French-made Louise Brooks vehicle *Prix de*

Beauté (1930) but also a trio of minor Italian classics—*Lo Squadrone Bianco/The White Squadron* (1936), *L'Assedio dell' Alcazar/The Siege of the Alcazar* (1940), and *Cielo Sulla Palude/Heaven Over the Marshes* (1949).

For the latter film, writer-director Genina moved with unexpected ease into the area of neorealism. As did his noted predecessors Roberto Rossellini and Vittorio De Sica, he opted to work here with a cast of nonprofessionals, chosen from the farm people of the bleak, malaria-ridden Pontine marshes near Rome, where the picture was filmed. This was the locale of the fact-based screenplay, which Genina, Suso Cecchi D'Amico, and Fausto Tozzi based on the story of Maria Goretti, a turn-of-the-century religious girl of fourteen who was murdered and, some fifty years later, canonized.

In the film, young Maria (portrayed by beatific-looking Ines Orsini) and her itinerant family settle in the Pontine countryside to eke out a sparse livelihood from the desolate land. Bereft of material possessions, the Gorettis raise their six children with love and a respect for God. Living and working closely with the farmer Luigi Serenelli (Francesco Tomolillo), Maria is friendly with his handsome son Alessandro (Mauro

Matteuci). The lad becomes obsessed with a passionate desire for the girl, pursuing and tormenting her with his advances. When Maria struggles against his attempted rape, the half-crazed Alessandro stabs her and is imprisoned. Following her death in the hospital, Maria is acclaimed a saint by her fellow villagers.

Enriched by G. R. Aldo's artful cinematography of the marsh country, *Heaven Over the Marshes* is truly a director's picture, reflecting Genina's wondrous success with his amateur actors, who look as correctly in character on film as they do in the accompanying still photographs. Perhaps it was their innate empathy with the movie's true-life subject—"method" acting at the simplest level. As one critic surmised: "To a Catholic audience, at least, this is likely to appear one of the most sincere and praiseworthy of the films on religious themes." But at two hours, the movie is really too long and slow moving. And it should be noted that it has been more popularly appreciated in a ninety-seven-minute cut.

Cielo Sulla Palude won Augusto Genina a Best Director citation at the 1949 Venice Film Festival.

CIELO SULLA PALUDE   Ines Orsini and Mauro Matteuci.

CIELO SULLA PALUDE.

Il Mulino del Po

(THE MILL ON THE PO)

A Lux Film Production / 1949

(U.S. release by Lux Films: 1951)

CREDITS

Director: Alberto Lattuada; *Producer:* Carlo Ponti; *Screenwriters:* Federico Fellini and Tullio Pinelli; *Adaptation:* Riccardo Bacchelli, Alberto Lattuada, Carlo Musso, Luigi Comencini, Mario Bonfantini, and Sergio Romano; *Based on the novel* Il Mulino del Po *by* Riccardo Bacchelli; *Cinematographer:* Aldo Tonti; *Editor:* Mario Bonotti; *Art Director:* Aldo Buzzi; *Costumes:* Maria De Matteis; *Music:* Ildebrando Pizzetti; *Running Time:* 105 minutes (*U.S. Running Time:* 96 minutes).

CAST

Carla Del Poggio *(Berta Scacerni)*; Jacques Sernas *(Orbino Verginesi)*; Mario Besesti *(il Clapasson)*; Leda Gloria *(la Sniza)*; Dina Sassoli *(Susanna Verginesi)*; Giulio Cali *(Smarazzacucco)*; Anna Carena *(L'Argia Verginesi)*; Giacomo Giuradei *(Princivalle Scacerni)*; Nino Pavese *(Raibolini)*; Isabella Riva *(Cecilia Scacerni)*; Domenico Viglione Borghese *(Luca Verginesi)*.

THE FILM

Writer-director Alberto Lattuada first came to the attention of U.S. audiences with the postwar dramas *Il Bandito/The Bandit* and *Senza Pieta/Without Pity*, filmed in the neorealist style and featuring his actress-wife Carla Del Poggio. Following those contemporary works, he chose to film an adaptation of *The Mill on the Po,* a period piece by novelist Riccardo Bacchelli about agrarian struggles and the beginnings of socialism in the northern Italy of 1876. Central to the film is a love story concerning a young couple victimized by family rivalries.

Berta Scacerni (Carla Del Poggio), the daughter of the miller Cecilia Scacerni (Isabella Riva), is engaged to Orbino Verginesi (Jacques Sernas), the son of a landowner. To avoid inspection of the mill's meter by

IL MULINO DEL PO   Carla Del Poggio, Jacques Sernas, Nino Pavese and Dina Sassoli.

tax officials, Berta's brutish, bullheaded brother Princivalle (Giacomo Giuradei) sets fire to the mill and is arrested. With the loss of their mill, the Scacernis are reduced to such dire circumstances that Berta accepts a servant's job in the Verginesi household. Luca Verginesi (Domenico Viglione Borghese) tries without success to impose his will on the local peasants, who take a militant position against certain social reforms. After he hands out eviction notices, the result is a general strike. Amid the confrontations, Berta, who fails to sympathize with the strikers, is publicly humiliated by Orbino's sister Susanna (Dina Sassoli). But her brother Princivalle is given to believe that it was Orbino who insulted Berta, resulting in tragedy for the star-crossed lovers.

Although some nine minutes were deleted from the movie prior to its American release (Lux Films executives must have paid heed to *Variety*'s review, commenting that "tighter editing would help its chances a lot"), the results brought some confusion to Bosley Crowther of the *New York Times*, who was nonetheless impressed with *The Mill on the Po*'s epic sweep. Certainly a generous budget and above-average production values are evident on the screen, from Aldo Tonti's beautiful location photography to the careful reconstruction of nineteenth-century period detail. Carla Del Poggio and Jacques Sernas make a handsome pair of tragic lovers, and there is a particularly effective performance by Giacomo Giuradei, the young

IL MULINO DEL PO.

IL MULINO DEL PO   Jacques Sernas and Carla Del Poggio.

54

nonactor (an actual farmer) whom director Lattuada discovered in the Po Valley and wisely took a chance on. *The Mill on the Po* may, as some critics have complained, have a surfeit of episodic detail and character incident, but its pictorial quality and richness of style would seem to make the film overdue for rediscovery.

Riso Amaro

(BITTER RICE)

A Lux Film Production / 1949

(U.S. release by Lux Films America: 1950)

CREDITS

Director: Giuseppe De Santis; *Producer:* Dino De Laurentiis; *Screenwriters:* Corrado Alvaro, Giuseppe De Santis, Carlo Lizzani, Carlo Musso, Ivo Perilli, and Gianni Puccini; *Cinematographer:* Otello Martelli; *Editor:* Giovanna Valeri; *Costumes:* Anna Gobbi; *Music:* Goffredo Petrassi; *Running Time:* 107 minutes.

CAST

Silvana Mangano *(Silvana)*; Vittorio Gassman *(Walter)*; Doris Dowling *(Francesca)*; Raf Vallone *(Marco)*; Checco Rissone *(Aristide)*; Nico Pepe *(Beppe)*; Adriana Sivieri *(Celeste)*; Lia Corelli *(Amelia)*; Maria Grazia Francia *(Gabriella)*; Dedi Ristori *(Anna)*; Anna Maestri *(Irene)*; Mariemma Bardi *(Gianna)*.

THE FILM

Before Gina, Sophia, Claudia and all the other Italian ladies whose vital statistics heralded their presence on international movie screens, there was Silvana Mangano. Not yet twenty when she created a sensation as the nubile star attraction of *Bitter Rice*, Mangano drew understandable critical comparisons—on a physical level—with both Rita Hayworth and Ingrid Bergman. Nor was her acting ability anything to be ashamed of. The daughter of an English mother and a Spanish-Sicilian father, Mangano had studied ballet for seven years, won the title of "Miss Rome 1946," became a top-echelon model, and played bit parts in several films prior to *Bitter Rice*. It is not difficult to understand what the newly formed production team of Carlo Ponti and Dino De Laurentiis saw in this sullen-faced, five-foot six-inch, 127-pound redhead when they were casting the central role of Silvana, the sensation-seeking rice-field worker in *Bitter Rice*. Not long thereafter, De Laurentiis married her, and they became parents of two daughters and a son, whose care subsequently took precedence over Mangano's acting career. Thus, Lollobrigida, Cardinale, and especially Loren soon surpassed Mangano in the Italian sexpot sweepstakes. When she tragically died of a heart attack in 1990 at the age of sixty, it is doubtful that the name Silvana Mangano meant very much to the average American moviegoer. And despite her various other film achievements, her obituaries understandably singled out *Bitter Rice* as the vehicle with which she remained most closely associated.

In 1950, with its provocative poster-art poses of Silvana standing in a rice field, her buxom figure clad in abbreviated shorts, thigh-length stockings and a tight sweater, *Bitter Rice* created a worldwide sensation. For American audiences, its advertised offer of "an earthy drama of human passions!" promised for-

RISO AMARO   Silvana Mangano.

bidden pleasures with which censor-restricted, U.S.-made movies couldn't hope to compete.

Following closely on the heels of such neorealistic Italian classics as *Shoeshine, Open City,* and *The Bicycle Thief, Bitter Rice* arrived with advance pretensions of social responsibility that soon dissipated into sexy melodrama. And so what ostensibly went into production as a serious drama about the exploitation of Italy's Po Valley women rice-field workers emerged as a steamy popular tale about an impressionable girl

(Mangano) who falls for the sinister glamour of a slick, sadistic crook (overacted by Vittorio Gassman), who plans to steal the rice crop. American actress Doris Dowling *(The Lost Weekend, The Blue Dahlia)* made an effective Italian debut as Gassman's reformed moll (and Mangano's fellow rice harvester), and Raf Vallone, as a virile army sergeant attracted to both Mangano and Dowling, inaugurated a long international film career.

Bitter Rice remains director Giuseppe De Santis's

most memorable contribution to the export of Italian films. As for Silvana Mangano—from her initial appearance, executing a brazenly erotic dance before entraining to the rice fields of the Po—it was the natural stepping-stone to 1952's popular triangle drama *Anna* (reuniting her with Gassman and Vallone) and what then seemed international fame had the actress not put her responsibilities as Signora De Laurentiis first.

RISO AMARO Raf Vallone, Vittorio Gassman and Silvana Mangano.

RISO AMARO Doris Dowling and Raf Vallone.

RISO AMARO Silvana Mangano.

Luci del Varietà

(VARIETY LIGHTS)

A Film Capitolium Production / 1951

(U.S. release by Pathe-Contemporary: 1965)

CREDITS

Directors: Alberto Lattuada and Federico Fellini; *Producer:* Alberto Lattuada; *Screenwriters:* Federico Fell-

57

ini, Ennio Flaiano, Alberto Lattuada, and Tullio
Pinelli; *Cinematographer:* Otello Martelli; *Editor:*
Mario Bonotti; *Art Director:* Aldo Bizzi; *Music:* Felice
Lattuada; *Running Time:* 93 minutes.

CAST

Peppino De Filippo *(Checco Dal Monte)*; Carla Del
Poggio *(Liliana Antonelli)*; Giulietta Masina *(Melina
Amour)*; Folco Lulli *(Adelmo Conti)*; John Kitzmiller
(Johnny, the Trumpet Player); Dante Maggio *(Remo,
the Comedian)*; Carlo Romano *(La Rosa, the Lawyer)*;
Silvio Bagolini *(the Journalist)*; Gina Mascetti *(Valeria
De Sole)*; Checco Durante *(the Theater Owner)*; Joe
Faletta *(Bill)*; Enrico Piergentili *(the Business Manag-
er)*; Mario De Angelis *(the Maestro)*; Fanny Marchio
(the Soubrette); Giacomo Furia *(the Duke)*; Vanja
Orico *(the Gypsy Singer)*.

THE FILM

Prior to directing this, his first film (in collaboration
with established director Alberto Lattuada), Federico
Fellini had spent years writing radio scripts and collab-
orating on movie screenplays—one of which offered
him the small but pivotal acting role of the shepherd
who seduces Anna Magnani in *The Miracle*, half of the
two-part Roberto Rossellini film entitled *L'Amore.*
Before *Variety Lights*, Fellini had worked as assistant
director to Lattuada, so this was a natural step up,

58

based as it was on Fellini's original story. Many have speculated as to just who did what in this collaborative effort—with the most educated guess presuming that Lattuada handled the overall action and the cameras, while Fellini guided the actors.

The film opens during a performance by a second-rate traveling vaudeville troupe, led by middle-aged Checco Dal Monte (Peppino De Filippo). Watching, enthralled, in the audience is a stagestruck, ambitious girl named Liliana Antonelli (director Lattuada's wife Carla Del Poggio), who turns up backstage at the next town. Her face and figure immediately impress the womanizing Checco, who auditions her. Liliana's song-and-dance talents are rudimentary, but her fresh beauty beguiles the show's audience at a near-disastrous performance, which she manages to rescue. And so Checco's showgirl mistress Melina Amour (codirector Fellini's wife Giulietta Masina), is shunted aside for the new star. Soon Liliana wants star billing above even Checco, so it is no loss when she abruptly leaves the troupe to join a bigger, flashier one—a job she gets via a wealthy businessman. Checco returns to the forgiving Melina, and both companies wind up heading for their next engagement on the same train—Liliana in a first-class sleeping car, while Checco and Melina share the close quarters of third-class. And when a pretty young thing sits nearby, Cheeco's wandering eye lights up. He is wondering whether she might be an actress. . . .

Loaded with wonderful comedy touches, *Variety Lights* owes much to the talents of De Filippo, Masina, and company, who help create a memorable little world of tacky, itinerant, small-town vaudevillians. The seamless efforts of Fellini and Lattuada, who apparently share not only talented actress-wives but also a witty eye for detail, contrast the seemingly

LUCI DEL VARIETA Dante Maggio, Giulietta Masina, Peppino De Filippo, Gina Mascetti and Checco Durante.

glamorous with the squalid realities of show business at its lowest level.

Variety Lights was not very successful in Italy, and Fellini returned, for a time, to assisting other directors. That the film did not reach the United States until fifteen years later reflects the mid-sixties box-office draw of Fellini and Masina.

Bellissima

A Bellissima Films Production / 1952

(U.S. release by Italian Films Export: 1953)

CREDITS

Director: Luchino Visconti; *Producer:* Salvo d'Angelo; *Assistant Directors:* Francesco Rosi and Franco Zeffirelli; *Screenwriters:* Suso Cecchi D'Amico, Francesco Rosi, and Luchino Visconti; *Based on a story by* Cesare Zavattini; *Cinematographers:* Piero Portalupi and Paul Ronald; *Editor:* Mario Serandrei; *Art Director:* Gianni Polidori; *Costumes:* Piero Tosi; *Music:* Franco Mannino; *Running Time:* 130 minutes.

CAST

Anna Magnani *(Maddalena Cecconi)*; Walter Chiari *(Alberto Annovazzi)*; Tina Apicella *(Maria Cecconi)*; Gastone Renzelli *(Spartaco Cecconi)*; Alessandro Blasetti *(Himself)*; Tecla Scarano *(the Acting Teacher)*; Lola Braccini *(the Photographer's Wife)*; Arturo Bragaglia *(the Photographer)*; Linda Sini *(Mimmetta)*.

THE FILM

As in *Stella Dallas, Imitation of Life,* and their derivatives, mother love and sacrifice have traditionally served a dramatic purpose on film. In *Bellissima*, Luchino Visconti's first movie since the failure of his much-admired *La Terra Trema* in 1948, that theme is employed for comedy, often of a bittersweet variety. This, then, was to be a perfect vehicle for Italy's beloved Anna Magnani, filmed in the wake of her split (both professional and personal) with the Ingrid Bergman–smitten Roberto Rossellini.

Offering a rare and interesting look behind the scenes of Italian moviemaking at Cinecittá, *Bellissima* ("most beautiful one") casts Magnani as Maddalena

Cecconi, the working-class mother of a plain, awkward little girl named Maria (Tina Apicella). When she hears that a film studio is looking for a child actress, the ambitious Maddalena hustles Maria off to the audition, where she meets Alberto Annovazzi (Walter Chiari), an opportunistic studio employee, who offers to help. When Maria is chosen for a screen test, Maddalena sacrifices everything to present the child at her best: She engages an elderly actress (Tecla Scarano) to give her acting lessons, and she subsequently visits costumers, photographers, and hairdressers—all with the savings with which her husband Spartaco (Gastone Renzelli) planned to buy them a house. She even agrees to give Alberto money to buy gifts for studio personnel who might favor the child. In one of *Bellissima*'s more entertaining sequences, during a sexually charged outing alone with Alberto, Maddalena almost succumbs to his persuasive charms—a scene made all the more believable by the expressive acting of Chiari and, especially, Magnani.

But *Bellissima*'s cruel highlight comes after little Maria's test, when the stagestruck mother and daughter sneak into a projection booth and witness the talentless results, which provoke derisive comments and laughter from the attendant studio personnel. Maddalena invades the screening room, upbraiding

BELLISSIMA   Gastone Renzelli, Tina Apicella and Anna Magnani.

BELLISSIMA   Anna Magnani
and Walter Chiari.

the executives for their meanness, before taking the
child home. Not even the subsequent offer of a contract
for Maria can change Maddalena's mind. Although her
dreams of being mother to an Italian Shirley Temple
are shattered, the child will always remain her "bellissima."

Under Visconti's sensitive direction, Magnani's depiction of a Roman *Gypsy*'s Mama Rose displays a
brilliant range of emotions. For her work here, she
received the Italian Film Critics "Silver Ribbon" as
1952's Best Actress.

Considering Visconti's well-known penchant for
length, one might carp at this "little" film's original
running time of two hours and ten minutes. And
although some character development may be lacking,
the reader might find greater enjoyment in either of the
two shorter versions reputed to exist at, respectively,
95 and 100 minutes.

61

BELLISSIMA   Tina Apicella and Anna Magnani.

Roma, Ore 11

(ROME, 11 O'CLOCK)

*A Transcontinental Films–Titanus Production / 1952
(U.S. release by Times Film Corp.: 1953)*

CREDITS

Director: Giuseppe De Santis; *Producer:* Paul Graetz;
Screenwriters: Cesare Zavattini, Giuseppe De Santis,
B. Franchini, R. Sonego, and Gianni Puccini; *Cinematographer:* Otello Martelli; *Art Director:* Leon Bar-
sacq; *Music:* Mario Nascimbene; *Running Time:* 101
minutes.

CAST

Carla Del Poggio *(Luciana)*; Massimo Girotti *(Nando)*;
Lucia Bosé *(Simona)*; Raf Vallone *(Carlo)*; Elena Varzi
(Adriana); Lea Padovani *(Caterina)*; Delia Scala *(An-
gelina)*; Irene Galter *(Clara)*; Paolo Stoppa *(Clara's
Father)*; Maria Grazia Francia *(Cornelia)*; Eva Van-
icek *(Gianna)*; Armand Francioli *(Romolo)*; Nando di
Claudio *(Ferrari)*.

THE FILM

Based on a tragic, newsworthy accident that occurred
in Rome in 1950, Giuseppe De Santis's neorealistic
Rome, 11 O'Clock was the second and better of two
Italian melodramas to exploit the incident. Augusto
Genina's earlier *Tre Storie Proibite/Three Forbidden
Stories* was more vulgarly recounted.

Answering a want ad for a single stenographer, more
than two hundred girls crowd the staircase of a Roman
office building. Luciana (Carla Del Poggio), the anx-
ious wife of an unemployed workman (Massimo Girotti), eagerly pushes ahead of the others. But when she
emerges from the interview, Luciana is verbally attacked by the other applicants, who become increasingly agitated as the departing young woman passes
them. Just as she reaches ground level, the weight of
their struggling bodies causes the staircase to collapse,
resulting in a great many casualties. Luciana runs off
in panic.

The story now flashes back to concentrate on the
lives of certain of those unfortunate girls and the
factors that led to their being on that staircase. Simona

ROMA, ORE 11 Delia Scala, Lea Padovani, Carla Del Poggio,
Elena Varzi and Lucia Bosé.

(Lucia Bosé) is the wife of Carlo (Raf Vallone), a
well-born but destitute artist whose relatives disap-
prove of her. Pregnant, unwed Adriana (Elena Varzi)
comes from a respectable, middle-class family and
determines to survive on her own. The prostitute
Caterina (Lea Padovani) hopes to start a new, self-
respecting life in an office job. Angelina (Delia Scala) is
determined to break away from her previous employment as a domestic servant.

Following the accident, a police investigation is held
at the damaged building, and the conscience-stricken
Luciana overhears the reasons for the stairway's collapse. Learning that one of the victims has died, she
considers suicide but is deterred by Nando. Confused
by Luciana's distress, combined with the innocent
protestations of both the building's architect and its
owner, the police terminate the case as "not proven."
Meanwhile, on the street outside, a girl who applied for
the typist position waits for the next round of interviews to begin.

De Santis stages the staircase disaster as well as the
rescue operations that ensue most convincingly. But, as
in his earlier *Bitter Rice*, the director's expression of
protest against the era's unemployment problems and
the social conditions that underlie the script's melodramatics result in overly familiar plot clichés. In a large
cast of well-known faces, the most believable performances are those of Carla Del Poggio, Lucia Bosé, and

ROMA, ORE 11.

ROMA, ORE 11   Massimo Girotti
and Carla Del Poggio.

Lea Padovani in the film's meatiest roles. Eschewing his customary flair for the flamboyant, De Santis sharply delineates the different stories involved, keenly pinpointing the script's moments of satire and humor while at the same time zeroing in on the more tragic and the sentimental. But neorealism is the thrust of *Rome, 11 O'Clock*, and obscure though the film has now become, it remains vivid in the memories of those who saw it forty-odd years ago.

Umberto D.

A Rizzoli-De Sica-Amato Production / 1952

(U.S. release by Edward Harrison: 1955)

CREDITS

Director: Vittorio De Sica: *Screenwriters:* Cesare Zavattini and Vittorio De Sica; *Cinematographer:* G. R. Aldo; *Editor:* Eraldo Da Roma; *Art Director:* Virgilio Marchi; *Music:* Alessandro Cicognini; *Running Time:* 89 minutes.

CAST

Carlo Battisti *(Umberto Domenico Ferrari)*; Maria Pia Casilio *(Maria)*; Lina Gennari *(Elena, the Landlady)*; Alberto Albani Barbieri *(the Landlady's "Fiancé")*; and Eleana Simova, Elena Rea, and Memmo Carotenuto.

THE FILM

Vittorio De Sica's modest classic has been called "the last great film of the postwar film renaissance in Italy," meaning, of course, that naturalistic black-and-white movement that brought us, most notably, Rossellini's *Open City* and *Paisan* and De Sica's *Shoeshine* and *The Bicycle Thief*. Frequently, those directors employed nonprofessional "actors" for not only their films' smaller roles but their leading ones as well. And such was the case with *Umberto D.*, whose protagonist, Umberto D. was portrayed by a college professor named Carlo Battisti, who had reportedly never acted before. Since his low-keyed character is not called upon to display any great array of bigger-than-life histrionics, Battisti is no less than perfect in everything

director De Sica asks of him. Laurence Olivier could not have performed the part any better.

Umberto D. is what is generally referred to as "a little film"—in its scope of physical dimensions and size of cast. But there its "littleness" ends, for *Umberto D.* is as big as the human spirit, as all-encompassing as life itself. Unfortunately, for its box-office value, it has little to attract the public: there are no "names" in its cast, and its themes of old age and loneliness have never been known to draw moviegoers. As such, it joins three other motion-picture gems that found enough financial support to tell stories of emotional truth among the elderly: Leo McCarey's *Make Way for Tomorrow*, Akira Kurosawa's *Ikiru*, and Bryan Forbes's *The Whisperers*.

The film's story is deceptively simple. Umberto D. Ferrari (Battisti) is an old-age pensioner who appears to have no surviving relatives and few friends aside from his little mongrel dog Flag. His pension has become insufficient to pay for his needs, and he owes his landlady (Lina Gennari) so much back rent that she heartlessly threatens to turn him out. She also makes use of his room, when she knows he is out, to rent to couples for daytime assignations, a fact Umberto is shocked to discover one day when he returns home too soon. His one ally in this household is the maid Maria (Maria Pia Casilio), who confides that she is pregnant by one of her two boyfriends (she isn't sure which) and fears the landlady will fire her as soon as she learns her secret.

To save himself money, Umberto embroiders on a chill he is suffering and gets an ambulance to take him to the hospital for a week. But during his absence the landlady not only throws Flag out on the street but also begins remodeling the house, tearing out the wall of his room to do so. His living conditions and the ever-threatening landlady turn Umberto inevitably to thoughts of suicide, for he cannot bring himself to beg on street corners. His feeble efforts to seek handouts from former business colleagues have proved to no avail. First, Umberto tries, in vain, to find a new home for Flag, whom he's found. And then he decides that they'll die together in front of a train. But when the dog struggles free of Umberto's arms and runs from the railroad tracks, the old man loses heart. In the final scene, he succeeds in convincing Flag to trust him again, that this time he won't try any such drastic means of solving their problems. And so, in an upbeat (if not quite "happy") ending, man and animal are together in love but little else.

De Sica refrains from preaching here, and the script he developed in collaboration with Cesare Zavattini sticks to the austere essentials and is devoid of the

UMBERTO D. Maria Pia
Casilio and Carlo Battisti.

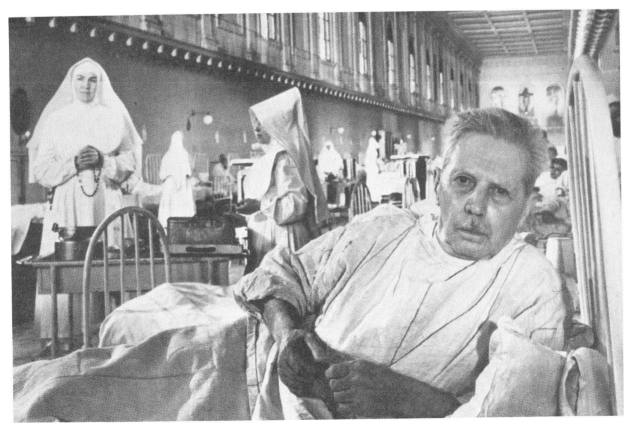

UMBERTO D. Carlo Battisti.

65

sentiment that usually accompanies man-and-his-dog stories.

Battisti's performance is totally honest; he is an impatient and slightly testy fellow, but he has his principles, and he has his pride. Maria Pia Casilio is equally right as the none-too-bright but good-hearted housemaid, and Lina Gennari is all self-satisfied heartlessness and calculated charm as the landlady, looking like an Amazon-sized Lana Turner. She's the one character De Sica tends to caricature.

Like many great films, *Umberto D.* was not a major award winner, but it brought Cesare Zavattini an Oscar nomination for his Original Story, and it tied among the New York Film Critics with Clouzot's *Diabolique* for Best Foreign Film of 1955.

Pane, Amore e Fantasia

(BREAD, LOVE AND DREAMS)

A Titanus Production / 1954

(U.S. release by Italian Films Export: 1954)

CREDITS

Director: Luigi Comencini; *Producer:* Marcello Girosi; *Screenwriters:* Luigi Comencini and Ettore Margadonna; *Based on a story by* Ettore Margadonna; *Cinematographer:* Arturo Gallea; *Editor:* Mario Serandrei; *Art Director:* Gastone Medin; *Music:* Alessandro Cicognini; *Running Time:* 90 minutes.

CAST

Vittorio De Sica *(Marshal Antonio Carotenuto)*; Gina Lollobrigida *(La Bersagliera)*; Marisa Merlini *(Annarella)*; Roberto Risso *(Carabiniere Pietro Stelluti)*; Virgilio Riento *(Don Emidio)*; Tina Pica *(Caramella)*; Vittoria Crispo *(the Mother)*; Maria Pia Casilio *(Paoletta)*; Memmo Carotenuto *(Carabiniere Baiocchi)*.

THE FILM

In Italy, where she was already justly celebrated—more for her peppery movie-star personality and 36-22-35 measurements than for her acting talent—the beautiful Gina Lollobrigida had perhaps her greatest

success in *Bread, Love and Dreams*, a pleasant rural comedy by Luigi Comencini, a director best known for exploitation melodramas like *Persiane Chiuse/Behind Closed Shutters* and *La Tratta della Bianche/Girls Marked Danger*. At a salary in the neighborhood of $100,000 per picture, Lollobrigida was enjoying the prestige of being among the world's then most highly paid actresses. In the U.S., she appeared in John Huston's unpopular Humphrey Bogart adventure, *Beat the Devil*, and art-house filmgoers initially knew her from a pair of Gérard Philipe movies, *Fanfan la Tulipe* and *Les Belles de Nuit/Beauties of the Night*, in which a sensational, partly censored bathing scene was actually—according to Gina—shot with a body double. But it was *Bread, Love and Dreams* that made the deepest inroads in establishing "La Lollo" as a box-office favorite among American men. On a visit to New York to help publicize the film's first-run engagement, she told an interviewer: "I am surprise [sic] so many people know me. In Italy, I expect this. Here, no. It is very nice."

Bread, Love and Dreams is stronger in characterization than in script, although Ettore Margadonna's original story received an Academy Award nomination. In an unnamed Italian mountain village, a handsome, middle-aged bachelor named Antonio Carotenuto (Vittorio De Sica) arrives as marshal of the local carabinieri. In the market for a wife, he is immediately attracted to a vivacious and independent orphan girl known as La Bersagliera (Lollobrigida). But she has serious eyes only for Stelluti (Roberto Risso), a young member of the carabinieri so shy that he can barely bring himself to speak to her. Annarella (Marisa Merlini), the village midwife, seems a more likely romantic prospect for Carotenuto, but he is warned by the priest (Virgilio Riento) that his behavior as a bachelor will be closely watched by the local gossips.

The spitfire Bersagliera gets into a brawl and is incarcerated for the night, suggesting to Carotenuto that she might be "easy." But that notion is disproved when she resists his advances. Romance eventually blooms for the girl and Stelluti after Carotenuto reassigns the young man to the forest area frequented by La Bersagliera. Finally, the marshal proposes to Annarella, and as the village celebrates the Feast of St. Anthony with a display of fireworks, it appears that wedding bells will soon toll.

Shooting on location, Luigi Comencini handled this screenplay he coauthored with Ettore Margadonna in a rather ordinary fashion, bypassing any and all social issues in the interest of pure escapist entertainment. But Lollobrigida responded to the story's opportunities with infectious, vivacious energy, and she played so well opposite the smooth old pro De Sica that the pair

PANE, AMORE E FANTASIA Maria Pia Casilio, Memmo Carotenuto, Vittorio De Sica, Gina Lollobrigida and Roberto Risso.

PANE, AMORE E FANTASIA   Roberto Risso and Gina Lollobrigida.

Luciano Trasatti, and Carlo Carlini; *Editor:* Rolando Benedetti; *Art Director:* Mario Chiari; *Costumes:* M. Marinari Bomarzi; *Music:* Nino Rota; *Running Time:* 109 minutes.

CAST

Franco Fabrizi *(Fausto)*; Franco Interlenghi *(Moraldo)*; Leonora Ruffo *(Sandra)*; Alberto Sordi *(Alberto)*; Leopoldo Trieste *(Leopoldo)*; Riccardo Fellini *(Riccardo)*; Jean Brochard *(Fausto's Father)*; Claude Farere *(Alberto's Sister)*; Carlo Romano *(Michele, Fausto's Employer)*; Lida Baarova *(Giulia, Michele's Wife)*; Enrico Viarisio and Paola Borboni *(Parents of Moraldo and Sandra)*; Arlette Sauvage *(Lady in Cinema)*; Vira Silenti *(Cinesina, Leopoldo's Date)*; Maja Nipora *(Soubrette)*; Achille Majeroni *(Old Comedian)*; Silvio Bagolini *(the Fool)*.

THE FILM

This dark-textured comedy-drama, satirizing the postwar generation of shiftless young males from mid-

teamed again with Comencini the following year for a popular sequel, *Pane, Amore e Gelosia* (called *Frisky* in the United States). A subsequent follow-up, directed by Dino Risi in 1955, replaced Gina with her closest rival, Sophia Loren, in a third comedy, inconclusively named simply *Pane, Amore e . . .* (Americans saw it retitled *Scandal in Sorrento.*)

I Vitelloni

(THE YOUNG AND THE PASSIONATE)

A Coproduction of PEG Films (Rome) and Cité Films (Paris) / 1953

(U.S. release by Janus Films: 1956)

CREDITS

Director: Federico Fellini; *Producer:* Lorenzo Pegoraro; *Screenwriters:* Federico Fellini, Ennio Flaiano, and Tullio Pinelli; *Cinematographers:* Otello Martelli,

dle-class families, was Fellini's second film as a solo director (following the Alberto Sordi comedy *The White Sheik*). Seeking a more marketable title, the movie's American distributor came up with *The Young and the Passionate*, which gives it a steamy implication not fulfilled by its content. But *I Vitelloni* (its title is drawn from Italian slang, referring to overgrown adolescents) isn't really that commercial a movie; Fellini never elects to capitalize on the film's more exploitable aspects at all. Indeed, producer Lorenzo Pegoraro even had trouble finding a distributor for his film.

The episodic story roughly covers a year in a small town on the Romagna coast where five middle-class young men in their twenties drift about, more concerned with male bonding than establishing any substantial goals for the future. Handsome, womanizing Fausto (Franco Fabrizi) has got his girlfriend Sandra (Leonora Ruffo) pregnant, a revelation that coincides with her winning the local Miss Siren contest—and fainting dead away. Sandra's introspective brother Moraldo (Franco Interlenghi, of De Sica's *Shoeshine*), is torn between family loyalty and his friendship with Fausto, whose circle also includes mama's boy and gambler Alberto (Alberto Sordi); the intellectual, aspiring playwright Leopoldo (Leopoldo Trieste); and would-be pop singer Riccardo (Riccardo Fellini, the director's brother).

A quiet but hasty marriage is arranged between Sandra and the irresponsible Fausto, whose suspicious

I VITELLONI Leonora Ruffo and Franco Fabrizi.

father prevents his running away to Milan. But marriage doesn't hamper Fausto's style, and he alternately pursues a sensuous-looking cinema neighbor (Arlette Sauvage) and the star soubrette (Maja Nipora) of a traveling variety show. Forced to seek employment because of his growing family responsibilities, Fausto is fired after making an unsuccessful play for his boss's wife (Lida Baarova).

At the film's close, Fausto at last appears to be settling down, after Sandra leaves home with their baby, forcing the young husband to seriously reconsider his values. When his working sister runs off with a married man, Alberto is faced with having to go to work to support their mother. Leopoldo's hopes are deflated when the old actor who takes an interest in his play apparently harbors an even *greater* interest in Leopoldo. And Moraldo (Fellini's own counterpart in this semiautobiographical film) faces the most positive future of all: He leaves family and friends to relocate in the big city.

Viewed from the nineties, *I Vitelloni* may look a bit quaint. Although these youths pursue irresponsible lives centering only on themselves, they dress immaculately in shirts, suits, and ties, and their manners are as respectable as their grooming. And despite such

digressions as Alberto's sporting female drag for a costume ball, none seems dangerously at odds with society. Nino Rota's very romantic background score tends to detract from whatever realism Fellini takes pains to establish in his narrative. But the acting is exemplary, with Fabrizi and Interlenghi particularly outstanding in their respective delineations of self-deluding narcissism and quietly maturing intelligence.

A relatively obscure early gem from a master filmmaker, *I Vitelloni* won a Silver Ribbon at the 1953 Venice Film Festival.

Aida

An OSCAR Film Production / 1953

(U.S. release by Italian Films Export: 1954)

CREDITS

Director: Clemente Fracassi; *Producers:* Ferrucio De Martino and Federico Teti; *Screenwriters:* Carlo Castelli, Anna Gobbi, Giuseppe Morelli, and Paolo Salviucci; *Ferraniacolor Cinematographer:* Piero Portalupi; *Editor:* Mario Bonatti; *Art Director:* Flavio Mogherini; *Costumes:* Maria De Matteis and Piero Tosi; *Choreographer:* Margherita Wallman; *Music:* from the opera by Giuseppe Verdi; *Musical Supervisor:* Renzo Rossellini; *Performed by* the Italian State Radio Orchestra and the Ballet of the Rome Opera House; *Running Time:* 95 minutes.

CAST

Sophia Loren (*Aida;* sung by Renata Tebaldi); Lois Maxwell (*Amneris;* sung by Ebe Stignani); Luciano Della Marra (*Radames;* sung by Giuseppe Campora); Afro Poli (*Amonasro;* sung by Gino Bechi); Antonio Casinelli (*Ramfis;* sung by Giulio Neri); Enrico Formichi (*the Pharaoh;* sung by himself); and dancers Alba Arnova, Victor Ferrari, and Ciro Pardo of the Rome Opera Ballet.

THE FILM

Until recently, under the artistic auspices of Franco Zeffirelli, opera on the screen has been problematic. In 1953, the Italians made several strides forward with the first color movie devoted to a single opera, *Aida*. Verdi's 1871 masterpiece had all of the suitable elements for the screen, but it would have to be condensed; after all, what movie audience would sit still for an operatic motion picture lasting over three hours? In addition to retaining the work's important musical highlights and adding some brief desert scenes of martial action, it was decided that an offscreen narrator would help advance the plot. And so the filmmakers managed to reduce all of Verdi's *Aida* to a then-average movie running time of ninety-five minutes. Although lovers of the original work probably felt sorely cheated, this *Aida* undoubtedly helped to spread the popularity of opera. Concert impresario Sol Hurok

thought enough of it to cosponsor its release in America, where it was sold as a prestige attraction. And, to aid that "sell," Hurok had the operatic names of Renata Tebaldi, Giuseppe Campora, and Ebe Stignani. For some, the drawback was that only those singers' glorious *voices*, emanating from the throats of actors chosen for their visual appeal, would be heard. So it was that a young Sophia Loren, in only her second leading role (following a long string of bits and supporting parts), came to the attention of the English-speaking public. In dark wigs and makeup, Loren's appearance was as strikingly beautiful as was Tebaldi's voice.

As the captive Ethiopian princess who has become a

AIDA   Sophia Loren.

AIDA Lois Maxwell and Sophia Loren.

AIDA "The Nile Scene" Sophia Loren.

slave to the Egyptian pharaoh's daughter Amneris, Aida shares a secret love with Radames, captain of the guard and the one man Amneris herself covets. The discovery of their love—and Radames's refusal to forsake Aida—results in his condemnation as a traitor to the Egyptians. He is sentenced to death by entombment, a fate shared by Aida, who has hidden herself away in the tomb before it is sealed. The opera closes as the lovers raise their voices in eternal love while Amneris bemoans her loss.

One wonders if those who have denounced this *Aida*'s acting performances as stiff and inept have actually seen this film. A recent viewing reveals that Sophia Loren, at eighteen, was already very much in touch with her dramatic sensibilities; one need only watch her in her scenes with the expressive Lois Maxwell and the handsome but wooden Luciano Della Marra to note a surprisingly mature range of emotions appropriate to her character. Considering that her *Aida* director is otherwise best known in this country for the steamy but inconsequential 1952 melodrama *Sensualitá* (with Eleonora Rossi-Drago and Marcello

AIDA   Sophia Loren and Luciano Della Marra.

Mastroianni), one wonders how much credit is due Clemente Fracassi for Loren's affecting portrayal. The actress has reported that she won the role by default, after Gina Lollobrigida had rejected the opportunity "because she felt that serving as a stand-in for a singer was beneath her star status."

Aida's lush atmosphere of star-crossed love in a warm climate belies the fact that it was shot in what Loren has described as "an unheated studio in the middle of winter." As she amusingly recalls: "Every time I opened my mouth to sing, puffs of steam would fill the air. To correct this, I chewed ice before each take, frosting my mouth, and an assistant stood just out of camera range with a powerful hair dryer, which he aimed at my lips."

Deservedly, *Aida* made an international star of Sophia Loren. But another decade would pass before her acclaim as an *actress* in Vittorio De Sica's powerful *Two Women*.

73

Senso

(THE WANTON CONTESSA / SUMMER HURRICANE)

A Lux Film / 1954

(U.S. release by Fleetwood Films of Mount Vernon: 1968)

CREDITS

Director: Luchino Visconti; *Producer:* Domenico Forges Davanzati; *Screenwriters:* Luchino Visconti, Suso Cecchi D'Amico, G. Prosperi, C. Alianello, and G. Bassanni; *From a novella by* Camillo Boito; *Technicolor Cinematographers:* R. R. Aldo and Robert Krasker; *Editor:* Mario Serandrei; *Art Directors:* Ottavio Scotti and Gino Brosio; *Costumes:* Marcel Escoffier and Piero Tosi; *Music:* Bruckner's Seventh Symphony and segments from Verdi's opera *Il Trovatore; Running Time:* 115 minutes.

CAST

Alida Valli *(Countess Livia Serpieri)*; Farley Granger *(Lieutenant Franz Mahler)*; Massimo Girotti *(Marquis Roberto Ussoni)*; Heinz Moog *(Count Serpieri)*; Rina Morelli *(Laura)*; Marcella Mariani *(the Prostitute)*; Christian Marquand *(Bohemian Officer)*; Tonio Selwart *(Colonel Kleist)*; Cristoforo de Hartungen *(Commander at Venetian Square)*; Tino Bianchi *(Meucci)*; Sergio Fantoni *(Patriot)*; Marianna Liebl *(Wife of Austrian General)*.

THE FILM

Of Luchino Visconti's two Risorgimento-era period pieces, set in Italy's 1860s, *Senso* is both the shorter and the lesser known. Nine years later, in *The Leopard*, the director would explore a larger canvas, representing the twilight of Sicily's mid-nineteenth-century aristocracy. *Senso* is simply concerned with Italian morals, ill-starred romance and a betrayed woman's vengeance in the Venice and Verona of that period. Both films are operatic in style, opulent in design, and artfully photographed, with suitably lush background

SENSO   Alida Valli.

music. But as one Italian critic wrote: "With *Senso*, we see the birth of the first true and authentic Italian historical film." Coming as it did between Visconti's *Bellissima* and *Le Notti Bianche/White Nights*, it later moved him to recall: "After *Senso*, everything was easier."

Opera literally sets the tone of *Senso*, which begins during an 1866 performance of Verdi's *Il Trovatore* at Venice's La Fenice. In the audience are a great many of the occupying Austrian officers, and after the tenor's impassioned rendition of "Di quella pira," the house virtually explodes in protest as Italian patriots shout for the foreigners to vacate Venice, bombarding them with leaflets from the upper balconies. In attendance, Countess Livia Serpieri (Alida Valli), the wife of a Venetian aristocrat, is introduced to Franz Mahler (Farley Granger), a handsome young Austrian officer known to be a Casanova. Intrigued and challenged, Livia finds herself falling in love with the younger Franz, despite her better judgment. Soon both family and patriotic duties take second place to romance as the countess risks her marriage and reputation. When liberation forces near Venice, she tries unsuccessfully to break off with him. But he persists, following her and the elderly Count Serpieri (Heinz Moog) when they leave the city for their country estate. When Franz invades her bedroom there, Livia is persuaded to help him buy his way out of the army by giving him a large sum of money intended for her cousin Roberto (Massimo Girotti) and the partisans. Later, when she seeks out Franz in his Verona barracks, she finds him

SENSO Alida Valli and Farley Granger.

dissolute with drink and apparently involved with a blond lady friend. Finally forced to see him for the faithless coward he really is, Livia realizes that it was her wealth and position with which he had really been infatuated and that he has betrayed not only her but her cousin as well. In retaliation, she coldly denounces his actions to the Austrians. As the story ends, Franz is shot by a firing squad as the humiliated Livia wanders off into the streets to face an uncertain future.

Visconti had originally wanted Ingrid Bergman and Marlon Brando for *Senso*'s leading roles. But the actress's then-husband, director Roberto Rossellini, would not allow her to work for anyone but himself, and the part went to the beautiful Alida Valli, who gave a much-praised performance of total conviction that may be her finest screen work. Farley Granger was cast opposite her because the movie's producers insisted on him over Brando. Granger vividly recalls Visconti's slow, painstaking perfectionism and utter disregard for production costs. The result is a visually striking, elegantly produced costume drama that took an astonishing fourteen years to reach New York City art cinemas. In the mid-fifties, American movie magazines had published illustrated reviews of *Senso* in an English-language version (boasting dialogue credited to none other than Tennessee Williams and Paul Bowles) entitled *Summer Hurricane*. This abridged edition of Visconti's film failed to open in the United States, although Great Britain witnessed its release under yet another title, *The Wanton Contessa*.

SENSO Alida Valli and Farley Granger.

75

La Strada

(THE ROAD)

A Carlo Ponti–Dino De Laurentiis Production / 1954

(U.S. release by Trans-Lux Films: 1956)

CREDITS

Director: Federico Fellini; *Producers:* Carlo Ponti and Dino De Laurentiis; *Screenwriters:* Federico Fellini, Tullio Pinelli, and Ennio Flaiano; *Based on a story by* Federico Fellini and Tullio Pinelli; *Cinematographer:* Otello Martelli; *Editors:* Leo Caffozo and Lina Caterini; *Art Director:* Mario Ravasco; *Costumes:* Margherita Marinari; *Music:* Nino Rota; *Running Time:* 115 minutes.

CAST

Anthony Quinn *(Zampanó);* Giulietta Masina *(Gelsomina);* Richard Basehart *(Il Matto, the Fool);* Aldo Silvani *(Columbiani, the Circus Owner);* Marcella Rovere *(the Widow);* Livia Venturini *(the Nun).*

THE FILM

Anyone familiar with this consummate classic of the Italian cinema's heyday might find difficulty in imagining how the movie might have turned out had Burt

Lancaster played the rough-hewn, itinerant strong-man Zampanó and Silvana Mangano interpreted the pathetic, endearing clown Gelsomina. For that was the casting originally ordained by a producing faction that agreed to come to the aid of Fellini, whose downbeat project initially met with no interest from any other potential underwriters. Quite likely, Lancaster would have done as fine a job as *La Strada*'s eventual male lead, Anthony Quinn. But it is impossible to imagine any actress more ideally cast than the plain but brilliant Giulietta Masina (offscreen, Signora Federico Fellini), a diminutive, natural clown in the Charlie Chaplin/Buster Keaton/Harry Langdon tradition and a far cry from the big-boned beauty of Silvana Mangano (despite the breadth of *her* acting talents). *La Strada* is one of those motion pictures that owes as much to its great director as to the uniform excellence of its cast.

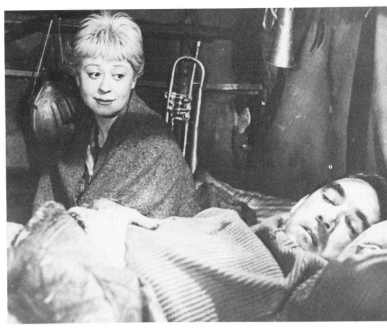

LA STRADA Giulietta Masina and Anthony Quinn.

LA STRADA Giulietta Masina and Anthony Quinn.

LA STRADA Giulietta Masina, Richard Basehart (center), and Anthony Quinn.

Much of *La Strada* is essentially a two-character story. The film begins with Zampanó, in need of an assistant for his chain-breaking, strongman circus act, literally buying from her impoverished mother the simpleminded Gelsomina, who becomes the servant of his every whim. Responding to his lessons, she displays talent on both drum and trumpet, with which she accompanies his performances. A brusque and uncommunicative womanizer, Zampanó mistreats Gelsomina shamefully as he hauls her about the country in a makeshift trailer attached to his motorcycle. More than willing to do his bidding, the lonely and neglected Gelsomina eventually finds a friend when their act is hired by a small traveling circus. But Zampanó and the playfully mocking, high-wire-walking clown Il Matto (Richard Basehart) take an immediate dislike to one another. A fight ensues, and Zampanó pulls a knife on the clown and is sent to jail. When he is released, the loyal Gelsomina is waiting for him, and fired from the circus, they take to the road again, only to encounter Il Matto, who is changing the flat tire on his car. Zampanó can't resist goading the clown into another vicious fight, accidentally killing him. Devastated by the loss of a gentle friend, Gelsomina recoils from her master and enters a prolonged period of mourning and depression. This so annoys Zampanó that he finally abandons her on the road, with only her trumpet for company. Time passes, and the strongman continues on the road alone until one day he learns that the obedient, adoring Gelsomina has died. The past and his memories of her overwhelm the uncommunicative brute as he collapses, sobbing, on a sandy beach.

As moving as *La Strada* remains on its own, it is Nino Rota's haunting score, with its plaintive, descending trumpet solo that stays with us—as unforgettable as Giulietta Masina's sweet, homely clown's face. The movie won a great number of international prizes, most notably Hollywood's Oscar for the Best Foreign Film of 1956 (the year of its U.S. release) as well as the New York Film Critics Award in that category. *La Strada*'s screenplay also garnered an Academy Award nomination. In Italy, the film was a Silver Ribbon winner at the 1954 Venice Film Festival; incredibly, however, there was *no* recipient in the Best Actress category!

La Strada may be considered, as one British critic put it, "a curious attempt at a kind of poetic neorealism," but the end result is a triumph of directorial style and performance artistry—including the fine work of Richard Basehart, who makes the most of his few but rich scenes as Il Matto. And for Fellini, *La Strada* finally and indelibly established his name outside Italy.

L'Oro di Napoli

(GOLD OF NAPLES / EVERY DAY'S A HOLIDAY)

A Carlo Ponti–Dino De Laurentiis Production / 1955

(U.S. release by Distributors Corporation of America: 1957)

CREDITS

Director: Vittorio De Sica; *Producers:* Dino De Laurentiis and Carlo Ponti; *Screenwriters:* Cesare Zavattini, Vittorio De Sica, and Giuseppe Marotta; *Adapted from the book* L'Oro di Napoli *by* Giuseppe Marotta; *Cinematographer:* Carlo Montuori; *Editor:* Eraldo Da Roma; *Art Director:* Gastone Medin; *Sets:* F. Ruffo; *Costumes:* Marcello Marchesi; *Music:* Alessandro Cicognini; *U.S. Running Time:* 118 minutes.

CAST (U.S. version)

"The Racketeer": Toto *(the Husband);* Lianella Carrell *(His Wife);* Pasquale Cennamo *(the Racketeer).*

"Pizza on Credit": Sophia Loren *(the Wife);* Gia-

L'ORO DI NAPOLI   Giacomo Furia, Sophia Loren and Alberto Farnese.

L'ORO DI NAPOLI   Vittorio De Sica.

wife and partner of a pizza maker who is upset about the disappearance of his wife's emerald ring (she left it in her lover's bedroom); "The Gambler," which has director De Sica waging all he owns in a card game with his porter's precocious little boy; and "Teresa," with top-billed (in America) Silvana Mangano as a prostitute duped into forsaking her protective brothel life for a marriage of convenience to a handsome businessman (Erno Crisa), who later confesses to her his undying love for a young woman who had killed herself for him.

Of the movie's four episodes shown in the United States, the first three provided varying degrees of Neapolitan amusement, while "Teresa" ended the quartet on a more serious note, a seemingly strange choice by the American distributor, Distributors Corporation of America (DCA). Later on, Paramount packaged an even more condensed version of the film that they called *Every Day's a Holiday*, unwisely omitting the "Gambler" segment as well as cutting character actor Paolo Stoppa entirely out of "Pizza on Credit." The unfortunate result, dubbed into "British English," ran a mere seventy-four minutes and met with such severe critical drubbing that it was shelved altogether.

Gold of Naples, however, drew its most favorable criticism for the De Sica sequence—and his brilliant comedy acting opposite scene-stealing little Piero Bilancioni—and for Silvana Mangano's serious acting,

como Furia *(the Husband)*; Alberto Farnese *(the Lover)*; Paolo Stoppa *(the Widower)*.

"The Gambler": Vittorio De Sica *(the Count)*; Mario Passante *(His Valet)*; Irene Montalto *(the Countess)*; Piero Bilancioni *(the Boy)*; Enrico Borgstrom *(His Father, the Porter)*.

"Teresa": Silvana Mangano *(Teresa)*; Erno Crisa *(the Husband)*; Ubaldo Maestri *(the Intermediary)*.

THE FILM

Originally a six-episode collection of vignettes adapted from a book of short stories by Giuseppe Marotta, *Gold of Naples* reached the United States minus two of its segments, opening as a four-part package that was met with considerable enthusiasm among both critics and cosmopolitan audiences. What was cut out was a sequence about a child's funeral procession with Teresa De Vita and nonprofessional actors and another that featured popular Italian character actors Eduardo De Filippo and Tina Pica in the story of a joke played on a snobbish nobleman. Remaining were "The Racketeer," in which Toto bests a former schoolmate turned mafioso who has become a permanent house guest; "Pizza on Credit," with Sophia Loren as the unfaithful

L'ORO DI NAPOLI   Erno Crisa and Silvana Mangano.

79

which won her a 1955 Silver Ribbon prize. But despite the movie's charm and humor, one might carp at the arrangement of its episodes: Had the Loren and Mangano episodes been juxtaposed, *Gold of Naples* would have delivered more balance as an entertainment. And its audiences would have left theaters on an "up" note.

A point of particular interest in *Gold of Naples* is the confident comedy performance of young Sophia Loren, directed for the first time by her future mentor De Sica. Already a seasoned ingenue, the nubile Loren makes a really major impression here, visibly blossoming under her director's considerate guidance. In a field of promising young Italian starlets of the early fifties, it is easy to understand why Sophia Loren became a big international star—and accomplished actress—who eventually copped an Academy Award (under De Sica's direction).

Finally, De Sica's knowing direction of this typically Neapolitan material is superbly enhanced by the sharp black-and-white photography of Carlo Montuori and especially the bouncy, indigenous music of Alessandro Cicognini.

Le Amiche

(THE GIRL FRIENDS)

A Trionfalcine Production / 1955
(U.S. release by Premiere Films: 1962)

CREDITS

Director: Michelangelo Antonioni; *Producer:* Giovanni Addessi; *Screenwriters:* Michelangelo Antonioni, Suso Cecchi D'Amico, and Alba de Cespedes; *Based on the story* "Tre Donne Sole," *included in* Cesare Pavese's book La Bella Estate; *Cinematographer:* Gianni di Venanzo; *Editor:* Eraldo da Roma; *Art Director:* Gianni Polidori; *Music:* Giovanni Fusco; *Running Time:* 104 minutes.

CAST

Eleonora Rossi-Drago *(Clelia)*; Yvonne Furneaux *(Momina)*; Valentina Cortese *(Nene)*; Madeleine Fischer *(Rosetta)*; Gabriele Ferzetti *(Lorenzo)*; Franco Fabrizi *(Cesare)*; Ettore Manni *(Carlo)*; Anna Maria Pancani *(Mariella)*; Maria Gambarelli *(Clelia's Employer)*.

THE FILM

Michelangelo Antonioni's fifth feature film, made five years before his international breakthrough with *L'Avventura*, paves the way for his later cinematic depictions of the privileged classes and their challenges in finding love, happiness, and the antidotes for ennui. Some critics, writing in retrospect, have seemingly found greater rewards in these early works of the fifties, before he allied himself with Monica Vitti and became fashionable among the intellectuals of film criticism. Among those early gems that unfortunately have not been widely seen in the United States is this study of a small group of women living in a closely knit community among the upper classes.

Traveling to Turin to establish a new branch of a successful Roman fashion salon, Clelia (Eleonora Rossi-Drago) encounters a near tragedy at her hotel when Rosetta (Madeleine Fischer), the unhappy rich girl in the next room, attempts suicide. This soon involves Clelia with the young woman's circle of friends: the superficial Momina (Yvonne Furneaux), separated from her husband and terminally bored with life; Lorenzo (Gabriele Ferzetti), the artist with whom Rosetta is emotionally involved; and his wife Nene (Valentina Cortese). Envious of Nene's greater success as a painter, Lorenzo carelessly permits himself an affair with Rosetta. Meantime, Clelia falls in love with an architect's assistant named Carlo (Ettore Manni), all the time realizing that a future with him would return her to the impoverished background she has determinedly put behind her. In a succession of gatherings and conversations, these complex relationships gradually work themselves out, reaching a turning point when Lorenzo tires of Rosetta's emotional demands and reveals his boredom with their relationship. The revelation drives her to kill herself. Clelia blames Momina for unthinkingly encouraging the affair, and

LE AMICHE   Valentina Cortese and Yvonne Furneaux.

80

LE AMICHE   Madeleine Fischer, Franco Fabrizi, Valentina Cortese and Gabriele Ferzetti.

she stages a scene at the dress shop that she assumes will result in her dismissal. Instead, her employer (Maria Gambarelli) offers her a position in Rome, and Clelia chooses her career over marriage to—and poverty with—Carlo. Lorenzo is reconciled with the loyal, forgiving Nene.

Antonioni is at his best in handling the subtleties of character in these interconnecting emotional relationships. And he gets the best work from Valentina Cortese and Gabriele Ferzetti as the troubled artist couple and Yvonne Furneaux as the most beautiful but least substantial of the "girlfriends." The director's signature use of the northern Italian landscapes (a factor in all of his later works) is particularly striking during a beach outing, with its attendant revelations of tensions and boredom. If the basic material, based on a story by Cesare Pavese, the Italian F. Scott Fitzgerald, verges on soap opera, it is left to the highly individualized talents of Antonioni to sidestep the clichés of the genre. He is immeasurably aided by the crisp black-and-white photography of Gianni di Venanzo and an inspired background score by Giovanni Fusco. *Le Amiche* was a Silver Lion winner at 1955's Venice Film Festival. But its U.S. release didn't come until seven years later, when *L'Avventura* and *La Notte* had established their director's credentials abroad.

For her performance in *Le Amiche*, Valentina Cortese was awarded the "Grollo d'Oro" in 1956 for Best Actress.

LE AMICHE   Ettore Manni and Eleonora Rossi Drago.

Amici per la Pelle

(FRIENDS FOR LIFE / THE WOMAN IN THE PAINTING)

A Cines Production / 1955

(U.S. release by Lopert Films: 1959)

CREDITS

Director: Franco Rossi; *Producer:* Elio Scardamaglia; *Screenwriters:* Ottavio Alessi, Leo Benvenuti, Piero de Bernardi, Giandomenico Giagni, Ugo Guerra, and Franco Rossi; *Cinematographer:* Gabor Pogany; *Editor:* Otello Colangeli; *Art Director:* Franco Lolli; *Costumes:* Maria Baroni; *Music:* Nino Rota; *Running Time:* 95 minutes.

CAST

Geronimo Meynier *(Mario)*; Andrea Scire *(Franco)*; Luigi Tosi *(Mario's Father)*; Vera Carmi *(Mario's Mother)*; Carlo Tamberlani *(Franco's Father)*; Paolo Ferrara *(Professor Martinelli)*; Marcella Rovena *(English Professor)*.

THE FILM

Franco Rossi's directorial career began with promise. Starting out as the dubbing voice for other actors, he moved on to become an assistant to directors like Mario Camerini and Renato Castellani before striking out on his own in the early fifties. Especially successful was *Amici per la Pelle*, a knowing study of childhood that attracted critical attention at the 1955 Venice Film Festival. But without exploitation angles for American distribution, four years passed before Lopert Films quietly brought the movie to U.S. theaters, albeit under the misleading title of *The Woman in the Painting* and with the equally misleading ad copy that read: "The story of a strange obsession!" The picture's new title made reference to a likeness of the dead mother of one of the story's two adolescent heroes. But a "strange obsession" would be difficult to substantiate here. So much for the ploys of American movie advertising!

In Rome, dark-haired, extroverted Mario (Geronimo

AMICI PER LA PELLE   Geronimo Meynier.

AMICI PER LA PELLE   Andrea Scire and Geronimo Meynier.

Meynier) and blond, shy Franco (Andrea Sciré) are thirteen-year-old classmates who, following a brief conflict, become close friends. Their mutual attraction arises chiefly from the very differences in their backgrounds and characters. Since the death of his mother, quiet, lonely Franco has lived with his diplomat-father in upscale hotels. Mario is the fun-loving son of a ceramics manufacturer. The boys become inseparable, competing in sports, sharing confidences, and going everywhere together. When Franco's father is transferred to the Middle East, it is arranged that his son will go to live with Mario's family. But the friendship is disrupted when Franco wins the school cross-country race, prompting the envious Mario to reveal to their classmates a secret that only he and Franco had shared. As a result, Franco decides to leave with his father, and he avoids further contact with Mario. But before the plane leaves, a desperately repentant Mario manages to reach the airport and achieve a reconciliation with Franco. As they part, the boys know they will now remain friends for life.

But this was only one of two endings shot for the film. In the version shown at the Venice Film Festival, a more downbeat denouement has Franco's plane departing before Mario can make up with him. Apparently, that ending was subsequently discarded for the more sentimentally pleasing finale familiar to those relative few who have discovered the rewards of this charming little movie.

The film is virtually a showcase for its two young male leads: Andrea Sciré, the better actor of the pair,

and the almost-too-beautiful Geronimo Meynier, who—true to motion-picture tradition—enjoyed the more successful film career, going on to play opposite Rosemarie Dexter in a 1964 Italian-Spanish adaptation of *Romeo and Juliet.* That film eventually reached U.S. shores in a poorly dubbed version that attempted unsuccessfully to compete in 1968 with the enormously popular Franco Zeffirelli film.

Where *The Woman in the Painting* succeeds best is in the tender, painful realities of adolescence, so well conveyed in the behavior of the two boys. Franco Rossi apparently found great rapport with his young actors, bringing him deserved acclaim as a director of considerable skill and promise. Unfortunately, his subsequent career—unlike that of Vittorio De Sica following *The Children Are Watching Us*—hasn't fulfilled that promise in any major fashion.

Il Ferroviere

(THE RAILROAD MAN / MAN OF IRON)

A Carlo Ponti–Dino De Laurentiis Cinematografica–ENIC Production / 1956

(U.S. release by Continental Distributing: 1965)

CREDITS

Director: Pietro Germi; *Producer:* Carlo Ponti; *Screenwriters:* Pietro Germi, Alfredo Giannetti, Luciano Vincenzoni, and [uncredited] Ennio De Concini; *Cinematographer:* Leonida Barboni; *Editor:* Dolores Tamburini; *Art Director:* Carlo Egidi; *Costumes:* Mirella Morelli; *Music:* Carlo Rustichelli; *Running Time:* 105 minutes.

CAST

Pietro Germi *(Andrea Marcocci)*; Luisa Della Noce *(Sara Marcocci)*; Sylva Koscina *(Giulia)*; Saro Urzi *(Liverani)*; Renato Speziali *(Renato)*; Carlo Giuffré *(Marcello)*; Edoardo Nevola *(Sandrino)*.

THE FILM

Reviewing from Rome in 1956, *Variety*'s critic called *The Railroad Man* "one of this country's top efforts of the season." And yet it took this final salute to the passing of neorealist drama all of nine years to reach

IL FERROVIERE Saro Urzi, Edoardo Nevola, and Pietro Germi.

IL FERROVIERE Sylva Koscina,
Renato Speziali and Saro Urzi.

IL FERROVIERE Pietro Germi and Edoardo Nevola.

the United States, due undoubtedly to its lack of either box-office names or sensational subject matter to help sell it to English-speaking audiences. Admittedly somewhat downbeat, *The Railroad Man* follows the declining fortunes of Andrea Marcocci (actor-director Pietro Germi, who also collaborated on the screenplay). Marcocci, a middle-aged family man, proudly works as a railroad engineer, spending much of his leisure time drinking with his friends and playing the guitar. In his absence, the rest of the family has become dysfunctional, to the dismay of his long-suffering wife Sara (Luisa Della Noce). His daughter Giulia (Sylva Koscina, in her film debut) has become pregnant by her casual boyfriend (Renato Speziali) and is soon pressured into a loveless marriage with him, from whom she eventually strays with an older man. Other family conflicts involve a nonachieving grown son (Carlo Giuffré) and a preadolescent one (the scene-stealing Edoardo Nevola), whose worship of his father makes him privy to Andrea's drinking bouts.

The "railroad man" suffers a major career setback when he is unable to brake in time to avoid hitting a suicide on the tracks, a traumatic experience that in turn causes a near accident when Andrea fails to stop his train for an important signal. He is then demoted to working on a yard-switch engine. At his favorite pub, where he has been shunned for turning scab during a strike, Andrea suffers a stroke.

What saves *The Railroad Man* from bathos, despite its story elements, is a warmly realistic, affectionate, but unsentimental approach that owes its success to director-writer-star Pietro Germi, a sort of Italian Spencer Tracy, who offers a wonderful portrait of a simple working man beset with the confusing conflicts of pride, conscience, love, and guilt. Little Edoardo Nevola gives a natural, ingratiating performance as the youngest Marcocci who attempts to understand the adult problems that are splitting the family apart all around him. And Sylvá Koscina makes her first screen mark as the unhappy daughter, anticipating a measure of international roles that were to come her way in the next decade. Luisa Della Noce is warmly sympathetic as her mother, and Saro Urzi does a fine job as Andrea's long-standing pal. No matter how obscure it may subsequently have become, *The Railroad Man* remains Pietro Germi's minor-league masterpiece.

Il Grido

(THE OUTCRY)

A Coproduction of S.P.A. Cinematografica (Rome) and Robert Alexander Productions (New York) / 1957

(U.S. release by Astor Pictures: 1962)

CREDITS

Director: Michelangelo Antonioni; *Producer:* Franco Cancellieri; *Screenwriters:* Michelangelo Antonioni, Elio Bartolini, and Ennio De Concini; *Cinematographer:* Gianni Di Venanzo; *Editor:* Eraldo da Roma; *Art Director:* Franco Fontana; *Music:* Giovanni Fusco; *Running Time:* 115 minutes.

CAST

Steve Cochran *(Aldo)*; Alida Valli *(Irma)*; Betsy Blair *(Elvia)*; Dorian Gray *(Virginia)*; Lyn Shaw *(Andreina)*; Gabriella Pallotta *(Edera)*; Mirna Girardi *(Rosina)*;

IL GRIDO   Steve Cochran, Mirna Girardi (in background) and Alida Valli.

IL GRIDO   Mirna Girardi and Steve Cochran.

IL GRIDO Steve Cochran and Alida Valli.

Guerrino Campanilli *(Virginia's Father)*; Gaetano Matteucci *(Edera's Fiancé)*; Pietro Corvelatti *(Old Fisherman)*.

THE FILM

Two years after American audiences discovered Michelangelo Antonioni's unusual filmmaking style in *L'Avventura*, they had the opportunity to explore one of his earlier works, this 1957 drama in which, for a change, a *man* was the central figure in a characteristically Antonionian odyssey of loneliness and isolation.

Antonioni was born in Ferrara; *Il Grido* was shot on the outskirts of that city as well as in the towns of Occhiobello and Portelogoscuro in the lower Po Valley, where the director finds psychological parallels to his characters in the misty, muddy desolation of overcast wintry landscapes. The late influences of the neorealist movement are more evident in this work than in any of the director's other movies, and yet the story elements are closer to the subsequent, so-called trilogy of his *L'Avventura, La Notte,* and *Eclipse.*

Aldo (Steve Cochran) has for seven years worked as a skilled laborer in the sugar refinery that dominates his small Italian town. During all that time, he has lived as the common-law spouse of Irma (Alida Valli), whose legal husband is (for reasons never made clear) living and working in Australia. They have a small daughter named Rosina (Mirna Girardi). But their relationship suffers an abrupt change when Irma learns that her husband has died and she tells Aldo, who had hoped to marry her, that she no longer loves him. Aldo tries to change her mind, but Irma is resolute, and following a stormy parting, he leaves and, with Rosina, sets out for an uncertain future as they wander through the Po Valley.

As they travel by foot and by thumb, three other women become a part of his life. First, there is Elvia (Betsy Blair), an old friend who offers temporary shelter and sympathy—until a visit from Irma (who leaves Aldo's clothes) makes it clear to her that he still loves the other woman. Next, Aldo and Rosina encounter Virginia (Dorian Gray), who operates a gas station where he finds interim employment as well as emotional solace. But Aldo realizes this environment is not good for an upset Rosina, and he sends her back to live with her mother. Moving on, he finds Andreina (Lyn Shaw), a prostitute who lives in a waterside shack and appears as desolate as Aldo.

Eventually, he returns to his village where he finds the residents gathered in protest over plans for the local construction of an airfield. Through a window, he sees Irma, now a mother of another child. Aldo goes back to the now-deserted refinery where he had worked and mounts the outside ladder on the refinery tower. As Irma, who has seen him, calls out his name, he reaches the top, dazedly looking down at her, and either deliberately—or unintentionally—falls to his death. It is Irma's horrified scream that provides the *"grido"* of the title.

One is briefly reminded of the melodramatic suicide wrap-ups that solved the problems of the heroines with loose morals of *Bitter Rice* and the more obscure Rossellini-Pagliero *Woman.* But *Il Grido* doesn't qualify as melodrama, and its acting is so sensitively rendered and truthfully conveyed that Aldo's death understandably leaves ambiguity in the minds of most viewers. What exactly motivates Irma to pursue him into the refinery yard with such frantic anxiety? Presumably, she has found a new and more satisfying life for herself. Or has she? We know enough not to expect facile answers from Antonioni, for whom the very word "elliptical" must have been originally coined.

Steve Cochran won much praise for his work here, underscoring the sensitivity displayed in some of this underrated actor's American television work. Alida Valli's quietly tortured Irma is everything one might expect from so fine a performer, and each one of the smaller roles is acted with naturalistic attention to detail. Nor does Antonioni sentimentalize little Rosina, who doesn't make her father's wanderings any easier.

Gianni Di Venanzo's dreary Po Valley photography isn't likely to attract tourists to the region, and Giovanni Fusco's piano-dominated background music would somehow sound more appropriate to a D. W. Griffith silent film.

Il Grido won the Critics' Grand Prize at the Locarno Film Festival in 1957.

Le Notti di Cabiria

(CABIRIA / NIGHTS OF CABIRIA)

A Coproduction of Dino De Laurentiis (Rome) and Les Films Marceau (Paris) / 1957

(U.S. release by Lopert Pictures: 1957)

CREDITS

Director: Federico Fellini; *Producer:* Dino De Laurentiis; *Screenwriters:* Federico Fellini, Ennio Flaiano, and Tullio Pinelli; *Additional Dialogue:* Pier Paolo Pasolini; *Cinematographer:* Aldo Tonti; *Editor:* Leo Catozzo; *Art Director:* Piero Gherardi; *Music:* Nino Rota; *Running Time:* 110 minutes.

CAST

Giulietta Masina *(Cabiria)*; François Périer *(Oscar)*; Amedeo Nazzari *(the Actor)*; Franca Marzi *(Wanda)*; Dorian Gray *(Jessy)*; Aldo Silvani *(the Hypnotist)*; Mario Passante *(the Cripple)*; Pina Gualandri *(Matilda)*.

THE FILM

Giulietta Masina's finest screen moments have always occurred in the pictures of her husband Federico Fellini, for which no accusatory charges of nepotism ever seem to have been made. With good reason, for Masina's performances—especially in this film and *La Strada*—remain among the finest in the annals of Italian film.

The actress first portrayed a streetwalker named Cabiria in *The White Sheik*, Fellini's 1952 comedy, in which that character was virtually a bit part on the sidelines. Apparently, there were elements both in the role and in Masina's characterization that struck the filmmaker as worthy of further development. Her performance in *Le Notti di Cabiria/Nights of Cabiria* afforded Masina perhaps her greatest role. Frequently likened in her performances to Charlie Chaplin, here she is literally a female "little tramp." Cabiria is an aging, cheerfully optimistic Roman prostitute whose luck always seems to have a way of running out on her. Respectability appears to be her unlikely goal; humiliation is more often the outcome.

LE NOTTI DI CABIRIA Giulietta Masina.

robs, beats, and betrays her. Alone and destitute, Cabiria wistfully but resolutely heads back to her old stomping grounds, as she does so falling in with a group of celebrant young people who serenade her as they walk.

In her compassionate hands, Masina brings Cabiria to vivid screen life, finding the pathos in a character at once both simple and complex—especially in her final scene. Some of the film's critics found fault with what they deemed Fellini's indulgence of Masina's "mannerisms," according her too many loving close-ups and allowing pathos to verge on bathos. Others, like the *New Yorker*'s Pauline Kael, disagreed. She called *Nights of Cabiria* "possibly Federico Fellini's finest film, and a work in which Giulietta Masina earns the praise she received for *La Strada.*"

LE NOTTI DI CABIRIA   François Périer and Giulietta Masina.

As her story begins, Cabiria is rescued from a pond where her lover has dumped her. Courageously, she picks up the pieces of her life and goes on, plying her trade on the outskirts of Rome. She is picked up by a famous movie star (Amedeo Nazzari), who has had a fight with his mistress. Cabiria is taken in a fancy car to his elegant villa, but she is hidden in a closet when his inamorata returns. With her dreams of high living dashed, Cabiria wistfully considers settling for an autographed picture of her host. Later, on a pilgrimage to a shrine, she prays for her lot to change, bring her a happy, permanent relationship. At a variety theater, Cabiria is persuaded to go onstage, where a hypnotist (Aldo Silvani) puts her in a trance, during which her dreams are made public. In the audience, a young man named Oscar (François Périer) is moved to seek her out afterward. In short order, he persuades Cabiria to marry him, and she gullibly agrees, selling her house and withdrawing her savings on his behalf. Their honeymoon exposes Oscar's ulterior motives, as he

The picture won an Academy Award for Best Foreign Film and the New York Film Critics Award, with Masina deservedly named Best Actress at the Cannes Film Festival.

In 1968, Bob Fosse developed the work into a musicalized Broadway vehicle for Gwen Verdon under the title *Sweet Charity*. And he later directed Shirley MacLaine in the movie version. But his prostitute-heroine, named Charity Hope Valentine, was a far cry from Fellini's less flashy little Cabiria.

Le Fatiche di Ercole

(HERCULES)

An OSCAR–Galatea Films Production / 1957
(U.S. release by Warner Bros.: 1959)

CREDITS

Director: Pietro Francisci; *Producer:* Federico Teti; *Screenwriters:* Pietro Francisci, Ennio De Concini, and

LE NOTTI DI CABIRIA Giulietta Masina and Amedeo Nazzari.

89

LE FATICHE DI ERCOLE   Steve Reeves.

Gaio Frattini; *Based on a story by* Pietro Francisci, *taken from* "The Argonauts"; *Eastman Color–Dyaliscope Cinematographer:* Mario Bava; *Editor:* Mario Serandrei; *Art Director:* Flavio Mogherini; *Costumes:* Giulio Coltellacci; *Music:* Enzo Masetti; *Running Time:* 107 minutes.

CAST

Steve Reeves *(Hercules)*; Sylva Koscina *(Iole)*; Gianna Maria Canale *(Antea)*; Fabrizio Mioni *(Jason)*; Ivo Garrani *(Pelias)*; Arturo Dominici *(Eurysteus)*; Mimmo Palmara *(Iphitus)*; Lidia Alfonsi *(the Sybil)*; Gina Rovere *(Amazon)*; Gabriele Antonini *(Ulysses)*; Andrea Fantasia *(Laertes)*; Afro Poli *(Chiron)*; Aldo Fiorelli *(Argos)*; Gino Mattera *(Orpheus)*; G. P. Rosmino *(Esculapius)*.

THE FILM

The reader may well wonder what a Steve Reeves picture is doing in a book called *The Great Italian*

Films. Simply put, *Le Fatiche di Ercole/The Labors of Hercules* was a landmark movie and a box-office blockbuster of colossal proportions for Boston-bred, self-styled showman Joseph E. Levine. At fifty-three, Levine enjoyed a minor reputation for what he called "the big, big sell"—acquiring the odd but exploitable and making the public want to see it via a media barrage of advertisements and publicity ploys that often cost him a small fortune.

Steve Reeves was a Montana-born bodybuilder whose quest for physical perfection took him to Southern California's Muscle Beach and the titles Mr. Pacific, Mr. America, Mr. World, Mr. Universe, and, in France, "Le Plus Bel Athlete du Monde." Subsequently, his handsome face and impressive form got him small roles in the Broadway musicals *Kismet* and *The Vamp* and supporting parts in several Hollywood pictures. At Metro-Goldwyn-Mayer, Reeves displayed his best assets in the Jane Powell vehicle *Athena* and caught the eye of Italian filmmakers looking for a superb physical specimen to portray the legendary Hercules in the sort of spectacular adventure movie that had not been attempted in many years. Director

LE FATICHE DI ERCOLE   Sylva Koscina and Steve Reeves.

90

LE FATICHE DI ERCOLE   Steve Reeves, Fabrizio Mioni (standing) and Afro Poli.

Pietro Francisci had previously turned out such minor-league pseudohistorical melodramas as *Attila* and *The Queen of Sheba*, but *The Labors of Hercules* was somewhat more ambitious. With a reported cast of six thousand and thirty-year-old Reeves performing the Labors (for the modest salary of $6,000), producer Federico Teti came up with an adventure-spectacle that several U.S. distributors screened and rejected before Levine flew to Rome and checked it out for himself. The showman's quoted reaction: "It had action and sex, a near shipwreck, gorgeous women on an island, and a guy tearing a goddam building apart. And where did you ever see a guy with a body like Reeves has?"

Levine paid $120,000 for the film, dubbed it into English (even including Reeves), retitled it simply *Hercules*, ordered six hundred prints of the color film, and then spent $1.2 million promoting it. Thus, what *Time* magazine called "a sort of Homeric Tarzan" became not only the summer of 1959's box-office champion but also the biggest surprise hit in Hollywood memory. Credited with being the man who initiated "saturation booking," Levine opened *Hercules* in 145 neighborhood theaters. In its first week, the movie brought in a then-astounding $900,000, and attendance snowballed.

Hercules's episodic plot scarcely requires discussion here. It has been critically dismissed variously as a motion picture "grounded in muddled mythology" and "a slow-paced and stilted affair, studded with routine spectacles that have been seen since movies immemorial." Nor did Steve Reeves, despite admiration for the musculature of his six-foot one-inch frame, two hundred pounds, and forty-eight-inch chest, win any acting laurels. But with Joseph E. Levine's promotional genius behind him, Reeves settled down in Italy and, at fees of $75,000 to $100,000 per picture, enjoyed stardom in a succession of adventure flicks over the next several years, begining with the sequel *Hercules Unchained* and encompassing *Goliath and the Barbarians*, *The Last Days of Pompeii*, *The Thief of Baghdad*, *Morgan the Pirate*, and *Duel of the Titans*. As his muscle-hero vogue waned, Reeves got his longtime wish to star in a Western. Unfortunately, *A Long Ride From Hell* (1968) was a colossal flop, and the actor decided to take his movie earnings and quietly retire at forty-two. But his *Hercules* has a place in movie history as the film that launched a flood of cheap sword-and-sandal imitations starrring names like Reg Park, Brad Harris, Mark Forest, and Kirk Morris.

91

Guendalina

*A Coproduction of Carlo Ponti Productions (Rome)
and Les Films Marceau (Paris) / 1957*

(U.S. release by Lopert Films: 1958)

CREDITS

Director: Alberto Lattuada; *Producer:* Carlo Ponti;
Screenwriters: Alberto Lattuada, Leo Benvenuti, Piero
di Bernardi, and Jean Blondel; *Based on a story by*
Valerio Zurlini; *Cinematographer:* Otello Martelli;
Editor: Eraldo Da Roma; *Art Director:* Maurizio Serra;
Costumes: Orietta Nasalli Rocca; *Music:* Piero Mor-
gan; *Running Time:* 100 minutes.

CAST

Jacqueline Sassard *(Guendalina);* Raf Vallone *(the
Father);* Raffaele Mattioli *(Oberdan);* Sylva Koscina
(the Mother); Patrizia Ralli *(Attilia);* Leda Gloria
(Oberdan's Mother).

THE FILM

Coming-of-age stories are such an old-fashioned cinema staple that one tends to dismiss them critically and
leave them for the superficial enjoyment of prepubes-
cent audiences. But once in a while, sufficient artistic
care and sensitivity go into the portrayal of adolescent
verities to make the jaded sit up and take notice. Such
is the excellence of *Guendalina,* a "little" black-and-
white picture with a small cast centering on a pair of
talented newcomers named Jacqueline Sassard and
Raffaele Mattioli. Of course, when film debuts are
outstanding, it is usually to the credit of a painstaking
director—in this case, veteran filmmaker Alberto Lattuada.

Set (and filmed) on the Italian Riviera at the end of
summer, *Guendalina* is all about the spoiled teenaged
daughter (Sassard) of wealthy but unhappily married
parents (Raf Vallone, Sylva Koscina) who summer at a
smart Mediterranean beach resort. With the season's

GUENDALINA   Jacqueline Sassard and Raffaele Mattioli.

close, Guendalina's mother seeks a divorce, deciding to stay on at the beach with the girl. Lonely without her summer friends, Guendalina flirts with a good-looking student named Oberdan (Mattioli), who neglects his studies for her. Platonic romance ensues, with Guendalina spending an entire night with the boy to help him prepare for his exams.

In her absence, Guendalina's father returns to discuss separation plans, and both parents become alarmed at the sight of her empty bed, reproaching themselves for setting so poor an example. Later, realizing the innocence of her love for Oberdan, they reconcile and prepare to leave the resort. Guendalina is forced to come to terms with the devastating possibility that she will likely never see Oberdan again. And that sadness marks the end of her childhood.

What makes *Guendalina* such a refreshing moviegoing experience is the subtle, unsentimental charm of the film's two young protagonists and the many moments of adolescent truth that director Lattuada manages to bring forth with such extraordinary sensitivity. For the strikingly attractive Sassard and Mattioli, *Guendalina's* promise was only partially fulfilled: She continued in important parts for another decade, most notably in the British-made *Accident*, before disappearing from films in her late twenties; Raf Mattioli (as he was subsequently billed) continued in supporting roles for several years but was the tragic victim of a heart attack in 1960, when he was only twenty-four.

Guendalina may be obscure to most readers of this book, but it is well worth the search.

I Soliti Ignoti

(THE BIG DEAL ON MADONNA STREET / PERSONS UNKNOWN / THE USUAL UNIDENTIFIED THIEVES)

A Lux-Vides Coproduction / 1958

(U.S. release by United Motion Picture Organization: 1960)

CREDITS

Director: Mario Monicelli; *Producer:* Franco Cristaldi; *Screenwriters:* Age (Agenore Incrocci), Scarpelli (Furio Scarpelli), Suso Cecchi D'Amico, and Mario Monicelli; *Cinematographer:* Gianni di Venanzo; *Editor:* Adriana Novelli; *Art Director and Costumes:* Piero Gherardi; *Music:* Piero Umiliani; *Running Time:* 105 minutes.

CAST

Vittorio Gassman *(Peppe)*; Marcello Mastroianni *(Tiberio)*; Totò *(Dante)*; Renato Salvatori *(Mario)*;

93

I SOLITI IGNOTI   Vittorio Gassman and Marcello Mastroianni.

Carla Gravina *(Nicoletta)*; Claudia Cardinale *(Carmelina)*; Memmo Carotenuto *(Cosimo)*; Tiberio Murgia *(Ferribotte)*; Rossana Rory *(Norma)*; Carlo Pisacane *(Capanelle)*; Gina Rovere *(Teresa)*.

THE FILM

Jules Dassin's French-made, mid-fifties thriller *Rififi* prompted Italian writer-director Mario Monicelli and his screenwriting colleagues Age, Scarpelli, and Suso Cecchi D'Amico to turn out this gentle spoof of that classic of its genre. They named it *I Soliti Ignoti*, after the police expression for "the usual unidentified persons." For some reason, it was a big hit in Italy and the United States, but not elsewhere.

With its ensemble cast and antic comic twists, *The Big Deal on Madonna Street*, as the film's American distributor renamed it, provides constant amusement as it follows some ambitious, cheerful, but easily distracted petty crooks as they plan a daring big-city crime. Their bungling leader Cosimo (Memmo Carot-

I SOLITI IGNOTI   Renato Salvatori and Claudia Cardinale.

enuto) is arrested for car theft as he is planning a major break-in: the safe of a Madonna Street loan bank, entered through a hole to be made in the empty apartment that adjoins it. To get off, he arranges for the hopeless amateur prizefighter Peppe (Vittorio Gassman) to admit blame for the auto heist instead. But his scheme fails, and they are both sent to jail. In prison, Peppe gets Cosimo to reveal the master robbery plan, and when he is released, Peppe sets out to stage the crime himself, with the aid of the gang: Mario (Renato Salvatori), who sells popcorn in a third-rate cinema; Tiberio (Marcello Mastroianni), an unsuccessful photographer whose wife (Gina Rovere) is serving time for smuggling; Ferribotte (Tiberio Murgia), a hot-tempered Sicilian who suspects every man around with intentions of seducing his sheltered sister Carmelina (Claudia Cardinale); and Dante (Totò), the elderly safecracker who will sell his expertise but refuses to participate in the caper.

With all the details carefully mapped out ahead of time, everything that *can* go wrong *does*. That adjacent apartment is now occupied by a pair of reclusive spinsters whose pretty maid (Carla Gravina) Peppe clumsily courts; Mario's interest in Carmelina foments trouble with her brother; and Tiberio sustains a fractured arm when he steals a camera. Cosimo gets out of jail, only to be killed when he bungles a holdup. (Perhaps because it lent an abruptly sobering note to this otherwise amusing comedy, that sequence and some fourteen other expendable minutes were excised from the American release print.)

Finally, the gang is more or less ready for the big heist, even though their watches cannot be synchronized, since only one of them owns a timepiece. Getting into the spinsters' temporarily deserted apartment, they stop to consume all the food in sight before spending hours knocking down the living-room wall— only to find themselves in the apartment's *kitchen!*

Chuckles and guffaws are well maintained by director Monicelli throughout this only slightly overlong spoof. And he doesn't give in to the sort of wild slapstick that might have seemed appropriate for this

I SOLITI IGNOTI   Marcello Mastroianni, Vittorio Gassman, Totò and Tiberio Murgia.

95

subject matter. Gassman, Mastroianni (playing a rare dimwit), and Salvatori all lend themselves easily to comedy, and that old master clown Totò (Italy's Buster Keaton) is marvelous as the enterprising break-in expert who nevertheless chooses not to get involved.

Under the title *The Usual Unidentified Thieves*, this picture was nominated for 1958's Best Foreign Language Oscar, which went to France's *Mon Oncle*. In 1984, Louis Malle filmed an English-language remake he called *Crackers*. It was not a success.

Two years later, the Italians released a sequel to the original film entitled *I Soliti Ignoti . . . Vent'Anni Dopo* that *Variety* called "more like a melancholy visit to the cemetery of Italian comedy than a worthy follow-up."

Estate Violenta

(VIOLENT SUMMER / THE WIDOW IS WILLING)

A Titanus-SGC Production / 1959

(U.S. release by Films Around the World, Inc.: 1961)

CREDITS

Director: Valerio Zurlini; *Producer:* Silvio Clementelli; *Screenwriters:* Valerio Zurlini, Suso Cecchi D'Amico, and Giorgio Prosperi; *Cinematographer:* Gino Santoni; *Editor:* Mario Serandrei; *Art Directors:* Dario Cecchi and Massimiliano Capriccioli; *Music:* Mario Nascimbene; *Running Time:* 107 minutes.

CAST

Eleonora Rossi-Drago *(Roberta Parmesa)*; Jean-Louis Trintignant *(Carlo Romanazzi)*; Jacqueline Sassard *(Rossana)*; Lilla Brignone *(Signorina Raluisa)*; Federica Ranchi *(Maddalena)*; Raf Mattioli *(Giorgio)*; Enrico Maria Salerno *(Carlo's Father)*; Cathia Caro *(Gemma)*.

THE FILM

Valerio Zurlini, who favorably impressed both critics and audiences with his first picture, *Un Giornata Balorda/From a Roman Balcony*, garnered equally favorable notices with this follow-up feature, a May-August love story set against a summer-resort background during wartime.

It is mid-1943, but the wealthy young vacationers at the Italian seaside town of Riccione refuse to let the faraway guns of World War II interfere with their carefree pursuit of fun and romance. Among them is Carlo Romanazzi (Jean-Louis Trintignant), who has been able to avoid conscription because of the rank of his father (Enrico Maria Salerno), a Fascist leader. Following a chance meeting at the beach with Roberta Parmesa (Eleonora Rossi-Drago), the well-to-do widow of a naval hero and mother of a four-year-old daughter, a captivated Carlo turns from his longtime girlfriend Rossana (Jacqueline Sassard) and quietly pursues the older woman.

Because of the difference in their ages and the fact that she shares a home with her disapproving mother-in-law (Lilla Brignone), Roberta does little to encourage Carlo. But their mutual attraction only increases, and the pair are inevitably drawn into a passionate affair that is eventually disrupted by the approach of Allied forces and the overthrow of the local government by an anti-Fascist faction. Guilt over his avoidance of military service forces Carlo to seek a safer haven in the south, and Roberta decides to go with him. But the horrors of war confront them when their train is strafed and bombed at the Bologna railroad station, and Carlo's conscience makes him resolve his relationship with Roberta. Insisting that she return home

ESTATE VIOLENTA   Eleonora Rossi-Drago and Jean-Louis Trintignant.

ESTATE VIOLENTA   Jean-Louis Trintignant and Eleonora Rossi-Drago.

without him, he stays behind to help care for the injured and the dying.

Hardly the "violent" drama promised by its title, the movie is essentially a routine love story between two people doomed never to realize more than temporary happiness. What gives it freshness and validity is the attention to setting and detail of Zurlini's direction, aided immeasurably by Gino Santoni's artfully composed camera setups. And, above all, there are the committed performances of France's Jean-Louis Trintignant and, in perhaps her finest acting, the Spanish-Italian star Eleonora Rossi-Drago, whose classic beauty recalls Ingrid Bergman in the forties. One might carp that Trintignant doesn't appear so youthful a boy, nor does Rossi-Drago look mature enough to make their love affair as impossibly ill matched as the screenplay requires. One must, of course, suspend a certain disbelief. Originally, Rossi-Drago appeared in a topless sequence that bothered some of the film's U.S. critics; the scene was later deleted from the ninety-five-minute general-release cut. In some areas, *Violent Summer* was shown under the more exploitative—and possibly more accurate, if cheapening—title *The Widow is Willing.*

Il Generale Della Rovere

(GENERAL DELLA ROVERE)

A Coproduction of Zebra Films (Rome) and Gaumont Films (Paris / 1959

(U.S. release by Continental Distributing: 1960)

CREDITS

Director: Roberto Rossellini; *Producer:* Morris Ergas; *Screenwriters:* Sergio Amidei, Diego Fabbri, and Indro Montanelli; *Cinematographer:* Carlo Carlini; *Editor:* Cesare Cavagna; *Art Director:* Piero Zuffi; *Music:* Renzo Rossellini; *Running Time:* 160 minutes *(U.S. Running Time:* 139 minutes).

CAST

Vittorio De Sica *(Emanuele Bardone)*; Hannes Messemer *(Colonel Mueller)*; Vittorio Caprioli *(Banchelli)*; Giuseppe Rossetti *(Fabrizio)*; Sandra Milo *(Olga)*; Giovanna Ralli *(Valeria)*; Anne Vernon *(Signora Fassio)*; Baronessa Barzani *(Contessa Della Rovere)*; Kurt Polter *(German Officer)*; Kurt Selge *(Schrantz)*; Mary Greco *(the Madam)*; Lucia Modugno *(the Prostitute)*; Linda Veras *(German Attendant)*; Luciano Picozzi, Nando Angelini, and Bernardino Menicacci *(Partisans)*.

THE FILM

With *General Della Rovere*, Roberto Rossellini at last won back the respect and admiration of the critics and

IL GENERALE DELLA ROVERE On the set: Vittorio De Sica, director Roberto Rossellini and Hannes Messemer.

the film community, which felt he had gone astray, both personally and professionally, during his respective alliances with Ingrid Bergman and Sonali Das Gupta. And in their critiques of this strong 1959 drama, many of the reviewers found cause to recall and compare it with the mid-forties Rossellini heyday of *Open City* and *Paisan*. In fact, some felt that *General Della Rovere* was almost an extension of material from those screen classics—set, like this one, amid German-occupied, World War II Italy. Others thought that the screenplay (by Sergio Amidei, Diego Fabbri and Indro Montanelli) was the best that Rossellini (famed for his improvisational story methods) had ever had to work with. But *General Della Rovere* was severely criticized for its original 160-minute length, and some even felt that the movie's 139-minute U.S. cut was too long, considering the material. Ironically, the picture had originally been filmed, edited, and packaged in a mere thirty-three intensive, cost-cutting days!

In 1943, a con artist named Emanuele Bardone (Vittorio De Sica) takes money from the families of captured Italian partisans by pretending to have sufficient influence to free their loved ones from Nazi internment. When the German SS commander in Genoa, Colonel Mueller (Hannes Messemer), eventually learns about these deceptions, he gets Bardone to take part in a much greater hoax. By promising the swindler both money and Swiss sanctuary, he arranges for Bardone to impersonate the famed partisan leader General Della Rovere. Unknown to the partisans, the real Rovere is dead, having been killed in an effort to contact another partisan leader named Fabrizio (Giuseppe Rossetti), who has assumed a pseudonym to prevent identification.

Convinced that Fabrizio is among the partisans confined to San Vittore prison, Mueller announces that Rovere has been apprehended. He then dispatches Bardone to that facility with orders to ferret out the real Fabrizio. Initially, Bardone has no problem following Mueller's orders, for years of practice have made him a good impersonator. Gradually, however, the trust of his cellmates, as they rely on him for leadership and guidance, eats away at his resolve, and almost without his knowing what is happening, Bardone starts to *become* the man he is impersonating. To protect "the general," a fellow prisoner submits to torture—and then commits suicide—before he'll undergo a follow-up interrogation. When Bardone protests that prisoner's treatment, he, too, is tortured. By this time, Bardone *is* General Della Rovere; the transformation is complete. By now he has learned Fabrizio's identity. But rather than betray the man, Bardone delivers an impassioned speech to his cellmates and is led away to face a firing squad.

IL GENERALE DELLA ROVERE Vittorio De Sica (center).

Even the critical minority who found fault with Rossellini's "comeback" film had nothing but the highest praise for the acting of Vittorio De Sica in what many felt was the finest work of his long screen career. In the *New York Times*, Bosley Crowther wrote: "Signor De Sica's performance, ranging from shifty and glib to dignified and laconic, is a beautiful thing." The *New York World-Telegram* critic Alton Cook theorized about the film's effectiveness: "The great steadying influence on the erratic Rossellini may have been the presence of De Sica, a wise old craftsman bursting with movie sagacity. With delicate perception, he makes clear and credible the gradual transformation of despicable coward to heroic stature."

Il Generale Della Rovere tied with *La Granda Guerra (The Great War)* for Best Picture at the 1969 Venice Film Festival, temporarily restoring Roberto Rossellini to the pantheon of revered cinema maestros. And the film won an Oscar nomination for Original Story and Screenplay.

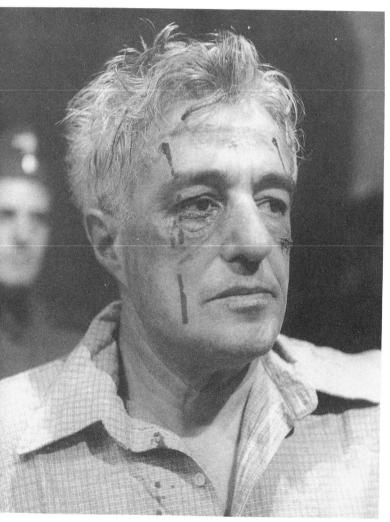

IL GENERALE DELLA ROVERE   Vittorio De Sica.

Kapò

A Coproduction of Vides-Zebra Film-Cineriz (Rome), Francinex (Paris), and Lovćen Film (Belgrade) / 1960

(U.S. release by Lionex Films: 1964)

CREDITS

Director: Gillo Pontecorvo; *Producer:* Morris Ergas; *Associate Producer:* Antonio Musu; *Screenwriters:* Gillo Pontecorvo and Franco Solinas; *Cinematographers:* Goffredo Bellisario and Alexander Sekulovic; *Editor:* Roberto Cinquini; *Art Director:* Piero Gherardi; *Music:* Carlo Rustichelli; *Running Time:* 116 minutes.

CAST

Susan Strasberg *(Edith)*; Laurent Terzieff *(Sascha)*; Emmanuelle Riva *(Therese)*; Didi Perego *(Sofia)*; Gianni Garko *(German Soldier)*; and Annabella Besi, Graziella Galvani, Mira Dinulovic, and Dragomir Felba.

THE FILM

Before Gillo Pontecorvo directed his best-known and deservedly lauded motion picture *The Battle of Algiers*, he had turned out a number of documentary shorts, a little-known feature debut called *La Grande Strada Azzurra/The Great Blue Road*, and a modest but hard-hitting World War II concentration-camp melodrama called *Kapò*. The latter took four years to reach U.S. screens, by which time it had racked up an Academy Award nomination as Best Foreign Film and a Best Actress trophy for its star, Susan Strasberg, at the 1961 Mar Del Plata Film Festival. Nevertheless, American critics had reservations about *Kapò*. Most could not refrain from comparing Strasberg's part—that of a Jewish girl sent to a death camp where she finds the means to survive—to her career-making Broadway lead in *The Diary of Anne Frank*. Some felt that this was sort of a poor man's sequel to the Frank story but with the star's performance no equal to her celebrated stage bow at fourteen.

Like Anne Frank, Edith (Strasberg) is a European teenager whose religion happens to be the wrong one

KAPO   Susan Strasberg and Emmanuelle Riva.

for that time and place in history. With her family, she is swept up by the Nazis and sent to a death camp, where her parents are exterminated. Edith is able to escape their fate with the help of the camp's doctor, who gives her the identification and clothing of a non-Jewish prisoner named "Nicole," who has died in the hospital. Under her new identity, she is transferred to a camp in Poland, where she suffers almost unbearable conditions and treatment; only the presence of her French partisan friend Therese (Emmanuelle Riva) affords her the will to survive. Because of her attractive appearance, Edith is chosen to "entertain" German soldiers, and eventually her fear of death motivates her to collaborate with the enemy and become a hated *Kapò*, or camp guard. Notwithstanding her hardened dedication to her new role, she falls in love with a Russian prisoner named Sascha (Laurent Terzieff).

When the Nazis cut back on the food rations, Therese is driven to kill herself, an event that profoundly shakes Edith, shocking her into regretting her collaboration with the Germans. Shifting to the side of

KAPO   Laurent Terzieff and Susan Strasberg.

the Russians, she suggests a plan of escape to her fellow prisoners as the Russian army approaches. Revealing herself to Sascha as a Jewess, Edith finds courage to sacrifice her own life in order to save the others.

While crediting the film's first third for "bringing us a time and place of tragedy in authentic and soul-wracking detail that is almost too painful to follow," Judith Crist, writing in the *New York Herald Tribune*, felt that *Kapò* "raises the question of where the recording of history ends and the exploitation of human tragedy begins." The British Film Institute's *Monthly Film Bulletin* reported that *Kapò* was "the favorite anti-Nazi film in Russia," with a backhanded compliment to its director: "Pontecorvo has certainly managed to find a fool-proof commercial formula for the most uncommercial subject of them all."

It can be argued that *Kapò* loses ground with the intrusion of its boy-girl romance; material of such strong content can only suffer by the trappings of melodramatic fiction. But so much of *Kapò* is powerful and impressive, and so much of its acting so dedicated, that one must accord credit where it is due. The camera work by a team of cinematographers frequently bears the look of a newsreel, and Pontecorvo obviously put to good use the lessons he learned here, for otherwise *The Battle of Algiers* would not be the masterpiece it would become six years later.

La Dolce Vita

(THE SWEET LIFE)

A Coproduction of Riama Film (Rome) and Pathé Consortium Cinema-Gray Film (Paris) / 1960

CREDITS

Director: Federico Fellini; *Executive Producer:* Franco Magli; *Producers:* Giuseppe Amato and Angelo Rizzoli; *Screenwriters:* Federico Fellini, Ennio Flaiano, Tullio Pinelli, and Brunello Rondi; *Totalscope Cinematographer:* Otello Martelli; *Editor:* Leo Cattozo; *Art Director:* Piero Gherardi; *Costumes:* Piero Gherardi; *Music:* Nino Rota; *Running Time:* 180 minutes.

CAST

Marcello Mastroianni *(Marcello Rubino)*; Yvonne Furneaux *(Emma)*; Anouk Aimée *(Maddalena)*; Anita

Ekberg *(Sylvia Rank)*; Alain Cuny *(Steiner)*; Annibale Ninchi *(Marcello's Father)*; Magali Noël *(Fanny)*; Lex Barker *(Robert)*; Nadia Gray *(Nadia)*; Jacques Sernas *(Film Star)*; Walter Santesso *(Paparazzo)*; Valeria Ciangottini *(Paola)*; Polidor *(Tabarin Clown)*; Mino Doro *(Nadia's Lover)*; Riccardo Garrone *(Riccardo)*; Harriet White *(Edna)*; Alain Dijon *(Frankie Stout)*; Giulio Girola *(Police Inspector)*; Nico Otzak *(Sophisticated Blonde)*; Audrey McDonald *(Sonia)*; Renée Longarini *(Signora Steiner)*; Carlo Di Maggio *(Toto Scalise)*; Adriana Moneta *(Prostitute)*; Sandra Lee *(Ballerina)*; Enrico Glori *(Nadia's Admirer)*; Gloria Jones *(Gloria)*; Lilli Granado *(Lucy)*; Laura Betti *(Laura)*; Ida Galli *(Debutante of the Year)*; Gio Staiano *(Effeminate Young Man)*.

THE FILM

Several years after the release of *La Dolce Vita*, Federico Fellini recalled its inspiration: "Rome had become

a big place in the 1950s. Life had become like a carnival—disordered and unreal. There was an unsettled climate. This is what I wanted to get in a film—this climate of activity, excitement, nervousness, and uncertainty. I had come to the point where I wanted to stop and inquire, 'What's going on?' "

The resultant film is an episodic series of sequences linked by the observations of a roving Roman journalist (Marcello Mastroianni), as corrupt and immature

LA DOLCE VITA   Anita Ekberg.

LA DOLCE VITA   Marcello Mastroianni, Adriana Moneta and Anouk Aimée.

an individual as those with whom he tirelessly mingles, often in the company of his paparazzo-pal (Walter Santesso). Marcello lives with his beautiful but neurotically possessive mistress Emma (Yvonne Furneaux) while continuing to romance friends like the self-possessed Maddalena (Anouk Aimée), a coolly glamorous nymphomaniac who frequents the clubs and sidewalk cafés of Rome's famed Via Veneto. One night, Marcello encounters Maddalena while nightclubbing, and they pick up a friendly prostitute (Adriana Moneta) whom they drive home, making love in her bed while she makes them coffee. Marcello returns home in the morning to find that Emma has attempted suicide, and he rushes her to a hospital. From there, he must go to the airport to cover the arrival of Sylvia Rank (Anita Ekberg), a buxom but childlike Hollywood actress from Sweden, in Rome to star in a movie. First,

however, she treats the press and photographers to a day-and-night photo shoot that encompasses interviews, a visit to St. Peter's and a Roman nightclub, and, finally—with Marcello still in fruitless amorous pursuit—a fully clothed predawn romp in the ornate Trevi Fountain pool.

Marcello next visits with his intellectual friend Steiner (Alain Cuny) before taking Emma along as he covers an alleged miracle involving two working-class children who are only too ready to restage the event—a visitation from the Madonna—for television cameras. At Steiner's house, Marcello attends a party and meets his young children. The next day, he takes his typewriter to a seaside restaurant, intent on writing that serious book he tells everyone he's working on, where he encounters a waitress whose innocent, "Ombrian angel" face haunts him. Back in Rome, he finds that his

LA DOLCE VITA   Yvonne Furneaux and Marcello Mastroianni.

LA DOLCE VITA   Annibale Ninchi, Marcello Mastroianni and Magali Noël.

rarely seen father (Annibale Ninchi) has come up from the provinces for a visit. Marcello and his paparazzo-pal take him to a nightclub, where they pick up good-natured Fanny (Magali Noël), a chorus girl to whom the father takes a shine. Later, the old man feels ill but insists on leaving on the dawn train. Though concerned, Marcello goes on to an upper-crust party at a suburban castle.

After a savage argument with Emma, they split, only to end up in bed together. The next day, Marcello learns that Steiner has shot himself after first killing his two children. Marcello is asked to break the sad news to Steiner's returning wife (Renée Longarini). At still another party—this one to celebrate the divorce of well-to-do Nadia (Nadia Gray)—Marcello is eyewit-

ness to a virtual orgy of wealthy, decadent Romans. At dawn, the party adjourns to a nearby beach, where a monstrous fish has been dragged ashore. Once again, across the channel, Marcello sees his "Ombrian angel." But the roar of the surf drowns out her words, and he can only guess what this intriguing innocent is trying to communicate to him.

For Fellini, *La Dolce Vita* was a virtual break-through film, moving into new cinematic territory in its portrayal of Rome at the advent of the "swinging sixties." Today, over thirty years later, it is difficult to perceive what might have given the censors pause. For the movie displays little sexuality in its sensual scenes and hardly any daring in its move into religious areas. Because *La Dolce Vita* is well made and well acted, it

105

still retains interest. But its "power" has diminished, and its air of moral freedom now seems almost amusing in its antiseptic purity.

Nino Rota's melodious music is so infectious an adornment to *La Dolce Vita* that one tends to believe that he is incorporating "standard" songs into his score—before realizing that *this* is where those familiar tunes *began*—and that Rota composed them!

After this film, "la dolce vita" became a part of the international language. In the United States, the movie was among those relative few foreign-language productions with sufficient popular appeal to merit turning out an alternate, English-dubbed version.

Despite its other nominations, *La Dolce Vita*'s sole Oscar was for the costume designs of Piero Gherardi. However, it won more respect at Cannes, where it was named Best Film. In the United States, similar accolades followed by way of the National Board of Review and the New York Film Critics.

L'Avventura

(THE ADVENTURE)

A Coproduction of Cino Del Duca and Produzione Cinematografiche Europée (Rome) and Société Cinématographique Lyre (Paris)/1960

(U.S. release by Janus Films: 1961)

CREDITS

Director: Michelangelo Antonioni; *Producer:* Amato Pennasilico; *Screenwriters:* Michelangelo Antonioni,

L'AVVENTURA   Gabriele Ferzetti and Lea Massari.

Elio Bartolini, and Tonino Guerra; *Cinematographer:* Aldo Scavardo; *Editor:* Eraldo Da Roma; *Art Director:* Piero Polletto; *Costumes:* Adriana Berselli; *Music:* Giovanni Fusco; *Running Time:* 145 minutes.

CAST

Monica Vitti *(Claudia);* Gabriele Ferzetti *(Sandro);* Lea Massari *(Anna);* Dominique Blanchar *(Giulia);* James Addams *(Corrado, Her Husband);* Renzo Ricci *(Anna's Father);* Esmeralda Ruspoli *(Princess Patrizia);* Lelio Luttazi *(Raimondo);* Dorothy De Poliolo *(Gloria Perkins);* Giovanni Petrucci *(Young Prince).*

THE FILM

Michelangelo Antonioni's motion pictures are not for everyone, nor do they pretend to be. His detractors have been as demonstrative, internationally, as his partisans. Significantly, *L'Avventura*'s initial public reception, at the 1960 Cannes Film Festival, was a mixture of jeers and bravos that culminated in the award of a Special Jury Prize for "a new screen language and beauty of its images." The movie went on to win numerous additional European honors both for itself and the performances of its stars, Monica Vitti and Gabriele Ferzetti. In the early seventies, *L'Avventura* remained sufficiently revered to take fifth place in a poll of international critics, conducted by Britain's *Sight and Sound* magazine, listing their all-time Top Ten Films.

A small group of mundane Italian socialites gathers for a party aboard the yacht of Princess Patrizia (Esmeralda Ruspoli), cruising off the northeast coast of Sicily. Included are Sandro (Ferzetti), a wealthy, fortyish architect; his fiancée Anna (Lea Massari), a former ambassador's daughter who deplores her role as little more than a sex object; and Claudia (Vitti), Anna's friend and only member of the party whose background is less than "privileged."

After anchoring the yacht for a Mediterranean swim, the group goes ashore on one of the region's many barren, volcanic islands. But a storm suddenly scatters the bathers, and afterward it is discovered that Anna has vanished. She is not to be found on the island, but Sandro and Claudia search hopefully and, in their grief, realize a mutual attraction. Fisherman in the area are questioned but without success. Both separately and together, Claudia and Sandro visit locales on the mainland where an unknown girl is reported to have been seen. But their hopes fade, replaced by guilt and remorse as they begin a sexual relationship of their own.

L'AVVENTURA Monica Vitti.

Eventually, the lovers meet their yachting friends again at a luxury hotel in Taormina. When Claudia awakens that night, she finds Sandro gone and is shocked to discover him in the arms of a stranger. Contrite and despairing, he can only weep quietly. And a forgiving Claudia follows him in compassion. Anna is never found.

If the film's story line dumbfounded some among its audiences, Antonioni knew his artistic intent all too clearly. As he told an interviewer for *L'Express:* "Superficially, *L'Avventura* may seem to be a love story, perhaps a somewhat mysterious one. During an excursion, a girl disappears. This fact creates a void which is immediately filled by other facts. For the fiancée and for one of the girl's friends, the search for her becomes a kind of sentimental journey, at the end of which they both find themselves in a new and quite unforeseen situation."

Thus, the filmmaker is concerned not with uncovering the mystery of Anna but with the behavior of Claudia and Sandro and their developing characters in

L'AVVENTURA Gabriele Ferzetti and Monica Vitti.

relation to their predicament—and one another. Not unexpectedly, many of the film's critics were put off by *L'Avventura*'s more than two and one-half hours of ambiguous uneventfulness. In the *New York Times*, Bosley Crowther wrote: "Watching *L'Avventura* is like trying to follow a showing of a picture at which several reels have got lost. What Antonioni is trying to get across is a secret he seems to be determined to conceal from the audience." *Time* magazine's uncredited reviewer was even more direct, calling the movie "a nightmarish masterpiece of tedium." But *Saturday Review*'s Hollis Alpert was a bit more generous: "*L'Avventura* is the work of a highly individualistic director. It all takes time, much time, but if you're willing to allow Antonioni his way, you may find yourself fascinated."

In Europe, *L'Avventura*'s distributor devised a clever advertising campaign, praising the film's champions for being among the elite and dismissing as ignorant fools those who found it otherwise. The results brought out the European intelligentsia, who flocked to attend it in respectful silence. In the United States, film buffs made *L'Avventura* a "must see," with the result that Michelangelo Antonioni now became a

household name. And if one were sufficiently naive to inquire of the director as to the missing Anna's fate, his standard answer was "It isn't important."

La Maschera del Demonio

(BLACK SUNDAY)

A Galatea–Jolly Film / 1960

(U.S. release by American International: 1961)

CREDITS

Director: Mario Bava; *Producer:* Massimo De Rita; *Screenwriters:* Ennio De Concini, Mario Bava, Marcello Coscia, and Mario Serandrei; *Based on the novel* The Vij *by* Nikolai Gogol; *Cinematographers:* Ubaldo Terzano and Mario Bava; *Editor:* Mario Serandrei; *Art Directors:* Giorgio Giovannini and Mario Bava; *Cos-*

LA MASCHERA DEL DEMONIO   Barbara Steele.

109

tumes: Tina Loriedo Grani; *Music:* Roberto Nicolosi *(English-language version:* Les Baxter); *Running Time:* 84 minutes.

CAST

Barbara Steele *(Princess Asa/Princess Katia)*; John Richardson *(Dr. Andrej Gorobek)*; Ivo Garrani *(Prince Vajda)*; Andrea Checchi *(Dr. Choma Kruvajan)*; Ar-turo Dominici *(Javutich)*; Enrico Olivieri *(Constantin)*; Mario Passante *(Nikita)*; Antonio Pierfederici *(the Priest)*; Clara Bindi *(the Innkeeper)*; Germana Domin-ici *(Her Daughter)*; Tino Bianchi *(Ivan)*.

THE FILM

Mario Bava had enjoyed a long career as a highly respected cameraman, with his directorial career spent

on movies perhaps less readily associated with the Italian cinema at its classic best: *Hercules in the Haunted World, Planet of the Vampires, Evil Eye,* and *Baron Blood* among them. But what distinguished Bava's films among others of the genre was his flair for visual style and his sense of humor in handling the cinematic clichés of horror.

In the cult horror classic *Black Sunday,* Bava also had a hand in writing, art direction, and camera work,

LA MASCHERA DEL DEMONIO   Barbara Steele and Arturo Dominici.

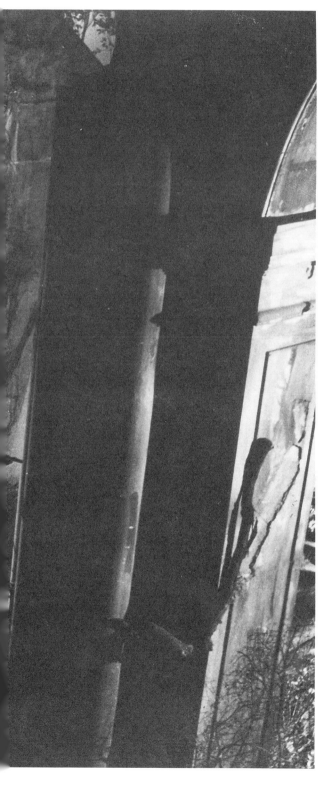

filming in black and white because he thought it more conducive to fright—as well as less exploitative of the movie's more gory elements, which were easier to accept thirty years ago, with this film's artfully moody lighting.

The story is loosely based on Gogol's 1835 novel *The Vij.* "Black Sunday" refers to the one day in each century when Satan purportedly moves among the living. In this case, it is in Moldavia, in 1830, where Dr. Choma Kruvajan (Andrea Checchi) is traveling to a medical conference with his assistant Dr. Andrej Gorobec (John Richardson). En route, he investigates the crypt of a seemingly deserted castle and accidentally cuts himself, dripping blood onto the tomb of one Princess Asa (Barbara Steele) of the House of Vajda. Two hundred years earlier, she had been branded a witch and burned at the stake with her lover Javutich

111

LA MASCHERA DEL DEMONIO   John Richardson and Andrea Checchi.

(Arturo Dominici), but not before putting a curse on her family—the very ones who had branded her a witch.

Now, revived by the scent of blood, she orders Javutich also to rise from his tomb and help her destroy the family's three remaining members by supplying her with the blood she needs to take over the body of her look-alike descendant Princess Katia (Steele again). Their first victim is Dr. Kruvajan, who has been sent for to look after old Prince Vajda (Ivo Garrani), both of whom Asa dispatches in standard vampire fashion.

The next day, Andrej arrives at Vajda castle to probe his colleague's disappearance, only to be immediately enchanted by the beautiful Katia, for whom he agrees to stay on and help protect her and her brother Constantin (Enrico Olivieri). The latter disposes of Javutich but is himself mortally wounded while Andrej hurries to the crypt, bent on destroying Asa. However, as he is about to destroy the supposedly lifeless body, he realizes that it is really Katia, not Asa, for she is wearing a crucifix, a religious symbol that could never adorn a vampire. Realizing Asa's trickery, Andrej, with the help of the local priest, puts Asa to permanent rest, and Katia is restored to life.

Italian filmmakers have long been more ready than their British and American counterparts to deal with the graphically explicit in matters of motion-picture horror. In fact, this film's original title translates as *The Mask of the Demon,* a reference to the metal adornment (with spikes on its *inside*) that is hammered onto the face of the witch Asa as she is burned at the stake in the opening sequence. That and a few other chilling moments—like the maggot-ridden face of Princess Asa's corpse as it slowly comes to life—were enough to discourage the British censors, who kept this film off their screens for eight years. In the United States, for reasons best known to distributor American International, Roberto Nicolosi's score was replaced by another, composed by Les Baxter; not everyone thought it an improvement.

For the wide-eyed English beauty Barbara Steele, in her film debut, her performance in this dual role effectively captured the imagination of moviegoers. *Black Sunday* paved the way for a succession of similar parts that made Steele the undisputed European cinematic horror queen and, eventually, a lasting cult figure. The actress later appeared in Fellini's *8½* but eventually chose to give up acting for a producing career.

Rocco e i Suoi Fratelli

(ROCCO AND HIS BROTHERS)

A Coproduction of Titanus Films (Rome) and Les Films Marceau (Paris) / 1960

(U.S. release by Astor Pictures International: 1961)

CREDITS

Director: Luchino Visconti; *Producer:* Goffredo Lombardo; *Screenwriters:* Luchino Visconti, Suso Cecchi

ROCCO E I SUOI FRATELLI   Annie Girardot and Alain Delon.

D'Amico, Pasquale Festa Campanile, Massimo Franciosa, and Enrico Medioli; *Partly inspired by the novel* Il Ponte della Ghisolfa *by* Giovanni Testori; *Cinematographer:* Giuseppe Rotunno; *Editor:* Mario Serandrei; *Art Director:* Mario Garbuglia; *Costumes:* Piero Tosi; *Music:* Nino Rota; *Running Time:* 180 minutes.

CAST

Alain Delon *(Rocco Parondi)*; Renato Salvatori *(Simone Parondi)*; Annie Girardot *(Nadia)*; Katina Paxinou *(Rosaria Parondi)*; Roger Hanin *(Morini)*; Paolo Stoppa *(Boxing Trainer)*; Suzy Delair *(Luisa)*; Claudia Cardinale *(Ginetta)*; Spiros Focas *(Vincenzo Parondi)*; Max Cartier *(Ciro Parondi)*; Rocco Vidolazzi *(Luca Parondi)*; Corrado Pani *(Ivo)*; Alessandra Panaro *(Ciro's Fiancée)*; Claudia Mori and Adriana Asti *(Dry-Cleaner Workers)*.

THE FILM

Of all the cinematic works of Luchino Visconti, *Rocco and His Brothers* remained his personal favorite. Epic both in scope and length, the picture remains uneven and episodic and has been much criticized for the violence and intensity of prolonged sequences involving prizefighting, rape, and murder.

In search of a better life, the widowed Rosaria Parondi (Katina Paxinou) and her four younger sons move from their impoverished Lucania farm in the

ROCCO E I SUOI FRATELLI   Renato Salvatori
and Roger Hanin.

south of Italy to Milan, where the eldest, Vincenzo
(Spiros Focas), has already settled. But their mass
arrival immediately has a disrupting influence on the
family of his fiancée Ginetta (Claudia Cardinale), and
Vincenzo secures cramped but serviceable quarters for
them elsewhere, introducing his siblings to the boxing
gym where he works out. For a boxing career, the most
likely prospect seems to be Simone (Renato Salvatori),
whose rugged good looks attract the trainer Morini
(Roger Hanin), who prepares him for a career in the
ring. The saintly Rocco (Alain Delon), who is clearly
the better boxer, has no interest in professional fighting
and finds employment at a dry cleaner's. Simone
makes a name for himself as a prizefighter, becoming
involved with a disillusioned prostitute named Nadia
(Annie Girardot), who fails to return his affections and
soon leaves him.

With the passage of time, Rocco serves in the military and one day encounters Nadia, recently released
from prison. Their immediate rapport gradually blossoms into a serious relationship. Rocco goes home to
find that his brother Ciro (Max Cartier) has found a
laborer's job with Alfa-Romeo and that Vincenzo has
had to marry the pregnant Ginetta. With a decline in
his boxing career, the dissipated Simone jealously
takes note of Nadia's relationship with Rocco and
tracks them down with his cronies. In a remote trysting
place, Rocco is roughed up and made to look on as
Simone rapes the defiant Nadia. But Rocco blames

ROCCI E I SUOI FRATELLI   Annie Girardot.

ROCCI E I SUOI
FRATELLI Annie Girardot
and Renato Salvatori.

himself for the brutal incident, breaking off with Nadia, whom he urges to stay with Simone. The latter affair resumes, but she eventually returns to her old profession.

Desperate for employment, Rocco turns to the ring, where his natural athletic skills bring him success and popularity. Meanwhile, Simone has turned to petty thievery, consorting with homosexuals for money. In a chance meeting with Nadia, he attempts to resume their old relationship. But she rejects him, and Simone savagely stabs her to death. Again Rocco attempts to protect his black-sheep brother, but the practical-minded Ciro turns Simone over to the police, explaining to the youngest brother Luca (Rocco Vidolazzi) that Simone was doomed and that the whole family—as well as the city of Milan—must share the responsibility. Perhaps one day Luca will be able to realize his dream of returning to their roots in the south.

Shot on location in and around Milan, *Rocco and His Brothers* makes good use of such landmarks as that city's magnificent wedding-cake cathedral. But above all, it is a fascinating character study, made all the more compelling by the painstaking care Visconti took with his handpicked cast, especially twenty-four-year-old Alain Delon, as the perhaps too-good Rocco; Renato Salvatori, who found in the multileveled torments of Simone the best role of his career; and the versatile Annie Girardot (who became Salvatori's off-screen wife).

The film's many awards and citations included a Special Jury Prize at the 1960 Venice Film Festival, reason enough to avoid bowdlerized versions of Visconti's masterpiece—especially the ninety-six minute cut that has circulated on American television!

La Ciociara

(TWO WOMEN)

A Coproduction of Champion Cinematografica (Rome) and Films Marceau-Cocinor-Société Générale de Cinématographie (Paris) / 1961

(U.S. release by Embassy Pictures: 1961)

CREDITS

Director: Vittorio De Sica; *Producer:* Carlo Ponti; *Screenwriters:* Cesare Zavattini and Vittorio De Sica; *Based on the novel by* Alberto Moravia; *Cinematogra-*

pher: Gabor Pogany; *Editor:* Adriana Novelli; *Art Director:* Gastone Medin; *Costumes:* Elio Costanzi; *Music:* Armando Trovajoli; *Running Time:* 110 minutes.

CAST

Sophia Loren *(Cesira)*; Eleanora Brown *(Rosetta)*; Jean-Paul Belmondo *(Michele)*; Raf Vallone *(Giovanni)*; Renato Salvatori *(Florindo)*; Carlo Ninchi *(Michele's Father)*; Andrea Checchi *(Fascist)*.

THE FILM

From Italian beauty-contest winner to major international movie star, ambitious Sophia Loren has, in her long career, starred in more than her share of forgettable flops. But she has also proven herself a strong, believable actress, especially under the direction of her beloved mentor Vittorio De Sica. In the fifties, he helped develop her comedic talents in the memorable "Pizza on Credit" episode of *Gold of Naples*, and Loren would later credit De Sica with teaching her everything she has learned about acting.

In 1960, plans were developed to film Alberto Moravia's *La Ciociara*, about a widow and her daughter in war-torn Italy, casting Anna Magnani as the mother of Sophia Loren. But apparently Magnani, at fifty-two, wasn't ready to play screen mama to Loren; by turning down the role, she paved the way for producer Carlo Ponti to move his wife (Loren) into the mother role and cast Italian-American teenager Eleanora Brown as the daughter. One can only wonder what the resultant

LA CIOCIARA Eleanora Brown and Sophia Loren.

movie about a young widow and her adolescent child
would have been had Magnani and Loren costarred.

It is 1943, and Cesira (Loren) is a Roman grocer's
widow who has married an older man to escape from
her impoverished peasant life in the mountainous
south. Terrified of the Allied bombings, she arranges to
have a neighbor Giovanni (Raf Vallone), with whom
she is intimate, look after the grocery while she takes
her twelve-year-old daughter Rosetta (Eleanora
Brown) to the safety of her mother's mountain village.
As they travel by train and on foot, Cesira protects
Rosetta from both enemy-aircraft gunfire and predatory Fascist soldiers, who desert at the news of Mussolini's capture. At the village, a disillusioned intellectual
named Michele (Jean-Paul Belmondo) falls for Cesira,
who cannot bring herself to take him seriously as she
forages for food. Rosetta, on the other hand, secretly
adores the unsuspecting man. Soon Cesira believes
they would survive better in Rome. On the way back,
she and Rosetta are brutally attacked and raped by
Moroccan troops in a bombed-out chapel. The next

day, the resilient Cesira is prepared to get on with her
life, but she finds Rosetta in an understandable state of
shock, now resentful of her mother's protectiveness.
After they are given a lift by the truck driver Florindo
(Renato Salvatori), Rosetta slips away to spend the
night dancing with him. The next day, Cesira rages at
the returning child, who defies her—until news of
Michele's death reunites them in sorrow and a new,
adult understanding.

In this demanding emotional role, with which she
obviously identified, Loren responded well to De Sica's
meticulous direction. In particular, the scene after her
rape comes alive with some of the most deeply felt
emotion ever recorded on film. As a result, there were
few arguments against the array of honors subsequently accorded the actress: the British Academy
Award as Best Foreign Actress; the Best Actress award
at Cannes; a similar accolade from Ireland's Cork
Festival; the New York Film Critics Award; and—
ultimately—Hollywood's very first Best Actress Oscar
ever given to a foreign-language performance. Loren's

competition that year included Audrey Hepburn *(Breakfast at Tiffany's)*, Piper Laurie *(The Hustler)*, Geraldine Page *(Summer and Smoke)*, and Natalie Wood *(Splendor in the Grass)*, Competition indeed!

Because *Two Women* was arguably Sophia Loren's finest screen performance, it is difficult to understand why she would consent to repeat the role in a 1989 Italian television film. Released in the United States on videocassette as *Running Away*, it teamed her with Sydney Penny (as the daughter) and Robert Loggia (as Loren's romantic interest). Perhaps the remake's current relative obscurity is as understandable as it is deserved. *Two Women* remains the film classic.

LA CIOCIARA   Sophia Loren and Eleanora Brown.

LA CIOCIARA Sophia Loren.

La Ragazza con la Valigia

(GIRL WITH A SUITCASE)

A Coproduction of Titanus (Rome) and SGC (Paris) / 1961

(U.S. release by Ellis Films: 1961)

CREDITS

Director: Valerio Zurlini; *Producer:* Maurizio Lodi-Fè; *Screenwriters:* Leo Benvenuti, Piero De Bernardi,

Enrico Medioli, Giuseppe Patroni Griffi, and Valerio Zurlini; *Cinematographer:* Tino Santoni; *Editor:* Mario Serandrei; *Art Director:* Flavio Mogherini; *Music:* Mario Nascimbene; *Running Time:* 135 minutes (*U.S. Running Time:* 111 minutes).

CAST

Claudia Cardinale *(Aida Zepponi)*; Jacques Perrin *(Lorenzo Fainardi)*; Corrado Pani *(Marcello Fainardi)*; Luciana Angelillo *(Aunt Marta)*; Gian Maria

Volonté *(Piero)*[*]; Romolo Valli *(Father Introna)*; Riccardo Garrone *(Romolo)*; Renato Baldini *(Francia)*; Ciccio Barbi *(Crosia)*; Nadia Bianchi *(Nuccia)*; Edda Soligo *(Teacher)*; Elsa Albani *(Lucia)*.

THE FILM

Claudia Cardinale began her long film career in the small role of Renato Salvatori's overprotected sister in

[*]U.S. sources mistakenly credit the role of Piero to Carlo Hintermann, a probable victim of the film's considerable editing.

The Big Deal on Madonna Street in 1958. At a time when the Italian movie industry needed replacements for Sophia Loren and Gina Lollobrigida, who had been lured away to English-speaking roles in London and Hollywood, Cardinale's well-proportioned, sultry good looks held great promise for a major career. And when producer Franco Cristaldi took her under his personal wing, she received careful grooming and placement in roles that would fulfill that promise. *Girl With a Suitcase*, in a role originally intended for Loren, provided Cardinale's most important break.

This unusual romantic melodrama casts her as a

LA RAGAZZA CON LA VALIGIA Claudia Cardinale.

voluptuous young vocalist named Aida Zepponi, who has been having an affair with Piero (Gian Maria Volonté), a small-time bandleader. As ambitious as she is amoral, Aida's head is turned by the smooth promises of Marcello Fainardi (Corrado Pani), a rich playboy who promises to help her get into motion pictures—until he becomes tired of her and summarily abandons her near Parma. Despairingly, she traces him to his home, which he shares with his straitlaced Aunt Marta (Luciana Angelillo) and his impressionable younger brother Lorenzo (Jacques Perrin). Before leaving the city, Marcello asks the boy to get rid of Aida, a task that the empathetic Lorenzo finds difficult. Appointing himself her unofficial protector, he not only sets her up in one of Parma's best hotels but buys her new clothes and gives her money. Worshipful friendship soon develops into love, although the more worldly Aida realizes that their affair has no future.

While Aida continues to attract the attentions of men who might fulfill her ambitions, Lorenzo's aunt learns of her relationship with Lorenzo and gets the family priest (Romolo Valli) to persuade Aida to leave Parma. Unable to effect a reconciliation with Piero, Aida determines to go away with Romolo (Riccardo Garrone), a musician eager to make her his mistress. But when she leaves his city, Lorenzo follows Aida to Riccione, where he is brutally beaten by Romolo. Realizing that their friendship can bring the boy no good, Aida insists that the heartbroken lad return home. Before he leaves, Lorenzo presents her with a parting gift—an envelope secretly filled with money (in the guise of a mere farewell letter).

Like many a foreign film, *La Ragazza con la Valigia*

122

was cut (by some twenty-four minutes!) before turning up on U.S. screens as *Girl With a Suitcase.* Edited out were all references to the illegitimate son Aida has by a man who has died. And in the original conclusion, it is Lorenzo's arrival in Riccione that keeps Aida from prostituting herself to feed the child. The omissions, of course, considerably alter her character's motivations.

IL POSTO   Sandro Panzeri.

But what makes the basic material work so beautifully is the sensitive direction of Valerio Zurlini, who obviously understands the painful anguish of youthful love, especially in light of young Lorenzo's privileged background. Fortunately, the cast is equal to his direction, for in Jacques Perrin, Zurlini had the perfect actor, capable of displaying all the requisite emotions with a subtlety remarkable for one so young (at twenty, Perrin—actually only two years younger than his leading lady—remained boyish enough to pass for sixteen). Cardinale, on the other hand, has the sexy aura of a young woman whose past has matured her beyond her years. Under Zurlini's careful guidance, they achieve an acting rapport that beautifully conveys this difficult material in such a way that it is always convincing.

Although Jacques Perrin emerged with the film's best critical notices, it was Claudia Cardinale who became the big international star. And she also wed her mentor Franco Cristaldi.

Il Posto

(THE JOB / THE SOUND OF TRUMPETS)

A 24 Horses–Titanus Production / 1961

(U.S. release by Janus Films: 1963)

CREDITS

Director: Ermanno Olmi; *Producer:* Alberto Soffientini; *Screenwriter:* Ermanno Olmi; *Cinematographer:* Lamberto Caimi; *Editor:* Carla Colombo; *Art Director:* Ettore Lombardi; *Music:* Pier Emilio Bassi; *Running Time:* 98 minutes (*U.S. Running Time:* 90 minutes).

CAST

Sandro Panzeri *(Domenico Cantoni)*; Loredana Detto *(Antonietta/"Magali")*; Tullio Kezich *(the Psychologist)*; Mara Revel *(the Old Woman).*

THE FILM

In the neorealist tradition of fifteen years earlier, documentary filmmaker Ermanno Olmi wrote and directed this quiet little autobiographical gem of a film, using nonprofessional actors. It was only his second feature, and although little transpires during its mod-

123

IL POSTO   Loredana Detto and Sandro Panzeri.

est ninety-odd minutes, there is a heartaching ring of truth in its every frame. Anyone who has ever applied for a first job cannot help but recall the attendant uncertainties and anxieties shared by young Domenico (portrayed by the plain, shy young Sandro Panzeri, an amateur who so eloquently enacts the film's leading role that one tends to accept *Il Posto* as Panzeri's own story).

Teenaged Domenico, who lives with his family in an apartment complex in a suburb of Milan, is sent forth to look for his first job. Along with many other candidates, he tests for a position with one of the city's large industrial firms. The interviews and exams are simplistic and undaunting; Domenico and the attractive girl Antonietta (Loredana Detto), whom he encounters there, both expect to pass, and indeed they do. She gets a typing job in the main office, while he is assigned to an outside section, where he must work as a messenger until a clerical position opens up for him. Later,

Domenico encounters Antonietta in the main building, and he shyly sends her a Christmas card, hoping to see her again at the company's New Year's Eve dance, which he awkwardly attends. She, however, never shows up. Then, after one of the clerks dies, room is made for Domenico in the office. And while the envious older clerks move toward the front of the office (an unspoken sign of prestige), the boy takes his seat at the back, secure in the job that his mother assures him will be "for life."

Olmi tells this simple story with the utmost charm, and the viewer is easily swept up by its disarming narrative. There are no stars here, no compelling drama, and no flashy directorial techniques. Indeed, it is the very truthfulness of the movie's content and the utter believability of all of its unsung nonprofessional players that make one forget it is not a documentary of one young man's entry into the work force. The details are all so correct, and Olmi's complete avoidance of

124

overdramatized anecdote or any sense of melodrama (even when informing us of the death of one of the senior clerks) is remarkable. Young Sandro Panzeri bears the uncertain reserve of many an introverted youth we've all known. (Olmi has said that Domenico is pure Olmi, as a youth.) Because so much of his "acting" is low-key, we continually seek out his big-eyed face for the telltale hint of expression that brings with it the recognition of memory. And our hearts ache for him when the pretty object of his admiration fails to attend that New Year's Eve party, leaving him to drink too much wine and laughingly join in a conga line to "Funiculi, Funicula." When, at the film's close, we see Domenico finally ensconced in the office job he had so much wanted, we wonder about his future, but at the same time we harbor safe feelings for him. His may be a lifetime of humdrum, uneventful routine, but we're cheered by the bright, hopeful expression on his very ordinary face.

Today Ermanno Olmi is better known for *The Tree of Wooden Clogs*, a film made seventeen years later. But *The Sound of Trumpets* (as this picture was curiously retitled for its U.S. release) remains a quiet early masterpiece and a classic coda to the much-touted period of Italian neorealist cinema.

Divorzio All'Italiana

(DIVORCE—ITALIAN STYLE)

A Coproduction of Lux, Vides and Galatea Films / 1961

(U.S. release by Embassy Pictures: 1962)

CREDITS

Director: Pietro Germi; *Producer:* Franco Cristaldi; *Screenwriters:* Ennio de Concini, Alfredo Giannetti, and Pietro Germi; *Cinematographers:* Leonida Barboni; *Editor:* Robert Cinquini; *Art Director:* Carlo Egidi; *Costumes:* Dina di Bari; *Music:* Carlo Rustichelli; *Running Time:* 108 minutes (*U.S. Running Time:* 104 minutes).

CAST

Marcello Mastroianni *(Ferdinando Cefalu)*; Daniela Rocca *(Rosalia Cefalu)*; Stefania Sandrelli *(Angela)*; Leopoldo Trieste *(Carmelo Patane)*; Odoardo Spadaro *(Don Gaetano)*; Agnela Cardile *(Agnese)*; Margherita Girelli *(Sisina)*; Bianca Castagnetta *(Donna Matilde)*; Lando Buzzanca *(Rosario Mule)*; Pietro Tordi *(Attorney De Marzi)*; Laura Tomiselli *(Zia Fifidda)*; Ugo Torrente *(Don Calogero)*; Antonio Acqua *(the Priest)*.

THE FILM

Director Pietro Germi (1914–74) initially studied for a nautical career before deciding to become an actor. And while studying acting and directing at Rome's Centro Sperimentale di Cinematografica, he supported himself as a film extra, assistant director, and occasional screenwriter. At thirty-one, he directed his first feature *Il Testimone* (1945), followed by *Gioventù Perduta/Lost Youth* (1947) and *In Nome della Legge/Mafia* (1949)—all realistic social dramas played out against Sicilian backgrounds. Combining an acting career with his film directing, Germi gradually turned away from serious themes and embraced comedy, albeit as a social satirist. Among the earliest, and probably the most popular worldwide, was *Divorce—Italian Style* (1961), starring Italy's second-most-popular movie actor, Marcello Mastroianni (Alberto Sordi then topped him by a narrow margin), in one of the best comic characterizations of his career. This performance brought him the rare accolade (for a foreign-language performance) of a Best Actor Oscar nomination. Pietro Germi (who also was nominated as Best Director), shared Best Story and Screenplay statuettes with his fellow *Divorce* scripters, Ennio de Concini and Alfredo Giannetti.

Their clever black comedy poked outrageous fun at the antiquated customs of southern Italy. Ferdinando Cefalu (Mastroianni) is a Sicilian nobleman, living near poverty in a few rooms in the now-run-down family mansion. Sharing his life, to Ferdinando's bored dismay, is his wife Rosalia (Daniela Rocca), whose constant nagging and state of sexual desire drive him to fantasize about her demise while quietly lusting after his teenaged cousin Angela (Stefania Sandrelli). One day, he concocts a scheme to solve his dilemma: Although Italian law forbids divorce, the crime of murder is punishable by only a light jail sentence—*if* the murderer acts in defense of his honor. And so Ferdinando seeks out a potential lover for the plump and mustachioed Rosalia, finally deciding upon one of her early admirers, timid Carmelo Patane (Leopoldo Trieste). But before he can catch them in flagrante, the couple run away together, disgracing Ferdinando throughout his village. With the avenging of honor now mandatory, he tracks down the lovers, dispatches the problematic Rosalia, and surrenders for a year and a half in prison. Upon release, Ferdinando happily re-

DIVORZIO ALL'ITALIANA Marcello Mastroianni.

DIVORZIO ALL'ITALIANA   Marcello Mastroianni and Daniela Rocca.

turns home to wed Angela. On their honeymoon trip, however, he is too complacent and content with the world to notice his bride flirting with a good-looking sailor.

And so Pietro Germi's sly comedy of Sicilian manners ends on a note of inconclusive mirth, promising a less tranquil future for the enterprising Ferdinando than he had imagined. To accomplish all of this with such perfection, Germi had just the right choice of actors in the marvelous Mastroianni, who offers a delightful parody of a small-town Casanova; Rocca, who is a bundle of hilarious contradictions as the unwanted wife; and Sandrelli, who needs only to display her natural physical attractions in contrast to those of her formidable rival.

A tremendous box-office hit in Italy, *Divorce—Italian Style* also won considerable praise and popularity abroad. In the United States, it did much to solidify appreciation for Mastroianni's acting talents, especially with those who had been heretofore merely impressed with his moody good looks in *La Dolce Vita*, *Il Bell' Antonio*, and *La Notte*.

DIVORZIO ALL'ITALIANA   Stefania Sandrelli and Marcello Mastroianni.

La Viaccia

(THE LOVE MAKERS)

A Coproduction of Titanus Films/Galatea Films/Arco Films (Rome), and Société Générale de Cinématographie (Paris) / 1961

(U.S. release by Embassy Pictures: 1962)

CREDITS

Director: Mauro Bolognini; *Producer:* Alfredo Bini; *Screenwriters:* Vasco Pratolini, Pasquale Festa Campanile, and Massimo Franciosa; *Based on the novel* L'Eredita (The Inheritance) *by* Mario Pratesi; *Cinematographer:* Leonida Barboni; *Editor:* Nino Baragli; *Art Director:* Flavio Mogherini; *Set Decorator and Costumes:* Piero Tosi; *Music:* Piero Piccioni, and Claude Debussy's "Rhapsody for Saxophone and Orchestra"; *Running Time:* 106 minutes.

CAST

Jean-Paul Belmondo *(Amerigo Casamonti)*; Claudia Cardinale *(Bianca)*; Pietro Germi *(Stefano Casamonti)*; Paul Frankeur *(Ferdinando Casamonti)*; Romolo Valli *(Dante)*; Gabriella Pallotta *(Carmelinda)*; Gina Sammarco *(the Madam)*; Marcella Valeri *(Beppa)*; Emma Baron *(Giovanna)*; Franco Balducci

LA VIACCIA Jean-Paul Belmondo and Claudia Cardinale.

LA VIACCIA   Claudia Cardinale and Jean-Paul Belmondo.

(Tognaccio); Claudio Biava (Harlequin); Duilio D'A-more (Bernardo); Paola Pitagora (Anna).

THE FILM

If director Mauro Bolognini is known at all in the United States, it may be for a pair of Marcello Mastroianni vehicles: Il Bell' Antonio (1960) and Per le Antiche Scale/Down the Ancient Stairs (1975). Or perhaps some will recall his youth-on-the-loose melodrama La Notte Brava/On Any Street (1959) or his costume drama with Anthony Quinn and Dominique Sanda, L'Eredita Ferramonti/The Inheritance (1976). Best known for his passionate interest in the Italian social scene, Bolognini has acquired a reputation as a stylist whose films occasionally offer more surface glitter than substance. One that has drawn critical

praise for its handsome attention to period detail is this tragic romantic drama, set in and around late-nineteenth-century Florence. Indeed, La Viaccia's back-alley exteriors and plush bordello interiors frequently take on the look of French Impressionist paintings, with credit largely due cinematographer Leonida Barboni's artful lighting of the respective sets and costumes of Flavio Mogherini and Piero Tosi. Britain's picky Monthly Film Bulletin termed this movie's period reconstruction "like a Toulouse-Lautrec come to life."

La Viaccia is the name of the Casamonti family farm, maintained for generations until the grandfather's death in 1885 sets off a power struggle among his heirs. One son, Ferdinando (Paul Frankeur), uses the profits from his Florentine wine business to buy out the others, offering his nephew Amerigo (Jean-Paul

Belmondo) a promising position in the city. The youth's father Stefano (Pietro Germi), who is now in charge of the farm, urges Amerigo to accommodate his uncle in the hope that Ferdinando will leave La Viaccia to the family and not to his mistress Beppa (Marcella Valeri) or her illegitimate son. In Florence, Amerigo happens to meet and fall desperately in love with a prostitute named Bianca (Claudia Cardinale), for whose favors he is driven to steal from his uncle. When his larceny is discovered, the young man is sent back to

the farm in disgrace. Obsessed with Bianca, Amerigo breaks from his family, returns to Florence, and takes a job in her brothel as a bouncer. In a dispute over one customer's attention to Bianca, Amerigo is stabbed but refuses to remain hospitalized until his wounds heal. And when he finds Bianca gone without a trace, he weakly staggers back to La Viaccia, only to die there from loss of blood. The Casamonti family also learns that Ferdinando has died, willing the farm to Beppa.

La Viaccia's critics carped at its screenplay's dra-

IL FEDERALE Georges Wilson and Ugo Tognazzi.

Il Federale

(THE FASCIST)

A Dino De Laurentiis–Cinematografica Film / 1961

(U.S. release by Embassy Pictures: 1965)

CREDITS

Director: Luciano Salcé; *Producers:* Isidoro Broggi and Renato Libassi; *Screenwriters:* Luciano Salcé, Pipolo, and Franco Castellano; *Cinematographer:* Erico Menczer; *Music:* Ennio Morricone; *Running Time:* 102 minutes.

CAST

Ugo Tognazzi *(Primo Arcovazzi)*; Georges Wilson *(Professor Bonafè)*; Stefania Sandrelli *(Lisa)*; Mireille Granelli *(Rita)*; Gianrico Tedeschi *(Baldacci)*; Elsa Vazzoler *(Baldacci's Wife)*; *and* Franco Giacobini, Renzo Palmer, Gianni Agus, and Luciano Salcé.

LA VIACCIA Jean-Paul Belmondo.

matic weaknesses while lauding the monochromatic movie's stunning graphic qualities and the excellence of its cast. Especially praised were the moody complexities of Cardinale's sexy, toughened prostitute and Belmondo's socially lacking, immorally driven, none-too-bright country boy. Frankeur and Germi shine briefly in lesser roles. Yet what *La Viaccia* ultimately offers its audience is a triumph of elegant style and rich nineteenth-century atmosphere. No small achievement!

IL FEDERALE Elsa Vazzoler and Ugo Tognazzi.

THE FILM

The Italian comic actor Ugo Tognazzi was best known in the United States for his role as a gay cabaret owner in the 1979 French film *La Cage aux Folles* as well as its two sequels. In the fifties, he became a popular character actor in Italian movies, moving into satirical vehicles in the sixties. Among them, one of his greatest successes was *Il Federale*, an intelligent political comedy-drama from writer-director Luciano Salcé, who never surpassed it in his later films.

It is set in the wartime Italy of 1944, where the Fascist high command dispatches fanatical Primo Arcovazzi (Tognazzi) to track down and capture Professor Bonafè (Georges Wilson), a celebrated anti-Fascist in hiding against the day of liberation from the Nazis. Following the professor's capture, a series of comic incidents ensue on the road to Rome as the pair travel by motorcycle-with-sidecar. Imprisoned by the Germans, they are caught up in an air raid and lose their clothing. Their arrival in Rome occurs just as the Eternal City is about to fall to the Americans. Since Arcovazzi is now attired in a Fascist officer's uniform, he is attacked and beaten by an angry crowd of

revenge-seeking citizens who want to shoot him. But he is saved in time by his prisoner, the professor, who offers Arcovazzi his civilian attire and aids his escape.

Luciano Salcé skillfully mixes thoughtful observances on the always-distant war with the antic cross-country adventures of the proudly strutting young Fascist and his gentle, elderly prisoner. An odd couple indeed, they are played splendidly to the hilt by Tognazzi and the French Wilson. The absurdity of Primo Arcovazzi's proud Fascist-uniformed arrival in a Rome overrun by liberating G.I.s superbly underscores a hopeless political cause that writer-director Salcé deftly satirizes with an offbeat, introspective approach. And the two leading actors play so well off each other: the wise old man (who could be a potential Italian president after the liberation) versus his boorish, dedicated Fascist captor, who expects to become a commissioned officer following the completion of this mission. The movie's fade-out leaves the fleeing Arcovazzi in an obvious political dilemma, his Fascist beliefs dwindling rapidly.

It took *The Fascist* all of four years to cross the Atlantic to American movie theaters. But without a sex angle to "sell" it or a star whose name might spell box office, the film could hope for little more than a modest run among urban audiences that might have noted the enthusiastic reviews and created word-of-mouth interest among their friends. Unfortunately but understandably, *The Fascist* has now faded into an obscurity that seems unlikely to be reversed.

IL FEDERALE Ugo Tognazzi and Georges Wilson.

132

L'Eclisse

(ECLIPSE)

A Coproduction of Interopa Film/Cineriz (Rome) and Paris Films (Paris) / 1962

(U.S. release by Times Film Corp.: 1962)

CREDITS

Director: Michelangelo Antonioni; *Producers:* Robert and Raymond Hakim; *Screenwriters:* Michelangelo Antonioni, Tonino Guerra, Elio Bartolini, and Ottiero Ottieri; *Cinematographer:* Gianni Di Venanzo; *Editor:* Eraldo Da Roma; *Art Director:* Piero Poletto; *Costumes:* Bice Bricchetto; *Music:* Giovanni Fusco; *Song* "Eclisse Twist" *sung by* Mina; *Running Time:* 130 minutes (*U.S. Running Time:* 123 minutes).

CAST

Alain Delon *(Piero)*; Monica Vitti *(Vittoria)*; Francisco Rabal *(Riccardo)*; Lilla Brignone *(Vittoria's Mother)*; Rossana Rory *(Anita)*; Mirella Ricciardi *(Marta)*; Louis Seigner *(Ercoli)*; Cyrus Elias *(the Drunk)*.

THE FILM

Existential despair and stylish ennui mark this characteristic excursion into Antonioni country, the closing entry in his trilogy about the lack of substantial emotion and communication in the world of the sixties. *Eclipse*, as in its predecessors *L'Avventura* and *La Notte*, also stars the director's then-favorite muse Monica Vitti, albeit as a character unrelated—other than thematically—to her roles in the earlier films.

Eclipse has little story line. Vittoria (Vitti) is a young, unmarried Roman who earns her living as a translator. As the movie begins, she is in the midst of breaking off her relationship with an older man named Riccardo (Francisco Rabal). Later, meeting her mother (Lilla Brignone) at the stock market's busy trading floor, Vittoria is introduced to her mother's energetic, handsome young broker Piero (Alain Delon). They soon enter into an affair, but when their initial mutual attraction fades, Vittoria again feels

hopeless and isolated. Alone, she walks away, enjoying a sense of kinship only with the unfamiliar sights and strange faces that she passes on the street. Antonioni ends his movie in an unusual fashion, offering a lengthy montage of empty streets and passing strangers as dusk settles over the Roman suburbs.

In Italy, Antonioni's films were never intended for the ordinary filmgoer; nor were they popular outside of Italian cities. But following the extraordinary *L'Avventura* in 1960, he gained a following that may have had its roots in cultism but gradually spread elsewhere, especially among the intelligentsia. If the critics were at first loath to admit their failure to understand Antonioni's motion pictures, by the arrival

L'ECLISSE Alain Delon.

133

L'ECLISSE Monica Vitti and Alain Delon.

of *Eclipse*, most were either empathetic to the director's intent or else so versed in intellectual rhetoric as to be both respected for their "insight" and quotable in the newspaper print ads.

In the handsome and charismatic faces of Vitti and Delon, Antonioni finds a magnetism that is capable of holding the attention of the uncommitted moviegoer who may (or may not) find food for thought in the hollow world in focus here. And Gianni Di Venanzo's luminous black-and-white photography makes the most of the film's visual starkness. Many have noted how Antonioni uses the method of tedium to explore tedium itself, and yet his filmmaking skills are such that boredom need not bore his audiences. Some have questioned the need for *Eclipse*'s bustling Roman stock-market sequence to go on at such length, and yet there is a method beyond Antonioni's "madness." Some point is always being made. But his audience must pay attention; Antonioni films are not for the passive. One needs to stay alert and perceptive.

Antonioni's pessimistic attitudes toward money and contemporary values bear examination. His despair enjoys an outlet through his muse, as *Eclipse*'s Vittoria

L'ECLISSE Monica Vitti.

escapes into fantasy by first taking a plane ride and fancying that she's a bird and then by painting her body and dancing like an African native. But her understandable attraction for Piero is not sufficient to share his worship of monetary values. This is not an easy film or a happy one. But it leaves room for reflection on contemporary values and sensibilities.

Eclipse took the Special Jury Prize at the 1962 Cannes Film Festival.

Il Mare

(THE SEA)

A Gianni Buffardi Production / 1962

(No official U.S. release)

CREDITS

Director: Giuseppe Patroni Griffi; *Producer:* Gianni Buffardi; *Screenwriters:* Giuseppe Patroni Griffi and Alfio Valdarini; *Cinematographer:* Ennio Guarnieri;

Editor: Ruggero Mastroianni; *Art Director:* Pierluigi Pizzi; *Music:* Giovanni Fusco; *Running Time:* 110 minutes.

CAST

Umberto Orsini *(the Actor)*; Françoise Prévost *(the Woman)*; Dino Mele *(the Boy)*.

THE FILM

Following in the wake of such spare and enigmatic films as *L'Avventura* and *La Notte*, it is not surprising that some critics drew comparisons between *Il Mare* and the works of Antonioni, particularly since the latter deals with such indigenous themes as boredom, loneliness, and lack of communication. And yet *Il Mare*, a first feature by writer-director Giuseppe Patroni Griffi, breaks new ground of its own as frequently as it suggests echoes of other filmmakers. Set against the unusual background of rain-lashed Capri in winter, *Il Mare* centers on the oddly interconnecting lives of three strangers brought together by fate. None of the trio is given a proper character's name; the audience never gets to know any of them that well.

In this episodic tale, a young actor (Umberto Orsini)

IL MARE   Umberto Orsini and Dino Mele.

135

arrives at a Capri that is "out of season." In an apparent effort at reconciliation, he places a call to Rome, but to little avail. In his disconsolate wanderings among the island's deserted streets and cafés, he repeatedly notices a sullen-faced adolescent (Dino Mele), who appears always to be alone and chiefly occupied with drinking. At first, there is little more than passing eye contact; later, they join in a whiskey-consuming outing that culminates at the hotel, where the boy forces eau de cologne down the actor's throat and deposits him in a water-filled bathtub.

When, the next day, the actor angrily confronts the youth, demanding an explanation, the lad charms the older man into extending a dinner invitation. At the restaurant, they are joined by yet another visitor to the island, an attractive woman (Françoise Prévost) who is there to sell a house that reminds her of an unhappy past marriage. Her immediate rapport with the boy and their subsequent wanderings through the streets visibly irritate the actor. The youth, in turn, is disturbed when a sexual attraction perceptibly grows between the woman and the older man. This naturally excludes the youth, who retaliates by attacking the actor in an alleyway.

In an effort at ridding himself of the boy, the actor gets him to admit he has family elsewhere and to telephone them to announce that he is coming home. After the boy disappears, the actor discovers that the phone is out of service. The actor and the woman spend a night together, but their liaison is less than satisfactory, and the next day she suddenly departs. Alone

IL MARE   Françoise Prévost and Umberto Orsini.

IL MARE   Françoise Prévost, Dino Mele and Umberto Orsini.

136

once more, the actor unhappily watches her boat leave the island.

With atmospheric assists from black-and-white cinematographer Ennio Guarnieri and composer Giovanni Fusco, Giuseppe Patroni Griffi tells us little about these puzzling characters, yet their backgrounds are as unimportant to his narrative as is the unrevealed fate of the vanished Anna in *L'Avventura*. Such character colorations are simply not on this writer-director's agenda. Why are these two males on Capri in the first place? What is the root of the boy's melancholy? Is he sexually attracted to the actor—or vice versa? Is the boy interested in the woman, aside from their game playing in the streets? Who was the actor attempting to phone? None of these points is of outward concern to the filmmaker. In the light of this array of noninformation, the performances of the three principals are impeccable. And one comes away from *Il Mare* with the knowledge of a brilliantly wrought study of three lonely, insecure individuals incapable of finding solace—or even love—in one another. And lest the wary fear that *Il Mare* might prove too angst ridden for their consideration, it should be added that Patroni Griffi's sardonic sense of humor is carefully maintained throughout the film, lending the narrative a detachment that nevertheless sustains the emotional power of *Il Mare*'s unfulfilled antagonists. Seldom shown in recent years, this unusual motion picture—occasionally seen on critics' all-time-best-film lists—may prove worth tracking down for those prepared for its enigmatic narrative.

Le Quattro Giornate di Napoli

(THE FOUR DAYS OF NAPLES)

A Titanus–Metro Production / 1962

(U.S. release by Metro-Goldwyn-Mayer: 1963)

CREDITS

Director: Nanni Loy; *Producer:* Goffredo Lombardo; *Screenwriters:* Pasquale Festa Campanile, Massimo Franciosa, Carlo Benari, Vasco Pratolini, and Nanni Loy; *Cinematographer:* Marcello Gatti, *Editor:* Ruggiero Mastroianni; *Art Director:* Gianni Polidori; *Music:* Carlo Rustichelli; *Running Time:* 124 minutes.

LE QUATTRO GIORNATE DI NAPOLI   Jean Sorel.

CAST

Lea Massari *(Maria)*; Frank Wolff *(Salvatore)*; Regina Bianchi *(Concetta)*; Jean Sorel *(Livornese)*; Aldo Giuffré *(Pitrella)*; Franco Sportelli *(Professor Rosati)*; Gian Maria Volonté *(Stimolo)*; Charles Belmont *(Sailor)*; Georges Wilson *(Reformatory Director)*; Raffaele Barbato *(Ajello)*; Domenico Formato *(Gennarino)*; Curt Lowens *(Sakau)*; Enzo Turco *(the Fascist)*.

THE FILM

Director Nanni Loy's powerful semidocumentary re-creates with astonishing verisimilitude a stirring episode of Neapolitan history. On September 8, 1943, Italy is close to defeat as the Allies approach the Italian front. But by the twelfth, the Nazis occupy Naples and in a public display of armed power take over the city's military installations. They order the public execution of an Italian sailor (Jean Sorel) and force the populace to applaud for the benefit of movie cameras. All of the city's males from five to fifty are forced to work in German labor camps. But when a group of partisans carry two of their dead through the streets, urging Neapolitans to rally and fight, the people are inspired to resist. Finally, on September 28, the city revolts. Without plan or organization and with makeshift

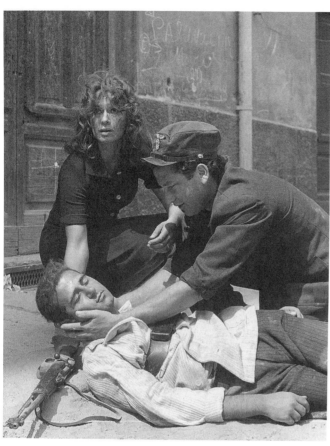

LE QUATTRO GIORNATE DI NAPOLI   Lea Massari, Frank Wolff and unidentified actor.

weapons and hidden arms, they fight back, building barricades in the streets and installing snipers on rooftops. On October 1, after four days of concentrated resistance, the Nazis withdraw from Naples, clearing the way for the approach of Allied troops.

Filming in the streets and houses of Naples, Loy enjoyed the full cooperation of its citizenry, who were proud to portray themselves in a permanent record of a turning point in their recent history. However, the documentary approach to this subject matter is punctuated with dramatic vignettes, which some critics felt lessened the newsreellike impact of much of the movie. The use of professional actors in those dramatized scenes made some critics feel that sentimental clichés had been introduced to compromise the material. Nevertheless, *The Four Days of Naples* was among the five foreign-language films nominated for 1962 Academy Awards. But it lost out to France's *Sundays and Cybele.*

138

LE QUATTRO GIORNATE DI NAPOLI.

Ti-Koyo e il Suo Pescecane

(TIKO AND THE SHARK)

A Coproduction of Titanus-Metro (Rome) and SNPC–SGC Films (Paris) / 1962

(U.S. release by Metro-Goldwyn-Mayer: 1966)

CREDITS

Director: Folco Quilici; *Producer:* Goffredo Lombardo; *Screenwriters:* Folco Quilici, Ottavio Alessi, Augusto Frassineti, and Giorgio Prosperi; *Based on the novel* Ti-Koyo et Son Requin *by* Clement Richer, *as adapted by* Italo Calvino; *Eastman Color Cinematographers:* Pier Ludovico Pavoni, Masino Manunza *(underwater photography)*, and Giovanni Scarpellini *(second-unit photography)*; *Editor:* Mario Serandrei; *Music:* Francisco de Masi; *Running Time:* 100 minutes *(U.S. Running Time:* 88 minutes).

CAST

Al Kauwe *(Tiko)*; Marlene Among *(Diana)*; Denis Pouira *(Tiko as a Child)*; Diane Samsoi *(Diana as a Child)*; Roau *(Cocoyo)*.

THE FILM

Shot in French Polynesia by documentary filmmaker Folco Quilici *(The Last Paradise)*, this strikingly pho-

TI-KOYO E IL SUO PESCECANE   Denis Pouira and Diane Samsoi.

140

TI-KOYO E IL SUO PESCECANE.

tographed Italian-French coproduction is essentially a movie best suited to children—especially in its reedited eighty-eight-minute, English-dubbed U.S. version. Its simplistic story concerns a young Polynesian lad named Tiko (in the American version) who finds a baby shark, which he raises in a sheltered lagoon on a less inhabited section of his native island. With the passage of time, Tiko's shark grows to maturity, and the boy is ordered to release his dangerous pet to deeper waters.

With the passage of the years, the island's peaceful simplicity is considerably changed by the intrusion of a business monopoly that takes control of the now-organized fisheries. Resisting the blandishments of "civilization," the grown-up Tiko maintains his living as a mother-of-pearl diver. But one day his shark returns to him, enabling the youth to dive in deeper and more dangerous areas via its protective vigil. When the business operation tries to kill the pet animal—and Tiko nearly dies protecting it—the young

141

TI-KOYO E IL SUO PESCECANE Al Kauwe and
Marlene Among.

man determines to find another island, unspoiled by
society. In the company of his childhood friend Diana,
Tiko sets sail for quieter waters, his shark following
protectively behind.

Italian filmmakers have seldom produced so charming a family film as this splendidly photographed
escapist fable. Its exotic locations are sufficient to
engage adult audiences despite its obvious appeal to
youngsters, who might more readily identify with
young Tiko and his friend Diana. In the title role, little
Denis Pouira proves engaging without recourse to the
cloying cuteness that so often spoils the acting of
juvenile newcomers. And Al Kauwe is equally effective
as Tiko the man.In a triumvirate of outstanding cinematographers, Masino Manunza contributes the most
footage, centering on the underwater world of Tiko's
unusual pet. Overall, however, audiences are not likely
to forget the breathtaking tropical seascapes and filter-
enhanced cloud formations captured in Eastman Color
by the movie's chief photographer, Pier Ludovico
Pavoni. *Tiko and the Shark* remains a masterpiece of
its kind.

Il Sorpasso

(THE EASY LIFE)

*A Coproduction of Fair Films, Incei Films, and Sancro
Films / 1962*

(U.S. release by Embassy Pictures: 1963)

CREDITS

Director: Dino Risi; *Producer:* Mario Cecchi Gori;
Screenwriters: Ettore Scola, Ruggero Maccari, and
Dino Risi; *Cinematographer:* Alfio Contini; *Editor:*
Maurizio Lucidi; *Art Director:* Ugo Pericoli; *Music:* Riz
Ortolani; *Running Time:* 105 minutes.

CAST

Vittorio Gassman *(Bruno Cortona)*; Jean-Louis Trin-
tignant *(Roberto Mariani)*; Catherine Spaak *(Lilly,
Bruno's Daughter)*; Luciana Angiolillo *(Bruno's Wife)*;
Linda Sini *(Aunt Lidia)*; Corrado Olmi *(Alfredo)*;
Claudio Gora *(Bibi, Lilly's Fiancé)*.

THE FILM

This absorbing comedy-drama might otherwise have
been called *Decadence Italian Style*, for writer-director Dino Risi's cynical look at upper-middle-class
self-indulgence focuses on the useless lives of sybarites
dedicated to the pleasures of Rome and the Italian
Riviera in the swinging sixties. The story's charming
nonhero is Bruno Cortona (Vittorio Gassman), a married but still active middle-aged playboy who, while
looking for a telephone to attempt to set up a date,
meets a young law student named Roberto Mariani
(Jean-Louis Trintignant). The mismatched pair have a
drink together, followed by a ride in Bruno's sports car.
And during the course of the following two days, the
fascinated but wary Roberto finds new excitement in
meeting the beautiful people in the extroverted Bruno's
carefree circle of beaches, dancing, drinking, and *la
dolce vita*. The young man also meets Bruno's patient
wife (Luciana Angiolillo) and vivacious teenaged
daughter (Catherine Spaak). The aimless life-style
quickly seduces him away from his studies and his
goals. As Bruno pursues another auto around the
curves of the Riviera heights in a reckless car chase,
Roberto is killed when their vehicle plunges over a cliff.

142

IL SORPASSO Catherine Spaak and Jean-Louis Trintignant.

IL SORPASSO Luciana Angiolillo, Catherine Spaak, Vittorio Gassman and Jean-Louis Trintignant.

IL SORPASSO Catherine Spaak and Vittorio Gassman.

Bruno, thrown clear and relatively unharmed, is left to reflect on his way of life—and the one that has just been lost.

Despite its dark underbelly, *The Easy Life*'s surface atmosphere is as carefree and devil-may-care as the twist-oriented background score of Riz Ortolani, the most indelible tune from which remains the bouncily insistent "Quando, Quando, Quando." And Vittorio Gassman's star performance as the irresponsible, eternal adolescent Bruno is everything the role calls for, explaining why he was long considered Italy's greatest actor (especially on the stage) despite his near eclipse on the international film scene by his more prolific compatriot Marcello Mastroianni. As the more sympathetic, not-unwilling victim of this hell-bent Don Quixote, Jean-Louis Trintignant always makes his impressionable *naif* credible, especially when in the company of beauties as captivating as Catherine Spaak. With its eye-catching images and Ortolani's head-nodding music, *The Easy Life* occasionally looks and sounds like a black-and-white Frankie Avalon–Annette Funicello entry. But then, the cumulative power of its more sophisticated dialogue and satirical attitudes remind us where we really are—and that it's not all fun and games here. Moreover, when it comes, the not totally unexpected impact of its climactic tragedy nevertheless shocks us. For Dino Risi, *The Easy Life* marks the high point of an uneven career more often given over to such sex comedies as *L'Ombrellone/Weekend Italian Style, Il Tigre/The Tiger and the Pussycat, La Moglie del Prete/The Priest's Wife* and *Profumo di Donna/ Scent of a Woman.*

Otto e Mezzo

(8 ½)

A Cineriz Production / 1963

(U.S. release by Embassy Pictures: 1963)

CREDITS

Director: Federico Fellini; *Executive Producer:* Clemente Fracassi; *Producer:* Angelo Rizzoli; *Screenwriters:* Federico Fellini, Tullio Pinelli, Ennio Flaiano, and Brunello Rondi; *Based on a story by* Federico Fellini and Ennio Flaiano; *Cinematographer:* Gianni Di Venanzo; *Editor:* Leo Catozzo; *Art Director and Costumes:* Piero Gherardi; *Music:* Nino Rota; *Running Time:* 138 minutes.

OTTO E MEZZO   Marcello Mastroianni.

OTTO E MEZZO Barbara Steele.

CAST

Marcello Mastroianni *(Guido Anselmi)*; Claudia Cardinale *(Claudia)*; Anouk Aimée *(Luisa Anselmi)*; Sandra Milo *(Carla)*; Rossella Falk *(Rossella)*; Barbara Steele *(Gloria Morin)*; Mario Pisu *(Mezzabotta)*; Guido Alberti *(the Producer)*; Madeleine Lebeau *(the Actress)*; Jean Rougeul *(Fabrizio Carini)*; Caterina Boratto *(Fashionable Woman)*; Annibale Ninchi *(Anselmi's Father)*; Giuditta Rissone *(Anselmi's Mother)*; Jan Dallas *(the Mind Reader)*; Edra Gale *(La Seraghina)*; Yvonne Casadei *(Aging Soubrette)*; Annie Gorasini *(Producer's Girlfriend)*; Tito Masini *(the Cardinal)*; Eugene Walter *(American Journalist)*; Gilda Dahlberg *(Journalist's Wife)*; Hedy Vessel *(the Model)*; Nadine Sanders *(Airline Hostess)*; Georgia Simmons *(Anselmi's Grandmother)*; Hazel Rogers *(Negro Dancer)*; Riccardo

Guglielmi *(Guido as a Farm Boy)*; Marco Gemini *(Guido as a Schoolboy)*; Jacqueline Bonbon *(Aging Dancer)*; Alberto Conochia *(Production Manager)*; Neil Robinson *(Agent)*; Mino Doro *(Claudia's Agent)*; Mario Tarchetti *(Claudia's Press Agent)*; Mary Indovino *(Mind Reader's Partner)*; Mario Conocchia *(a Director)*; Bruno Agostini *(Production Secretary)*; John Stacy *(Accountant)*; Mark Herron *(Luisa's Admirer)*; Elisabetta Catalano *(Luisa's Sister)*; Alfredo De Lafeld *(Cardinal's Secretary)*; Frazier Rippy *(Lay Secretary)*; Maria Tedeschi *(College President)*; Rosella Como, Francesco Rigamonti, and Matilde Calnam *(Luisa's Friends)*.

THE FILM

For those who ponder deeper meanings in this motion picture's unusual title, let it be explained up-front:

OTTO E MEZZO Claudia Cardinale.

Anouk Aimée and Marcello Mastroianni.

since Federico Fellini had previously made six full-length movies as well as three shorter segments of other films, it was simply selected for want of a better title. Later still, it would become a Broadway musical entitled *Nine*.

In *8 ½*, Fellini takes an obviously autobiographical look at the fantasies and frustrations of a forty-three-year-old movie director named Guido Anselmi (Marcello Mastroianni), who is beginning an ambitious new motion picture without fully knowing what he wants to express. Overtired and prone to nightmares, he visits a health spa near his film's location site. Suddenly, his blowsy mistress Carla (Sandra Milo) turns up, followed by his long-suffering wife Luisa (Anouk Aimée). The pressures occasioned by production executives and ambitious actresses drive Guido to escape into both memories of his childhood and sexual daydreams involving whores, religious figures, his late mother, his wife, and his mistress. At last, his ideal woman turns up

in the form of the actress Claudia (Claudia Cardinale), but he is disillusioned to find her vain, hard, and solely career-oriented. Returning to the fantastic giant spaceship ramp that is his movie set, Guido discovers that he is utterly unable to cope with the picture. After having a fantasy in which he commits suicide, the director is miraculously freed of his doubts and fears and commences to shoot a story concerning himself, his family, and friends. As it begins, all of those characters materialize to join hands in a joyful panoramic dance.

If this original masterpiece of self-reflective cinema eluded the appreciation of certain art-house moviegoers, it nevertheless charmed many of its critics. England's demanding *Monthly Film Bulletin* called it "a dazzling entertainment," and America's Judith Crist thought the film "among the most brilliant cinema works of our time" and "an intellectual and artistic exercise of the first rank."

Along with its Academy Award for Piero Gherardi's

147

costumes, *8 ½* also copped an Oscar for 1963's Best Foreign Language Film as well as the New York Film Critics Award. Thirty years later, the movie frequently turns up on international critics' all-time-ten-best lists.

Il Gattopardo

(THE LEOPARD)

A Titanus/SNPC/SGC Production / 1963

(U.S. release by 20th Century-Fox: 1963)

CREDITS

Director: Luchino Visconti; *Producer:* Goffredo Lombardo; *Executive Producer:* Pietro Notarianni; *Screenwriters:* Suso Cecchi D'Amico, Pasquale Festa Campa-nile, Massimo Franciosa, Enrico Medioli, and Luchino Visconti; *Based on the novel by* Giuseppe Tomasi de Lampedusa; *Technicolor/Technirama Cinematographer:* Giuseppe Rotunno; *Editor:* Mario Serandrei; *Art Director:* Mario Garbuglia; *Set Decorators:* Giorgio Pes and Laudomia Hercolani; *Costumes:* Piero Tosi; *Music:* Nino Rota; *Unpublished Waltz by* Giuseppe

IL GATTOPARDO Burt Lancaster.

148

Verdi; *Running Time:* 205 minutes (*U.S. Running Time:* 165 minutes).

CAST

Burt Lancaster *(Don Fabrizio Corbera, Prince of Salina)*; Claudia Cardinale *(Angelica Sedara/Bertriana)*; Alain Delon *(Tancredi Falconieri)*; Paolo Stoppa *(Don Calogero Sedara)*; Rina Morelli *(Maria Stella)*; Serge Reggiani *(Don Ciccio Tumeo)*; Romolo Valli *(Father Pirrone)*; Leslie French *(Cavalier Chevally)*; Ivo Garrani *(Colonel Pallavicino)*; Mario Girotti *(Count Cavriaghi)*; Pierre Clementi *(Francesco Paolo)*; Lucilla Morlacchi *(Concetta)*; Giuliano Gemma *(the Gara-*

IL GATTOPARDO Claudia Cardinale, Burt Lancaster and Alain Delon.

IL GATTOPARDO   Rina Morelli and Burt Lancaster.

baldino General); Ida Galli (Carolina); Ottavia Piccolo (Caterina); Carlo Valenzano (Paolo); Anna Maria Bottini (Governess Mlle. Dombreuil); Marino Masè (Tutor); Lola Braccini (Donna Margherita); Howard Nelson Rubien (Don Diego); Olimpia Cavalli (Mariannina); Sandra Chistolini (Youngest Daughter); Brook Fuller (Little Prince); Giovanni Melisendi (Don Onofrio Rotolo).

THE FILM

Arguably, Luchino Visconti's masterpiece (some prefer to cite the director's earlier Rocco and His Brothers), The Leopard has sometimes been alluded to as "the Italian Gone With the Wind" due to its similar depiction of the changing of an extravagant way of life in a parallel era—the 1860s. While America's South underwent irrevocable change as the result of the devastating Civil War, Italy's inevitable move toward unification sent Garibaldi's Redshirts into Sicily to crush the Bourbon monarchy in the interests of forming the United Kingdom of Italy. Most affected by the invasion in this story is the aristocratic Prince of Salina, Don Fabrizio Corbera (Burt Lancaster), known locally as Il Gattopardo (the Leopard), who is aware that the sweeping changes of the Risorgimento signify the twilight of the privileged class as Italy's middle class rises up. When his favorite nephew Tancredi (Alain Delon) falls in love with Angelica (Claudia Cardinale), the beautiful daughter of nouveau riche Don Calogero (Paolo Stoppa), Don Fabrizio encourages their union. This, despite the jealous dismay of his own daughter Concetta (Lucilla Morlacchi), for whom

150

her father arranges a financially expedient marriage to Angelica's tradesman father. At a lavish ball designed to introduce Angelica to Sicilian society, Don Fabrizio witnesses her successful assimilation into Tancredi's world before leaving the festivities to wander off into the night, a lonely, saddened figure, unable to visualize any place for himself in a world of change.

Bringing Giuseppe Tomasi de Lampedusa's international bestseller to the screen in authentic style was a costly move, requiring American participation. Director Luchino Visconti's casting of Burt Lancaster for the leading role in this long, lavish film brought backing from 20th Century-Fox, with the actor's own voice heard in *The Leopard*'s English-language edition but dubbed in its French and Italian versions. Not unexpectedly, Visconti was displeased with Fox's 165-minute cut, which omitted a full forty minutes of his slow-moving but carefully crafted epic—the insult compounded by printing the film on inferior color stock.

Like most cinema artisans, Visconti refused to pander to the masses by tightening or pacing his film for popular consumption, with the result that *The Leopard* bored some critics while confusing and irritating others. American audiences failed to make the picture a hit. Yet *The Leopard* has its partisans, who argue in favor of the full three-hour, twenty-five-minute Technicolor/Technirama Italian version.

The Leopard meticulously re-creates a long-past period of the upper-crust, mid-nineteenth-century Sicilian landed gentry; Piero Tosi's costumes blend felicitously with the film's careful hairstyles and makeup, and the attendant sets of Mario Garbuglia (and his meticulous set decorators) are eloquently captured by Giuseppe Rotunno's camera. Striking set pieces, like the Corbera family at mass, the country picnic, and the clan's dusty journey to their summer home, linger in the memory as a collective prelude to the lengthy, climactic dress-ball sequence that takes up most of *The Leopard*'s final hour, underscored by Nino Rota's

IL GATTOPARDO   Alain Delon and Claudia Cardinale.

151

infectious background music, which incorporates what has been called a "lost" waltz by Giuseppe Verdi, Italy's opera king.

Following in the tradition of his *Senso*, Visconti's subsequent depiction of Risorgimento Italy reflects his love of opera in its sweep and grandeur, unfolding at a measured pace more closely related to the director's La Scala assignments than to the popular cinema. One must admire Visconti's artistic integrity and at the same time understand a popular culture's disinterest in so uncompromising an entity as *The Leopard*'s uncut edition. For Burt Lancaster (Visconti's third choice, after Russia's Nikolai Cherkassov and Britain's Laurence Olivier), the film marked a career milestone for the actor and for the poise and dignity of his portrayal—perhaps more acceptable in its Italian-dubbed foreign version because of his New York accent. *The Leopard* remains among Lancaster's proudest personal achievements.

Although far more popular in Europe, *The Leopard* was voted one of the five-best foreign films of 1963 by the National Board of Review. In France, it won the Golden Palm Award at Cannes that year.

I Compagni

(THE ORGANIZER)

A Coproduction of Lux-Vides (Rome), Mediterranée Cinema Production (Paris) and Avala Film (Belgrade) / 1963

(U.S. release by Continental Distributing: 1964)

CREDITS

Director: Mario Monicelli; *Producer:* Franco Cristaldi; *Screenwriters:* Age (Agenore Incrocci), Scarpelli (Furio Scarpelli), and Mario Monicelli; *Cinematographer:* Giuseppe Rotunno; *Editor:* Ruggero Mastroianni; *Art Director:* Mario Garbuglia; *Costumes:* Piero Tosi; *Music:* Carlo Rustichelli; *Running Time:* 130 minutes (*U.S. Running Time:* 126 minutes).

CAST

Marcello Mastroianni *(Professor Sinigaglia)*; Renato Salvatori *(Raul)*; Annie Girardot *(Niobe)*; Gabriella Giorgielli *(Adele)*; Folco Lulli *(Pautasso)*; Bernard Blier *(Martinetti)*; Raffaella Carra *(Bianca)*; François Périer *(Maestro Di Meo)*; Vittorio Sanipoli *(Baudet)*; Giuseppe Cadeo *(Cenerone)*; Elvira Tonelli *(Cesarina)*; Giampiero Albertini *(Porro)*; Pippo Starnazza *(Bergamasco)*; Pippo Mosca *(Cerioni)*; Franca Ciolli *(Omero)*; Antonio Casa Monica *(Arrò)*; Gino Manganello *(Uncle Spartaco)*; Edda Ferronao *(Maria)*; Anna Di Silvio *(Gesummina)*; Sara Simoni *(Cenerone's Wife)*; Anna Glori *(Signora Cravetto)*; Antonio Di Silvio *(Pietrino)*; Enzo Casini *(Antonio)*; Kenneth Kove *(Luigi)*; Mario Pisu *(Manager)*.

THE FILM

Writer-director Mario Monicelli made his international mark with the gangland satire *I Soliti Ignoti/The Big Deal on Madonna Street* (1958), incidentally the first of supporting actor Marcello Mastroianni's pictures to enjoy wide success abroad. Five years later, director and now-star teamed again in the far more sober trade-union period piece *I Compagni/The Organizer*—this time with Mastroianni as the male lead. Long associated with comedies starring the popular Italian funnyman Totò, Monicelli had earlier worked as a writer on the neorealist melodrama *Riso Amaro/Bitter Rice*.

Many of *The Organizer*'s critics were reminded, in its striking visual images and rich content, of such proletarian film classics as Sergei Eisenstein's silent *Strike* and Rene Clement's *Gervaise*. Yet Monicelli's motion picture stands very much on its own, portraying with sympathetic detail and occasional humor the plight of exploited textile workers in late-nineteenth-century Turin. In a rare excursion into character acting, the thirty-nine-year-old Mastroianni essays the title role of a political refugee from Genoa who, during a visit to an old Turin friend, stays on to organize the workers in strike after strike—frequently at risk to his own safety—until, by the story's end, the mill workers have at last found their strength in a union.

Mastroianni's performance won him renewed critical respect. Appearing bearded and often bespectacled, Italy's reigning cinema favorite had already displayed top-notch professional competence in the roles assigned him. But now many sat up and took new notice of his acting skills. In the *New York Herald Tribune*, Judith Crist wrote: "Mastroianni's creation of this complex man is masterly. . . . I defy you to find a trace of the matinee idol in this scrawny, stooped, scraggly bearded, myopic man."

And there was much praise as well for the black-and-white cinematography of Giuseppe Rotunno, who managed to give *The Organizer* the look of old da-

I COMPAGNI   Marcello Mastroianni.

I COMPAGNI   Annie Girardot and Marcello Mastroianni.

I COMPAGNI   Marcello
Mastroianni and Renato
Salvatori.

154

guerreotype photographs, recalling the nineteenth-century works of Atget, Brady, and Riis.

The Organizer was Oscar- nominated for its Original Story and Screenplay by Age-Scarpelli and director Monicelli, and the National Board of Review cited it among the best foreign-language imports of 1964. At Argentina's International Film Festival, *The Organizer* won the Critics Prize and the Catholic Film Office Prize as well as awards for Best Picture and Best Screenplay.

Una Storia Moderna: L'Ape Regina

(THE CONJUGAL BED / QUEEN BEE)

A Coproduction of Sancro Films (Rome) and Les Films Marceau and Cocinor Films (Paris) / 1963

(U.S. release by Embassy Pictures: 1963)

CREDITS

Director: Marco Ferreri; *Producers:* Henryk Chrosicki and Alfonso Sansone; *Screenwriters:* Goffredo Parise, Marco Ferreri, and Raphael Azcona, *in collaboration with* Pasquale Festa Campanile, Massimo Franciosa, and Diego Fabbri; *Based on an idea by* Goffredo Parise; *Cinematographer:* Ennio Guarnieri; *Editor:* Lionello Massobrio; *Art Director:* Massimiliano Capriccioli; *Set Decorator:* Rosa Sansone; *Costumes:* Luciana Marinucci; *Music:* Teo Usuelli; *Running Time:* 95 minutes.

CAST

Ugo Tognazzi *(Alfonso)*; Marina Vlady *(Regina)*; Walter Giller *(Father Mariano)*; Linda Sini *(Mother Superior)*; Riccardo Fellini *(Riccardo)*; Achille Maieroni *(Aunt Mafalda)*; Pietro Tattanelli *(Uncle Don Giuseppe)*; Jusupoff Ragazzi *(Aunt Jolanda)*; Igi Polidoro *(Igi)*; Melissa Drake *(Maria Costanza)*; Sandrino Pinelli *(Maria Costanza's Fiancé)*; Mario Giussani *(Count Ribulsi)*.

THE FILM

Thirty-four-year-old Marco Ferreri was an unknown director when his first big success reached the United States in 1963 as *The Conjugal Bed*. Presaging the outrageous studies in sex and social consciousness *(La Grande Bouffe, L'Ultima Donna/The Last Woman)* that he would turn out in years to come, this sharply satiric comedy-drama offered a human variant on the insect world that met with mixed critical reaction. There were those who applauded its audacious, stylish humor and another faction that found its content tasteless and its exposition overdone.

Middle-aged businessman Alfonso (Ugo Tognazzi) is an Italian bachelor who thinks it is time he must marry. Bypassing the women he has known in his single years, he selects a much younger bride named Regina (Marina Vlady) who is both religious and a virgin. After the wedding, the couple settle down with her family—a beehive of cousins and widowed aunts, all of whom anxiously await Regina's anticipated pregnancy. Brought up to believe that a wife's primary function is motherhood, she concentrates on concep-

UNA STORIA MODERNA: L'APE REGINA   Marina Vlady.

155

UNA STORIA MODERNA: L'APE REGINA Ugo Tognazzi and Marina Vlady.

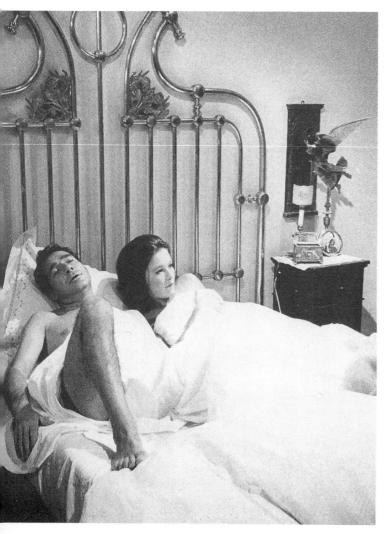

tion, even paying a conjugal visit to her Alfonso in his office. Suffering from a troublesome heart condition, he manages to evade her aggressive tactics by going on a week's retreat to a monastery. But as soon as he returns, Regina resumes her sexual aggressiveness. Alfonso even resorts to painful hormone shots, and finally Regina finds herself pregnant. But now that Alfonso is able to meet her sexual demands, Regina denies herself to him; with child at last, she believes her wifely obligations temporarily fulfilled. Recuperating from his heart problems at a rest home, Alfonso is visited by his wife, who, though pregnant, is no less amorous than before. A sexual act results, causing Alfonso to have a fatal heart seizure. Not long after Alfonso's death, Regina triumphantly becomes a mother.

Feminism ahead of its time? Perhaps, for one of the film's satiric central themes appears to be man's diminishing status in life as women rise not only in business life but also in sexual and social importance. Ugo Tognazzi, reaching international stardom here in a wonderful portrayal of harassed frustration, is well matched by the beautiful Marina Vlady, with her portrait of an innocent-seeming kitten's transition into tigress. Her performance won her the Golden Palm Award as Best Actress at the 1963 Cannes Film Festival.

UNA STORIA MODERNA: L'APE REGINA Ugo Tognazzi and Marina Vlady.

Ieri, Oggi, Domani

(YESTERDAY, TODAY AND TOMORROW)

A Coproduction of Champion Films (Rome) and Les Films Concordia (Paris) / 1963

(U.S. release by Embassy Pictures: 1964)

CREDITS

Director: Vittorio De Sica; *Producer:* Carlo Ponti; *Screenwriters:* "Adelina" *by* Eduardo De Filippo and Isabella Quarantotti; "Anna" *by* Cesare Zavattini and Billa Billa Zanuso, *based on the story* "Troppo Ricca" *by* Alberto Moravia; "Mara" *by* Cesare Zavattini; *Technicolor Cinematographer:* Giuseppe Rotunno; *Editor:* Adriana Novelli; *Art Director:* Ezio Frigerio;
Set Decorator: Ezio Altieri; *Costumes:* Piero Tosi; *Miss Loren's "Mara" wardrobe:* Christian Dior; *Choreographer for "Mara":* Jacques Ruet; *Music:* Armando Trovajoli; *Running Time:* 120 minutes.

CAST

"Adelina": Sophia Loren *(Adelina)*; Marcello Mastroianni *(Carmine)*; Aldo Giuffré *(Pasquale Nardella)*; Agostino Salvietti *(Lawyer Verace)*; Lino Mattera *(Amadeo Scapece)*; Tecla Scarano *(Bianchina Verace)*; Silvia Monelli *(Elvira Nardella)*; Carlo Croccolo *(Auctioneer)*; Pasquale Cennamo *(Police Captain)*.

"Anna": Sophia Loren *(Anna)*; Marcello Mastroiani *(Renzo)*; Armando Trovajoli *(the Other Man)*.

"Mara": Sophia Loren *(Mara)*; Marcello Mastroianni *(Augusto Rusconi)*; Tina Pica *(Grandmother)*; Giovanni Ridolfi *(Umberto)*; Gennaro Di Gregorio *(Grandfather)*.

THE FILM

As fellow actors, Sophia Loren, Marcello Mastroianni, and Vittorio De Sica first teamed in a pair of popular

IERI, OGGI, DOMANI
"Adelina." Sophia Loren, Marcello Mastroianni and Silvia Monelli.

157

IERI, OGGI, DOMANI "Anna." Sophia Loren and Marcello Mastroianni.

mid-fifties comedies: *Peccato Che Sia una Canaglia/ Too Bad She's Bad* and *La Bella Mugnaia/The Miller's Beautiful Daughter.* But even more successful was their collaboration on the three-part anthology film *Ieri, Oggi, Domani/Yesterday, Today and Tomorrow,* with Loren and Mastroianni each playing three different roles under De Sica's clever direction. Set, respectively, in the cities of Naples, Milan, and Rome, it is essentially a showcase for the talents of its attractive stars. Loren, in particular, gets to display her versatility—and breathtaking figure—in roles ranging from enterprising black marketeer to cool, wealthy matron to sexy professional mistress.

Each of the three stories is self-contained, without any need for a linking element. "Adelina" opens in the streets of Naples, where the police arrive to arrest the beautiful Adelina (Loren) for peddling contraband cigarettes to support her unemployed husband Carmine (Mastroianni). He, in turn, comes up with an "only-in-Italy" loophole whereby no expectant mother can be jailed until six months after her baby's birth (to allow for the usual nursing period). The concept works so smoothly that Adelina and Carmine find an ongoing solution to avoid prison. By managing a series of chain

pregnancies, she avoids incarceration altogether. When their brood has grown to seven offspring, Carmine becomes physically debilitated, unable to produce the needed eighth pregnancy. Adelina is jailed. But all is saved when her fellow citizens raise the lire to pay her fine, and her sentence is commuted.

In Milan, the elegant "Anna" (Loren) is married to a prestigious businessman while romantically involved with a hopeful young writer (Mastroianni). One day he wrecks her convertible, trying to avoid hitting a child. Upset by the damage to her vehicle, Anna chooses her car over her lover, accepting a lift from an apparently rich stranger to return to Milan.

While awaiting the return of her lover Rusconi (Mastroianni), Roman call girl "Mara" (Loren) becomes aware of the admiration of a lovelorn young and naive seminary student named Umberto (Giovanni Ridolfi). Although appreciative of his attention, she nevertheless resists his awkward overtures, only to have the boy's grandmother (Tina Pica) accuse her of corrupting a minor. Umberto decides on a solution: He'll leave the seminary to join the Foreign Legion. This leads Mara to confront her young admirer with the truth about herself and her profession, convincing

IERI, OGGI, DOMANI   "Mara." Marcello Mastroianni and Sophia Loren.

him to keep to his chosen calling. She then takes a week's vow of chastity in his honor, much to the dismay of the frustrated Rusconi.

Earthy, funny, and beautifully played, *Yesterday, Today and Tomorrow* is the perfect Sophia Loren vehicle—under the guidance of her *Two Women* mentor De Sica. Perhaps as compensation for appearing as second banana to Loren, Marcello Mastroianni plays his assignments very broadly, bordering on caricature sufficient to impress those British Film Academy members who named him the year's Best Foreign Actor.

With most prior Italian films—outside of historical spectacles—having been shot in black and white, American critics marveled at the opportunity to enjoy the Technicolored sights of Naples, Milan, and Rome—where location scenes were filmed. And Hollywood's motion picture academy voted *Yesterday, Today and Tomorrow* an Oscar—director De Sica's third—as Best Foreign Language Film of 1964. The trio immediately reconnoitered for *Matrimonio All'Italiana/Marriage Italian Style*.

Sedotta e Abbandonata

(SEDUCED AND ABANDONED)

A Coproduction of Lux-Ultra-Vides (Rome) and Lux Cie Cinématographique de France (Paris) / 1964

(U.S. release by Continental Distributing: 1964)

CREDITS

Director: Pietro Germi; *Executive Producer:* Antonio Musu; *Producer:* Franco Cristaldi; *Screenwriters:* Pietro Germi, Luciano Vincenzoni, Age (Agenore Incrocci), and Scarpelli (Furio Scarpelli); *Cinematographer:* Aiace Parolin; *Editor:* Roberto Cinquini; *Art Director:* Carlo Egidi; *Set Decorator:* Andrea Fantacci; *Costumes:* Angela Sammaciccia; *Music:* Carlo Rustichelli; *Running Time:* 123 minutes (*U.S. Running Time:* 118 minutes).

SEDOTTA E ABBANDONATA   Stefania Sandrelli.

CAST

Stefania Sandrelli *(Agnese Ascalone)*; Aldo Puglisi *(Peppino Califano)*; Saro Urzi *(Vincenzo Ascalone)*; Lando Buzzanca *(Antonio Ascalone)*; Leopoldo Trieste *(Baron Rizieri)*; Rocco D'Assunta *(Orlando Califano)*; Lola Braccini *(Amalia Califano)*; Paola Biggio *(Matilde Ascalone)*; Umberto Spadaro *(Cousin Ascalone)*; Oreste Palella *(Police Chief Potenza)*; Lina La Galla *(Francesca Ascalone)*; Roberta Narbonne *(Rosaura Ascalone)*; Rosetta Urzi *(Consolata, the Maid)*; Adelino Campardo *(Policeman Bisigato)*; Vincenzo Licata *(Profumo, the Undertaker)*; Italia Spadaro *(Aunt Carmela)*; Gustavo D'Arpe *(Ciarpetta, the Lawyer)*; Salvatore Fazio *(Father Mariano)*.

THE FILM

If the comedy of manners is a film genre not readily identified with Sicily, then the acclaimed writer-director Pietro Germi helped change that situation, first with the sardonic *Divorce—Italian Style* (1961) and then with this totally unrelated follow-up that, for once, had nothing to do with the Mafia. *Seduced and Abandoned* is not a perfect film; it takes a half hour too long to etch its portrait of a small town's foibles in establishing family "honor" and justice. But in so doing, it offers humorous insights into the old-fashioned mores that apparently still prevailed in southern Italy when this film was made.

During the afternoon siesta in a small Sicilian village, Peppino Califano (Aldo Puglisi) seduces Agnese Ascalone (Stefania Sandrelli), the fifteen-year-old sister of his fiancée Matilde (Paola Biggio). When the teenager is later found to be pregnant, her father Vincenzo (Saro Urzi) is moved to terminate Matilde's engagement to Peppino and find her a new and more respectable fiancé, the penniless but titled Baron Rizieri (Leopoldo Trieste). Peppino, of course, is pressured by Papa Ascalone to marry Agnese, but he objects to the idea of taking an unchaste bride! Fearing for his safety, he takes his family's advice and goes into hiding. But the code of honor rules the Ascalone family, and Papa Vincenzo takes his lawyer's advice that his son Antonio (Lando Buzzanca) must kill Peppino in an act of sudden and justifiable rage. For such a crime the maximum prison sentence can only be five years. But Agnese warns the local carabinieri, and everyone winds up at a private hearing at which Peppino is ordered to marry Agnese or face prison on the charge of seducing a minor. With the girl's family now eager for his consent, Peppino's arrogant behavior turns Agnese against him, and she refuses to marry him.

Now all hell breaks loose in the village, whose inhabitants openly ridicule the dishonored girl and her family. The baron breaks his engagement to Matilde, and Vincenzo suffers a fatal heart attack. As if that weren't enough for the Ascalones, Matilde becomes a nun, and the baron attempts suicide. Finally, Agnese saves the family honor by agreeing to wed Peppino.

Germi, who coauthored the screenplay with three other writers, based his film on an Italian statute that absolves a man of criminal charges if he weds the woman he has seduced. Such social hypocrisy is a perfect setup for the considerable humor that Germi mines from this material, and the director makes good use of a largely unfamiliar cast to do so. As Agnese,

SEDOTTA E ABBANDONATA   Saro Urzi, Stefania Sandrelli and Aldo Puglisi.

SEDOTTA E
ABBANDONATA   Aldo Puglisi
and Stefania Sandrelli.

161

Stefania Sandrelli—the young beauty for whom Marcello Mastroianni killed his wife in *Divorce–Italian Style*—makes the perfect target for a lusty young man like Peppino, who is played to the hilt by the rather sinister looking Aldo Puglisi, a previously little-known Sicilian actor. Indeed, the entire cast is colorfully right for this grotesque comedy. Carlo Rustichelli's rousing, lilting musical score merits praise for reminding us that this is all in fun.

Some critics found *Seduced and Abandoned* lacking when compared to *Divorce–Italian Style*. But the *New York Herald Tribune*'s Judith Crist dubbed it "a hilarious and ferocious film, seething with anger and sparkling with scorn of the hypocrisies—nay, the crimes—that are committed in the name of honor and the sanctity of the family and society."

Prima della Rivoluzione

(BEFORE THE REVOLUTION)

An Iride Cinematografica Production / 1964

(U.S. release by New Yorker Films: 1965)

CREDITS

Director: Bernardo Bertolucci; *Screenwriters:* Bernardo Bertolucci and Gianni Amico; *Cinematographer:* Aldo Scavarda; *Editor:* Roberto Perpignani; *Music:* Gino Paoli and Ennio Morricone; *Songs:* "Ricordati" and "Vivere Ancora" *by* (and *sung by*) Gino Paoli, and "Avero 15 Anni" *sung by* Ennio Ferrari; *Running Time:* 112 minutes.

CAST

Adriana Asti *(Gina)*; Francesco Barilli *(Fabrizio)*; Allen Midgette *(Agostino)*; Morando Morandini *(Cesare)*; Domenico Alpi *(Fabrizio's Father)*; Giuseppe Maghenzani *(Fabrizio's Brother)*; Cecrope Barilli *(Puck)*; Cristina Pariset *(Clelia)*; Emilia Borghi *(Fabrizio's Mother)*; Iole Lunardi *(Fabrizio's Grandmother)*; Evelina Alpi *(Girl)*; Gianni Amico *(Friend)*; Goliardo Padova (the *Painter)*; Guido Fanti *(Enore)*; Salvatore Enrico *(Sacristan)*; Ida Pellegri *(Clelia's Mother)*.

THE FILM

Years before writer-director Bernardo Bertolucci inspired reams of both negative and positive criticism with such pictures as *The Conformist, Last Tango in Paris, 1900,* and *The Last Emperor,* he attracted the attention of young cinema intellectuals with his second feature, *Before The Revolution* (1964). Bertolucci's somber debut film *La Comara Secca / The Grim Reaper* failed commercially. But *Before The Revolution*—released when Bertolucci was only twenty-four—had occupied fully two years of his life and reflected the obvious influences of his older contemporaries Jean-Luc Godard, Michelangelo Antonioni, and Pier Paolo Pasolini. When *Before The Revolution* played the New York Film Festival in the autumn of 1964, *New York Times* critic Eugene Archer called it both "a beauty" and "the revelation of the Festival."

The story centers on twenty-year-old Fabrizio (Francesco Barilli), a fervent Marxist whose ideology leads him to reject the Parmesan middle-class background he shares with fiancée Clelia (Cristina Pariset). Encouraging the young man in his beliefs are the schoolteacher Cesare (Morando Morandini) and Agostino (Allen Midgette), the headstrong son of a wealthy manufacturer. Fabrizio's first revolutionary

PRIMA DELLA RIVOLUZIONE Francesco Barilli and Adriana Asti.

162

PRIMA DELLA
RIVOLUZIONE Adriana
Asti and Francesco
Barilli.

act is to break off with Clelia, which so upsets his parents that they invite his young Milanese aunt Gina (Adriana Asti) to stay with them in the hope that she might help bridge the communication gap with their son. When Agostino tragically drowns, Fabrizio is suddenly left without a confidant and draws closer to Gina, who warmly reciprocates his friendship. So warmly that they soon become lovers. But he finds his aunt's neurotic moodiness difficult to cope with, and their relationship changes rapidly after he sees her emerge from a transient hotel with a chance pickup. As Gina prepares to return to Milan, the politically disillusioned Fabrizio reconciles with Clelia, whose acceptance offers him the security he needs. Later, he encounters Gina at the opera, but despite his continuing fascination with her, Fabrizio marries Clelia. And while Cesare goes on preaching revolution to a new generation of students, the unstable Gina tearfully embraces her nephew's younger brother (Giuseppe Maghenzani).

Of its leading players, only the stunningly expressive Adriana Asti seems to have resurfaced in several less memorable French and Italian imports, namely, *Disorder, Ludwig,* and *Down the Ancient Stairs.*

Bertolucci, of course, has proven of more durable substance. And notwithstanding the obvious signs of influence from his older European predecessors, he paints a cinematic canvas with his own original strokes, crowding the screen with images as striking as they are overstated. And yet he already possesses the astonishing artistry to get away with it. His frank handling of the film's sexual scenes are a precursor of the furor to come with his ground-breaking *Last Tango in Paris.* But in the final analysis, Bertolucci's *Before The Revolution* continues to impress with the remarkable maturity of its early promise of a major filmmaker on the rise.

Il Vangelo Secondo Matteo

(THE GOSPEL ACCORDING TO ST. MATTHEW)

A Coproduction of Arco Films (Rome) and Lux Cie Cinématographique de France (Paris) / 1964

(U.S. release by Continental Distributing: 1966)

163

IL VANGELO SECONDO
MATTEO Otello Sestili and
Enrique Irazoqui.

CREDITS

Director: Pier Paolo Pasolini; *Producer:* Alfredo Bini;
Cinematographer: Tonino Delli Colli; *Editor:* Andrea
Fantucci; *Art Directors:* Niño Baragli and Luigi Scac-
cianoce; *Costumes:* Danilo Donati; *Music:* Luis E.
Bacalov *and selections from the works of* Johann
Sebastian Bach, Wolfgang Amadeus Mozart, Sergei
Prokofiev, and Anton Webern, *as well as the spiritual*
"Sometimes I Feel Like a Motherless Child" *sung by*
Odetta; *Running Time:* 142 minutes.

CAST

Enrique Irazoqui *(Jesus Christ)*; Margherita Caruso
(Young Mary); Susanna Pasolini *(Older Mary)*; Mar-
cello Morante *(Joseph)*; Mario Socrate *(John the Bap-
tist)*; Settimo di Porto *(Peter)*; Otello Sestili *(Judas)*;
Ferruccio Nuzzo *(Matthew)*; Giacomo Morante *(John)*;
Alfonso Gatto *(Andrew)*; Enzo Siciliano *(Simon)*; Gior-
gio Agamben *(Philip)*; Guido Cerretani *(Bartho-
lomew)*; Luigi Barbini *(James, Son of Alpheus)*; Mar-
cello Galdini *(James, Son of Zebedee)*; Elio Spaziani
(Thaddeus); Rosario Migale *(Thomas)*; Rodolfo
Wilcock *(Gaipha)*; Alessandro Tasca *(Pontius Pilate)*;
Amerigo Bevilacqua *(Herod I)*; Francesco Leonetti
(Herod II); Franca Cupane *(Herodiade)*; Paola Te-
desca *(Salome)*; Rosana di Rocco *(Angel of the Lord)*;
Elseo Boschi *(Joseph of Arimathaea)*; Natalia Gins-
burg *(Mary of Bethany)*; Renato Terra *(Pharisee)*.

IL VANGELO SECONDO
MATTEO The miracle of the
loaves and fishes.

THE FILM

Unlike most dramatizations of the life of Jesus, Pier Paolo Pasolini's most admired movie employed no actual screenplay. Instead, the idiosyncratic film-maker confined himself strictly to the account by Matthew, employing only those words written by the saint. (The picture's English subtitles follow the English edition by Msgr. Ronald Knox.) No additional dialogue was devised, and only events described by Matthew are depicted.

In the director's words: "I liked the Christ of Matthew. He was rigorous, demanding, absolute. This is the Christ who says, 'I came not to send peace, but a sword,' the Christ who will 'burn up the chaff with unquenchable fire,' and who calls his contemporaries 'a generation of vipers'!"

With *The Gospel According to St. Matthew*, Pasolini sought to avoid the customary clichés of reverential treatments seen in costly Hollywood productions like *King of Kings* and *The Greatest Story Ever Told*. Especially, he was intent on finding a storytelling style

that would avoid the picture-postcard piety that had discouraged sincere men of the cloth each time a filmmaker had dealt with the life of Christ.

Nor did Pasolini want the usual star-studded cast. On the contrary, he decided to employ only nonprofessionals. For Jesus, he selected a young Spanish student named Enrique Irazoqui, who had contacted the director, during a visit to Rome, to discuss a Pasolini novel he had read. The filmmaker was immediately struck by Irazoqui's resemblance to El Greco's painting—the look Pasolini wanted (although the young man's voice later had to be replaced by the dubbing of a professional actor). For the older Mary, who would suffer through the Passion, Pasolini chose his own mother Susanna, while the young Mary was portrayed by a student. The director's friends filled out the rest of the cast. A music critic was cast as St. Matthew, a writer as Simon, and a poet as Andrew. A lawyer became Joseph; a truck driver played Judas. What Pasolini sought was the look of primitive, rough-hewn faces—the faces he felt that the peasants of Nazareth and Palestine and the fishermen of Galilee must surely have possessed.

Nor did he go for glamorously picturesque settings. "I did not want a historical or archaeological film," the director later explained. "With authentic costumes and scenery, it would have had a facile commercial aspect I was trying to avoid. I proceeded by analogy. I chose Calabria in southern Italy as the settings because, like Jerusalem, it is close to the Mediterranean and there are many humble people there. My Bethlehem is a village abandoned by Calabrian peasants seeking better jobs in industry. Herod's palace is a twelfth-century castle, still standing in Calabria. The costumes are based on frescoes by Piero della Francesca." All of these bleakly striking locations were artfully captured by the black-and-white camera work of Tonino Delli Colli, with an emphasis on grayish tones.

Taking the Son of God through the familiar stages of his life from the manger to the cross, Pasolini presents him not in the customary immaculate white robes but as an ordinary-looking man garbed in homespun clothing as he travels the countryside, preaching his words of exhortation. Indeed, this Jesus is a severe and dedicated revolutionary whose life and times were intentionally presented in a fashion designed to make him relevant to today's world. Coming from an acknowledged Marxist and atheist like Pasolini, this is truly an extraordinary motion picture, utterly unlike any of the "Biblicals" Hollywood has ever turned out.

Reflecting the general level of American reaction to *The Gospel According to St. Matthew*, Robert Salmaggi, of the *New York Herald Tribune*, called it "a lean, clean honest film," while *Time* magazine's anonymous critic, though lamenting its surfeit of "interminable closeups and sermons," summed it up as "a modest, unadorned movie that should satisfy the yearnings of anyone who has ever suffered through the pretentious piety of multimillion-dollar orgies of Scripturama."

Dedicated to the memory of Pope John Paul XXIII, the controversial Pasolini's least shocking film won the Special Jury Prize of the 1964 Venice Film Festival as well as being named one of America's best foreign films of 1966 by the National Board of Review.

Matrimonio All'Italiana

(MARRIAGE ITALIAN STYLE)

A Coproduction of Champion Films (Rome) and Les Films Concordia (Paris) / 1964

(U.S. release by Embassy Pictures: 1964)

CREDITS

Director: Vittorio De Sica; *Executive Producer:* Joseph E. Levine; *Producer:* Carlo Ponti; *Screenwriters:* Eduardo de Filippo, Renato Castellani, Antonio Guerra, Leo Benvenuto, and Pier de Barnardi; *Based on the play* Filumena Marturano *by* Eduardo de Filippo; *Eastmancolor Cinematographer:* Roberto Gerardi; *Editor:* Adriana Novelli; *Art Director:* Carlo Egidi; *Set Decorator:* Dario Michell; *Costumes:* Piero Tosi and Vera Marzot; *Music:* Armando Trovajoli; *Running Time:* 120 minutes.

CAST

Sophia Loren *(Filumena Marturano)*; Marcello Mastroianni *(Domenico Soriano)*; Aldo Puglisi *(Alfredo)*; Tecla Scarano *(Rosalie)*; Marilù Tolo *(Diane)*; Pia Lindstrom *(Cashier)*; Giovanni Ridolfi *(Umberto)*; Vito Moriconi *(Riccardo)*; Generoso Cortini *(Michele)*; Raffaelo Rossi Bussola *(Lawyer)*; Vincenza Di Capua *(Mother)*; Vincenzo Aita *(Priest)*.

THE FILM

Marriage Italian Style reunited the award-winning team of Sophia Loren, Marcello Mastroianni, and director Vittorio De Sica in still another box-office hit.

MATRIMONIO ALL'ITALIANA Sophia Loren.

young girlfriend (Marilù Tolo), Filumena reacts accordingly, pretending to be dying so that he will save her from mortal sin by marrying *her* instead. But Domenico learns that he has been tricked, and he gets the union annulled. However, Filumena has another card up her sleeve: informing him that she wants to legitimize her three sons, whom she has secretly supported in foster homes. She admits that one of the boys (she won't tell him which one) is *his*. Domenico now becomes obsessed with discovering which son he has fathered, resorting to every possible trick and threat until, after a fight that culminates in lovemaking, he realizes that he indeed cares deeply for her. With the three boys in attendance, the pair are married again,

MATRIMONIO ALL'ITALIANA   Marcello Mastroianni and Sophia Loren.

One of its five screenwriters, Eduardo de Filippo, had written the play *Filumena Marturano* on which it was based and had also starred opposite Tamara Lees in an earlier movie version, filmed under its original title in 1951.

In mid-sixties Naples, wealthy, middle-aged playboy-businessman Domenico Soriano (Mastroianni) is tricked into marrying Filumena Marturano (Loren), a former prostitute who had been his mistress for the past twenty years. They had met in 1943 in a Neapolitan brothel when she was seventeen, beginning a courtship that resulted in her acquiring her own apartment and eventually moving into the Soriano home. For years Filumena has run her lover's bar and pastry shop as well as his household, and had looked after his senile mother until her death.

When she discovers that Domenico intends to wed a

MATRIMONIO ALL'ITALIANA   Marcello Mastroianni and Sophia Loren.

168

after which each of the youths begins calling Domenico "Papa." Doubtless, he will spend the rest of his life trying to find out which one of them is his own flesh and blood.

Although De Sica intensely disliked the film's title ("Distributors always have bad taste"), neither could he agree on producer Carlo Ponti's suggestion of *Three Women.* If they had to echo the sound of a past box-office winner, perhaps *Marriage Italian Style* rather than *Filumena Marturano,* which might present unnecessary problems for English-speaking audiences. At any rate, the resultant movie scored as big a hit as the prior *Yesterday, Today and Tomorrow,* especially for its stars. Sophia Loren enjoyed an actor's field day as she progressed (via flashback) from teenaged tart to flamboyant streetwalker to bossy housekeeper to devoted mother, while at the same time gracefully aging from an exuberant seventeen to a tired thirty-seven. As Bosley Crowther observed in his *New York Times* review: "Whenever Vittorio De Sica gets together with Sophia Loren to make a motion picture, something wonderful happens." Having asked De Sica why Loren is always at her best under his guidance, the great director once replied: "She has confidence in me. She is a *filodrammatica;* with beauty, with talent, but she needs to be handled."

Loren again evinces perfect on-screen rapport with Mastroianni, incomparable as the born womanizer who tries in vain to outwit her but inevitably succumbs to her wiles.

Marriage Italian Style garnered an Academy Award nomination as Best Foreign Film of 1964.

La Battaglia di Algeri

(THE BATTLE OF ALGIERS)

A Coproduction of Igor Films (Rome) and Casbah Films (Algiers) / 1966

(U.S. release by Rizzoli Films through Allied Artists: 1967)

CREDITS

Director: Gillo Pontecorvo; *Producers:* Antonio Musu and Yacef Saadi; *Screenwriter:* Franco Solinas; *Based on a story by* Gillo Pontecorvo and Franco Solinas; *CinemaScope Cinematographer:* Marcello Gatti; *Editors:* Mario Serandrei and Mario Morra; *Second-Unit*

Director: Giuliano Montaldo; *Art Director:* Sergio Canevari; *Music:* Ennio Morricone and Gillo Pontecorvo; *Running Time:* 135 minutes (*U.S. release:* 120 minutes).

CAST

Jean Martin *(Colonel Mathieu);* Yacef Saadi *(Saari Kader);* Brahim Haggiag *(Ali La Pointe);* Tommaso Neri *(Captain Dubois);* Fawzia El-Kader *(Halima);* Michele Kerbash *(Fathia);* Mohamed Ben Kassen *(Little Omar);* Ugo Paletti *(the Captain).*

THE FILM

Gillo Pontecorvo's on-location re-creation of hostilities as they transpired in the Algerian rebellion against the French from 1954 to 1957 was staged with such apparent authenticity that *The Battle of Algiers* found it necessary to state in an on-screen forword that no newsreel footage had been used in the movie. Nor, to any appreciable degree, were professional actors used for the principal characters, one of whom is portrayed by Yacef Saadi, the film's coproducer. Subsidized by the Algerian government, with the people of Algiers reenacting their struggles of a decade earlier, *The Battle of Algiers* was, not unexpectedly, cold-shouldered by the French, who kept it off their screens until 1971. They also boycotted its showing at the 1966 Venice Film Festival, where this docudrama won the Golden Lion for Best Picture, among its ten other international prizes.

In 1954, 130 years of French colonialism in Algeria ends in revolt as the secret organization called the FLN (Front de Liberation Nationale) strikes for independence. Led by Saari Kader (Saadi), the Arabs initiate a reign of terror against Algiers's European community, targeting in particular the city's policemen. By sealing off the notorious Casbah, refuge for the FLN, the governor hopes to quell the uprising. But the attacks persist. A French newspaperman gains professional entry into the Casbah to plant a bomb that kills scores of Arab families, and Kader strikes back in kind. Sending three Arab women into the city in European guise, Kader orders bombings of an air terminal, a café, and a dance bar. The French then bring in a paratroop division under the leadership of hard-hitting Colonel Mathieu (Jean Martin), who tortures captured terrorists into naming their compatriots.

The United Nations debates the hostilities, finally deciding against intervention. By then, Mathieu has wiped out all FLN leaders save one, the obsessively militant ex-thief Ali La Pointe (Brahim Haggiag), who

LA BATTAGLIA DI ALGERI.

LA BATTAGLIA DI ALGERI   Gillo Pontecorvo directing.

LA BATTAGLIA DI ALGERI.

fights on for the liberation of Algeria—until, finally, he is trapped behind the bedroom wall of his hideout. Mathieu demands that Ali surrender or be blown up with the house. The rebel leader refuses and dies. But despite the defeated FLN, thousands of the Algerian populace riot, taking over the city, and on July 3, 1962, they achieve their independence.

Recalling the documentary-like realism of such predecessors as *Open City* and *The Four Days of Naples*, American critics recognized a throwback to neorealism in Pontecorvo's intensely detailed direction, and they praised his remarkable objectivity in depicting the fight for liberation without resorting to the use of star actors or glamorized dramatics.

Pontecorvo had, several years earlier, mixed near-documentary realism with melodrama in the stark but uneven prison-camp story *Kapò*. But *Kapò*'s hard-hitting moments almost pale in comparison to *The Battle of Algiers*, the motion picture with which Pontecorvo is still most readily identified.

Il Buono, Il Brutto, Il Cattivo

(THE GOOD, THE BAD AND THE UGLY)

*A P.E.A. (Produzioni Europée Associates)
Production / 1966*

(U.S. release by United Artists: 1968)

CREDITS

Director: Sergio Leone; *Producer:* Alberto Grimaldi;
Screenwriters: Luciano Vincenzoni and Sergio Leone;
Based on a story by Age (Agenore Incrocci), Scarpelli
(Furio Scarpelli), Leone, and Vincenzoni; *Techni-
color-Techniscope Cinematographer:* Tonino Delli
Colli; *Editors:* Nino Baragli and Eugenio Alabiso; *Art*

Director and Costumes: Carlo Simi; *Music:* Ennio
Morricone; *Running Time:* 180 minutes *(U.S. Running
Time:* 161 minutes).

CAST

Clint Eastwood *(Joe);* Eli Wallach *(Tuco);* Lee Van
Cleef *(Setenza); and* Aldo Giuffré, Chelo Alonso, Mario
Brega, Luigi Pistilli, Rada Rassimov, Enzo Petito,
Claudio Scharchilli, Al Mulock, Livio Lorenzon, Anto-
nio Casale, Sandro Scarchilli, Angelo Novi, Benito
Stefanelli, Silvana Bacci, Antonio Casas, and Aldo
Sambrell.

THE FILM

Based largely on the cult popularity of this film,
followed by *Once Upon a Time in the West,* the late
Sergio Leone will always be a legendary part of Italian
movie history as the king of all so-called spaghetti-
western directors. Leone had started in the business as

IL BUONO, IL BRUTTO, IL CATTIVO   Eli Wallach and Clint Eastwood.

IL BUONO, IL BRUTTO, IL
CATTIVO Clint Eastwood.

an assistant on other directors' pictures. His first full-fledged directorial credit was *The Colossus of Rhodes* (1961), a surprisingly well-made historical adventure yarn. It was Leone who not only revitalized the western genre but also afforded American television actor Clint Eastwood *(Rawhide)* big-screen European stardom in a pair of "sleeper" westerns known in the United States as *A Fistful of Dollars* (1964) and *For a Few Dollars More* (1965). Before his continental fame could spread to American cinema audiences, Eastwood returned there in 1966 to star in the third, biggest, and last of his Leone series, *The Good, the Bad*

and the Ugly, for which he was paid a then-impressive salary of $250,000. Bypassing its immensely popular predecessors, this violent, three-hour Civil War oater went on to become one of its decade's highest-grossing Italian films.

It took the first of this trio all of three years to reach America, and although the critics weren't impressed, movie audiences loved them—especially the epic-length third entry. More violent than the earlier pair and more operatic in scope and pace, *The Good, the Bad and the Ugly* boasted slam-bang shoot-outs, elaborate cinematic set pieces, terrific photography by

Tonino Delli Colli of the striking locations, and what many consider the best score ever composed by the prolific Ennio Morricone. And while critics decried its display of cinematic overkill, western devotees saw it again and again, belatedly establishing a stateside Leone cult that made Eastwood a top *movie* star on his *home* turf.

The film is set in the Civil War Southwest where a cashbox containing $200,000 is stolen and concealed in an unmarked grave. A mysterious gunslinger known only as "Joe" (Eastwood, as the "Good" part of the title) has formed a nervous friendship with the Mexican bandit Tuco (Eli Wallach, the "Ugly" one). To collect the bounty money, Joe hands Tucco over to a succession of sheriffs, from whom he proceeds to rescue the outlaw before a hanging can take place. They subsequently share the reward monies. Eventually, however, Tuco decides to betray his friend and

hires three men to kill Joe. When the latter's fast draw decimates his would-be assassins, Tuco retaliates by capturing him and nearly dragging Joe to his death in the dry desert heat—until Joe tells the Mexican that he knows the whereabouts of the buried cashbox. With Tucco thus motivated to give him water and shade, they once again join together—in a hunt for the treasure.

In the meantime, the sadistic Setenza (the "Bad" Lee Van Cleef) conducts his own search for the cashbox, having joined the Union army to track down the one soldier who knows its burial spot. Attired in Confederate uniforms, Joe and Tuco are taken prisoner by the Union soldiers and brought to Setenza. When Tuco lets it be known that it is he who knows the location of the treasure, he is brutally beaten until he reveals that it is buried in a graveyard. In the film's climactic shoot-out in Sad Hill Cemetery, Joe kills Setenza, while sparing Tuco, whom he leaves with his share of the gold—if he can free himself from the rope Joe has tied around his neck.

What most American critics failed to appreciate was Leone's dark sense of humor, the film's cynical lack of sentiment, and the director's delicious stylishness, from the bigger-than-life close-ups of its often stone-faced trio to the realistic buzz of flies around corpses. Underscoring it all is Morricone's persistent music, with its orchestrated Indian cries. If the critics have been slow to come around in favor of *The Good, the Bad and the Ugly*, a knowing body of fans has long since established the movie as a classic of its kind.

A Ciascuno il Suo

(WE STILL KILL THE OLD WAY)

A Cemo Film Production / 1967
(U.S. release by Lopert Films: 1968)

CREDITS

Director: Elio Petri; *Producer:* Giuseppe Zaccariello; *Associate Producer:* Luigi Millozza; *Screenwriters:* Elio Petri and Ugo Pirro; *Based on the novel by* Leonardo Sciascia; *Technicolor Cinematographer:* Luigi Kuveiller; *Editor:* Ruggero Mastroianni; *Art Director:* Sergio Canevari; *Costumes:* Luciana Marinucci; *Music:* Luis Enrique Bakalov; *Running Time:* 99 minutes (*U.S. Running Time:* 92 minutes).

CAST

Gian Maria Volonté *(Paolo Laurana)*; Irene Papas *(Luisa Roscio)*; Gabriele Ferzetti *(Rosello)*; Salvo Randone *(Professor Roscio)*; Luigi Pistilli *(Arturo Manno)*; Mario Scaccia *(the Priest)*; Laura Nucci *(Laurana's Mother)*; Leopoldo Trieste *(Parliament Member)*;

IL BUONO, IL BRUTTO, IL CATTIVO   Eli Wallach, Clint Eastwood and Lee Van Cleef.

A CIASCUNO IL SUO   Irene Papas, Gabriele Ferzetti and Gian Maria Volonté.

Franco Tranchina *(Dr. Antonio Roscio)*; Luciana Scalise *(Rosina)*; Anna Rivero *(Manno's Wife)*; Giovanni Pallavicino *(Ragana)*; Orio Cannarozzo *(Police Inspector)*; Carmelo Oliviero *(the Archpriest)*.

THE FILM

Much of director Elio Petri's work evokes references to Kafka in the evaluation of the former's often-elliptical style, especially with regard to *Investigation of a Citizen Above Suspicion* (1970) and its predecessors, the futuristic *The Tenth Victim* (1965) and *We Still Kill the Old Way*. Essentially a political thriller, the latter film also infuses elements of contemporary Sicilian observation, anti-Mafia sentiments, and even marital comedy, albeit with a darkly sinister tone to its humor. With Italy's current, murderous struggle between Sicily's Cosa Nostra and the law's efforts to defeat the crime lords' tenacious hold, the ever-timely *We Still Kill the Old Way* would seem worthy of rescue from its relative obscurity and deserving of reevaluation.

Murdered while on a hunting trip, Arturo Manno (Luigi Pistilli) and Dr. Antonio Roscio (Franco Tranchina) are assumed by their fellow Sicilians to have been the victims of a crime of honor, since the married Manno had been illicitly involved with a local peasant named Rosina (Luciana Scalise). However, the idealistic professor Paolo Laurana (Gian Maria Volonté) remains unconvinced that the killings were carried out by the girl's father and two brothers, and he embarks on an investigation of his own. The professor believes that the actual motive for murder was to silence Dr. Roscio's criticism of the Mafia, with Manno slain only as a cover-up. His intensive inquiries net little as he is confronted with Sicily's *omerta* (code of silence). With the help of Roscio's attractive widow

A CIASCUNO IL SUO   Gian Maria Volonté and Irene Papas.

176

Luisa (Irene Papas), Laurana uncovers a diary left by her husband in which he maps out his plan to denounce a powerful but unnamed political figure whom Laurana suspects is Luisa's politician-cousin Rosello (Gabriele Ferzetti). The professor then begins to receive anonymous letters threatening his life, and although drawn into an ambush by Rosello, he is freed when he reveals that he has in his possession Roscio's incriminating diary. Luisa, whom he now loves, lures Laurana to a remote beach, where he discovers that she is actually Rosello's mistress. There the professor is brutally set upon by hired assassins and burned alive in a sandstone quarry. His death clears the way for Luisa and Rosello to wed, and also allows the village to bury its chilling secrets about the three murders.

Behind the camera, director Petri and his cinematographer Luigi Kuveiller make evocative use of the Palermo locations of Cefalù and the Villa Floria, although black-and-white photography might have served this sinister plot's purposes more appropriately than the Technicolor hues that so glorify the natural beauty of this Sicilian terrain. Finally, there's the sprightly, Calypso-flavored background music of Luis Enrique Bakalov, with its occasional, ominous drum obbligato to remind us that serious "Family" business is, after all, afoot here.

C'Era una Volta il West

(ONCE UPON A TIME IN THE WEST)

A Coproduction of Rafran Cinematografica and San Marco Films / 1969

(U.S. release by Paramount Pictures: 1969)

CREDITS

Director: Sergio Leone; *Executive Producer:* Bino Cicogna; *Producer:* Fulvio Morsella; *Screenwriters:* Sergio Leone and Sergio Donati; *Based on a story by* Dario Argento, Bernardo Bertolucci, and Sergio Leone; *Technicolor-Techniscope Cinematographer:* Tonino Delli Colli; *Editor:* Nino Baragli; *Art Director:* Carlo Simi; *Set Decorator:* Carlo Leva; *Music:* Ennio Morricone; *Running Time:* 165 minutes.

CAST

Henry Fonda *(Frank)*; Claudia Cardinale *(Jill McBain)*; Jason Robards *(Cheyenne)*; Charles Bronson *(the Man/Harmonica)*; Frank Wolff *(Brett McBain)*; Gabriele Ferzetti *(Morton)*; Keenan Wynn *(Sheriff of Flagstone)*; Paolo Stoppa *(Sam)*; Marco Zuanelli

C'ERA UNA VOLTA IL WEST Charles Bronson.

(Wobbles); Lionel Stander (Barman); Jack Elam (Knuckles); John Frederick (Frank's Henchman); Woody Strode (Stony); Enzo Santianello (Timmy McBain); Dino Mele (Harmonica as a Boy); Aldo Sambrell (Man from Cheyenne); Benito Stefanelli (Station Manager); Marilu Carteny (Maureen McBain); Michael Harvey (Frank's Aide).

THE FILM

Director Sergio Leone—that Cecil B. DeMille of the Italian sagebrush—had initially sought character actor Charles Bronson for his increasingly ambitious trio of box-office-hit spaghetti westerns: *A Fistful of Dollars, For a Few Dollars More,* and *The Good, the Bad and the Ugly,* but Bronson was skeptical enough to sidestep the assignments, to the respective benefit of Clint Eastwood, Lee Van Cleef, and Eli Wallach, who took the roles Bronson had rejected. Leone finally broke down Bronson's resistance with an overblown script he called *Once Upon a Time in the West.* It was by far the longest, most expensive picture the filmmaker had thus far attempted. Perhaps to underscore his admiration for the westerns of John Ford, the director took his Italo-American cast and crew—headed by Claudia Cardinale, Henry Fonda, Jason Robards, and Gabriele Ferzetti—to Ford-favored locales in Utah and Arizona as well as Spain, all artfully captured by the color cameras of the great Tonino Delli Colli. Ennio Morri-

C'ERA UNA VOLTA IL WEST Claudia Cardinale and Charles Bronson.

178

cone's plaintive, harmonica-flavored score added the final horse-operatic touch.

For cult-minded Americans, *Once Upon a Time in the West* remains Leone's masterpiece, a triumph of style and flair over familiar content. Its story centers on the vicious rivalry over a piece of land in the American West of the 1870s. The railroad wants the property for its water well, but it belongs to the recently widowed Jill McBain (Claudia Cardinale), a lady with a New Orleans past who is new to the area. In the employ of the crooked railroad magnate Morton (Gabriele Ferzetti), black-clad Frank (Henry Fonda) is the hired gun who has killed her husband and will do what he

has to do to get her land. Meanwhile, an outlaw named Cheyenne (Jason Robards) is determined to help Jill, as well as clear his own name. And Harmonica (Bronson) is a mysterious stranger out to settle an old personal score against Frank: When Harmonica was fifteen, Frank had forced him to play his namesake instrument while participating in the torture and hanging of his older brother. In one of the film's most effective climactic scenes, Harmonica coolly shoots Frank before he can draw his gun. While the killer lies dying, the laconic stranger reveals his motivation for hunting him down, stuffing his ever-handy harmonica into Frank's mouth as an epitaph. (Leone's casting is unique here,

presenting that all-American hero Henry Fonda as one of the most relentless villains in cinema history.) The ugly/handsome Bronson, a rugged and quietly enigmatic fellow for whom death is a natural part of living, is the movie's true hero.

Faced with a 165-minute superwestern, Paramount, the film's cofinancier and U.S. distributor, nervously kept its *American* release a virtual secret. Its New York run was short, with Paramount cutting the film by thirty minutes before booking it elsewhere. This indiscriminate reediting only made the already intricate story confusing, and moviegoers were apathetic. In France, however, Leone's epic was a great success, playing continuously for *four years* and setting a record as that country's all-time box-office champion.

During the seventies, *Once Upon a Time in the West* became a U.S. cult classic among those who appreciated Leone's cinematic excesses. For this violent tale of vengeance is a sprawling tribute to Hollywood westerns by an Italian who grew up with reverence for the genre.

In 1980, director Martin Scorsese initiated a campaign to preserve deteriorating color films, since many post-1950 pictures exist on inferior stock that quickly fades. To illustrate his cause, the director selected for restoration *Once Upon a Time in the West*, most prints of which were in poor condition. The restored version met with acclaim at that year's New York Film Festival.

Romeo e Giulietta

(ROMEO AND JULIET)

A Coproduction of British Home Entertainments Productions, Verona Produzione, and Dino De Laurentiis Cinematografica / 1968

(U.S. release by Paramount Pictures: 1968)

CREDITS

Director: Franco Zeffirelli; *Producers:* Anthony Havelock-Allan and John Brabourne; *Associate Producer:* Richard Goodwin; *Screenwriters:* Franco Brusati, Masolino D'Amico, and Franco Zeffirelli, *adapted from the play by* William Shakespeare; *Technicolor Cinematographer:* Pasquale De Santis; *Editor:* Reginald Mills; *Production Designer:* Renzo Mongiardino; *Art Director:* Luciano Puccini; *Set Decorator:* Christine Edzard; *Costumes:* Danilo Donati; *Music:* Nino Rota; *Song* "What Is a Youth?" *by* Nino Rota and Eugene Walter; *Prologue and Epilogue Spoken by* Laurence Olivier [uncredited]; *Running Time:* 152 minutes.

CAST

Olivia Hussey *(Juliet);* Leonard Whiting *(Romeo);* Milo O'Shea *(Friar Laurence);* Michael York *(Tybalt);* John McEnery *(Mercutio);* Pat Heywood *(Nurse);* Robert Stephens *(Prince of Verona);* Natasha Parry *(Lady Capulet);* Keith Skinner *(Balthazar);* Richard Warwick *(Gregory);* Dyson Lovell *(Sampson);* Ugo Barbone *(Abraham);* Bruce Robinson *(Benvolio);* Paul Hardwich *(Lord Capulet);* Antonio Pierfederici *(Lord Montague, with voice dubbed by* Laurence Olivier*);* Esmeralda Ruspoli *(Lady Montague);* Robert Bisacco *(Count Paris);* Roy Holder *(Peter);* Aldo Miranda *(Friar John);* Dario Tanzini *(Page to Tybalt).*

THE FILM

Following the success of his Anglo-Italian film production of *The Taming of the Shrew* with Elizabeth Taylor and Richard Burton, Franco Zeffirelli set his sights on a relatively low-budget version of *Romeo and Juliet*— but this time *without* big-name stars. Admittedly a box-office risk, Zeffirelli's idea was to cast the title roles with teenagers who would approximate the actual ages of Shakespeare's classic characters, with more seasoned actors in the supportiing roles. As the director said at the time: "I wanted to bring the story to the attention of young people. The story is of two urchins crushed by a stupid, banal quarrel, with origins even the adults don't know. In love the young couple found an ideal—one they could die for—and youth today is hungry for ideals."

Shooting entirely in Italy, Zeffirelli worked wonders with his two young British leads, Olivia Hussey and Leonard Whiting. *Time* magazine's critic reflected the general consensus: "Both look their parts and read their lines with a sensitivity far beyond the limitations of their age."

With astute editing of the text, Zeffirelli tailored his *Romeo and Juliet* to the tastes of the sixties, emphasizing constant movement. Without destroying his feeling for the bard's poetry, the director nevertheless refrains from any inclination to halt the action for the word. The turbulent—often violent—activities of the warring Capulets and Montagues afford this romantic classic a contemporary look akin to the musical modernization that won fifties acclaim under the title of *West Side Story.*

Zeffirelli's youth-oriented approach to *Romeo and Juliet* was a complete international success, winning a large adolescent audience as well as the appreciation of

ROMEO E GIULIETTA   Leonard Whiting, Olivia Hussey and director Franco Zeffirelli on the set.

181

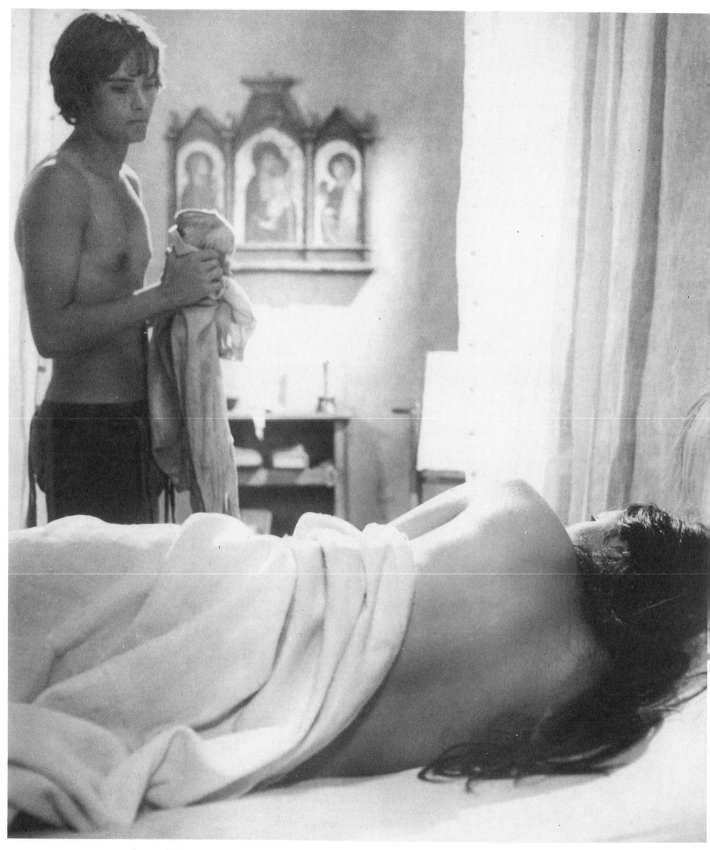

ROMEO E GIULIETTA   Leonard Whiting and Olivia Hussey.

182

ROMEO E GIULIETTA   Michael York (left), Christian Roberts (center) and Leonard Whiting (right).

an older generation. In fact, the movie virtually res-cued Paramount from closing down. Cinematographer Pasquale De Santis won an Academy Award for his artistry both on the actual Italian locations and on the sets built on the soundstages of Cinecittá. And the film took another deserved Oscar for Danilo Donati's luxu-rious costumes. *Romeo and Juliet* also owes a great deal of its success to the musicianship of Nino Rota, whose haunting background score features a song ("What Is a Youth?") that won separate acclaim on its own. It is also worth noting that the movie lost a Best Picture Oscar to *Oliver!*, while Zeffirelli saw the Best Director award go to Carol Reed for that same movie. In New York, the National Board of Review named Franco Zeffirelli 1968's Best Director.

ROMEO E GIULIETTA   Olivia Hussey and Leonard Whiting.

Il Giorno della Civétta

(MAFIA / THE DAY OF THE OWL)

A Coproduction of Panda Cinematografica (Rome) and Les Films Corona (Paris) in association with Corona Cinematografica (Rome) / 1968

(U.S. release by American International Pictures: 1969)

CREDITS

Director: Damiano Damiani; *Producers:* Ermanno Donati and Luigi Carpentieri; *Screenwriters:* Ugo Pirro and Damiano Damiani; *Based on the novel by* Leonardo Sciascia; *Eastmancolor-Techniscope Cinematographer:* Tonino Delli Colli; *Editor:* Nino Baragli; *Art Director:* Sergio Canevari; Costumes: Marilu Carteny; *Music:* Giovanni Fusco; *Running Time:* 113 minutes (*U.S. Running Time:* 98 minutes).

CAST

Claudia Cardinale *(Rosa Nicolosi)*; Franco Nero *(Cap-* *tain Bellodi)*; Lee J. Cobb *(Don Mariano Arena)*; Nehemiah Persoff *(Pizzuco)*; Serge Reggiani *(Parrinieddu)*; Rosanna Lopapero *(Caterina)*; Gaetano Cimarosa *(Zecchinetta)*.

THE FILM

Writer-director Damiano Damiani began his professional career turning out documentary shorts before graduating to feature films as an assistant director and screenwriter in the mid-fifties. In 1960, his first full-length directing job won him a prize at the San Sebastian Film Festival for *Il Rosseto/Lipstick*. Dramas and melodramas were his forte, although U.S. audiences took little note of *L'Isola di Arturo/Arturo's Island* (1962). The following year's *La Noia/The Empty Canvas*, because it costarred an amusingly over-the-top Bette Davis in her first Italian picture, was seen by more Americans than its predecessors.

But dramatically strongest of all is Damiani's 1968 crime melodrama *Il Giorno della Civétta/The Day of the Owl*, an adaptation by the director and Ugo Pirro of the Sicilian writer Leonardo Sciascia's 1961 novel of that same name.

When a construction supplier is murdered in a Mafia-dominated Sicilian town, Bellodi (Franco Nero), a police captain from northern Italy, is dis-

IL GIORNO DELLA CIVETTA Lee J. Cobb and Claudia Cardinale.

IL GIORNO DELLA CIVETTA Franco Nero.

patched to investigate. He is met with the decades-old *omerta* of the villagers in this heart of mobster country. No one is willing to run the risk of crossing the powerful Don Mariano Arena (Lee J. Cobb) by talking—until one witness agrees to testify and is killed in retaliation. His widow Rosa (Claudia Cardinale), in an attempt to discredit her, is accused of adultery by the Mafia and is torn between helping Bellodi or remaining silent. The law officer manages to identify the killers and gets them and Don Mariano imprisoned. But it is only a matter of time before justice, Sicilian style, triumphs, with the Mafia henchman freed to once again take his place in the village square. By then, Bellodi has been transferred to a remote part of the country. In the town, things are once again as they were.

Critics were pleasantly surprised at the film's strength of purpose and impressed with the properly sinister performance of visiting star Lee J. Cobb (typifying a sixties trend to attract overseas audiences with international casting). Also worthy of note was the serious dramatic acting of Claudia Cardinale, reinforcing her increasingly worthy body of work in *Bell' Antonio*, *Girl With a Suitcase*, *La Viaccia*, and *The Leopard*. And if the strikingly handsome, blue-eyed Franco Nero appeared too youthful as the Mafia-hunting police captain, his sincere and committed acting works in his favor.

Above all, Damiani's directorial flair makes much of the colorful Sicilian backgrounds, resulting in a film of more social significance than might have been expected.

IL GIORNO DELLA CIVETTA Franco Nero and Claudia Cardinale.

185

Incidentally, U.S. audiences should not confuse this movie with Pietro Germi's *In Nome della Legge* (1949). Though separated by twenty years, both it and this picture were renamed *Mafia* for their American distribution.

La Caduta Degli Dei

(THE DAMNED / GÖTTERDÄMMERUNG)

A Coproduction of Pegaso Film (Rome) and Praesidens Film (Zürich) / 1969

(U.S. release by Warner Bros.–Seven Arts: 1969)

CREDITS

Director: Luchino Visconti; *Executive Producer:* Pietro Notarianni; *Producers:* Alfredo Levy and Ever Haggiag; *Screenwriters:* Nicola Badalucco, Enrico Medioli, and Luchino Visconti; *Eastmancolor Cinematographers:* Armando Nannuzz and Pasquale de Santis; *Editor:* Ruggero Mastroianni; *Art Directors:* Pasquale Romano and Enzo Del Prato; *Costumes:* Piero Tosi; *Music:* Maurice Jarre; *Running Time:* 164 minutes (*U.S. Running Time:* 155 minutes).

CAST

Dirk Bogarde *(Friedrich Bruckmann)*; Ingrid Thulin *(Baroness Sophie von Essenbeck)*; Helmut Griem *(Aschenbach)*; Helmut Berger *(Martin von Essenbeck)*; Charlotte Rampling *(Elisabeth Thallmann)*; Florinda Bolkan *(Olga)*; Rene Kolldehoff *(Baron Konstantin von Essenbeck)*; Umberto Orsini *(Herbert Thallmann)*; Albrecht Schönhals *(Baron Joachim von Essenbeck)*; Renaud Verley *(Günther von Essenbeck)*: Nora Ricci *(Governess)*; Irina Wanka *(Lisa Keller)*; Valentina Ricci *(Thilde Thallmann)*; Karin Mittendorf *(Erika)*.

THE FILM

Luchino Visconti's wealth of experience in directing for the opera house can only have increased his natural appetite for the romantic, the melodramatic, and the epic-proportioned in motion-picture subject matter. And none of his major films is more operatic than *The Damned*, the American title for this depraved portrait of Germany's Third Reich in its earlier stages. Much of Europe saw it as *Götterdämmerung*, a fitting allusion to the final work in Wagner's grandiose *Ring* cycle.

Some have thought that *The Damned*'s power-hungry, back-stabbing von Essenbeck steel dynasty must represent the Krupps. But Visconti's source material was far less concentrated, with reference not only to the Krupp family but to all of the industrialists who supported Hitler. In the maestro's words: "What was most important to us, our point of departure and a book in which we could always find references to all the people or episodes we needed, was William L. Shirer's *The Rise and Fall of the Third Reich: A History of Nazi Germany*. It really became our Bible throughout the making of the film."

The screenplay focuses on the Germany of 1933–34, that brief period when it still might have been possible to stop Hitler. In the elegant home of steel baron Joachim von Essenbeck (Albrecht Schönhals), his family has gathered to celebrate the old man's birthday. But while his grandson Martin (Helmut Berger) offers a sinister transvestite impersonation of Marlene Dietrich, their entertainment is disrupted by news of the burning of the Reichstag. Politically divided, the family soon engages in an intense power struggle for succession. Martin's mother Sophie (Ingrid Thulin), widow of Joachim's eldest son, and Friedrich Bruckmann (Dirk Bogarde), her longtime lover and the company's manager, form an alliance with Aschenbach (Helmut Griem), Joachim's nephew and an SS leader, to get control of the firm. That night, the opportunists denounce Herbert (Umberto Orsini), an anti-Fascist and the firm's former vice president. Helping him to escape a political purge, they then use his gun to kill old Joachim, paving the way for Friedrich to be made president. But Vice President Konstantin (Rene Kolldehoff) discovers Martin's sexual proclivity for young children, which has precipitated the suicide of one victim, and he blackmails the young man to gain control. Martin, the company's major stockholder, switches his support to Konstantin.

However, Konstantin's power is short-lived. A member of the homosexually disposed SA troops, he is present when they hold an overnight orgy at the lakeside resort of Wiesee, and is slaughtered with his colleagues when the SS stage their Night of the Long Knives massacre. Sophie and Friedrich are now in control, refusing to accept the fact that they need the support of Aschenbach, who wants the steel industry under SS control. Seeking to destroy the couple, he informs Martin that it was Friedrich who killed Joachim, playing upon the boy's hatred of his domineering mother.

LA CADUTA DEGLI DEI   Albrecht Schönhals (left foreground), Helmut Griem, Renaud Verley, Rene Kolldehoff, Ingrid Thulin, Dirk Bogarde, Helmut Berger and Charlotte Rampling.

LA CADUTA DEGLI DEI   Ingrid Thulin and Dirk Bogarde.

187

Herbert returns to Germany to disclose that his wife Elisabeth (Charlotte Rampling) and his children were sent to Dachau, where she died. In exchange for his children's release, he surrenders to the police. In a drug-induced state, Martin now takes the upper hand, raping Sophie and forcing her to marry a Nazi-uniformed Friedrich in a bizarre ceremony, culminating in the presentation of Martin's wedding gift: cyanide tablets! Aschenbach, who completely dominates Martin, is now undisputed heir to the von Essenbeck Steelworks.

Superbly acted, particularly by Ingrid Thulin and newcomer Helmut Berger as that lethal mother and son, Helmut Griem as the blond Nazi charmer, and Dirk Bogarde (although his footage was reputedly trimmed before the final cut), the film was considered so strong in content that it was rated "X" in the United States.

LA CADUTA DEGLI DEI   Rene Kolldehoff (right) amid the "Night of the Long Knives."

LA CADUTA DEGLI DEI Helmut Berger.

Not all of the critics were impressed by *The Damned*. But The *New York Times* saw fit to list it among 1969's ten-best films, and the National Board of Review named it one of the year's five-best foreign imports. In Italy, the movie was as successful with the public as with the press, establishing box-office records.

Fellini-Satyricon

A Coproduction of P.E.A. (Rome) and Les Productions Artistes Associés (Paris) / 1969

(U.S. release by United Artists: 1970)

CREDITS

Director: Federico Fellini; *Producer:* Alberto Grimaldi; *Screenwriters:* Federico Fellini and Bernardino Zapponi, *with the collaboration of* Brunello Rondi; *Freely adapted from* "Satyricon" *by* Caius Petronius Arbiter; *DeLuxe Color-Panavision Cinematographer:* Giuseppe Rotunno; *Editor:* Ruggero Mastroianni; *Production Designer:* Danilo Donati; *Art Directors:* Luigi

189

FELLINI-SATYRICON   Max Born (left) and Hiram Keller.

Scaccianoce and Giorgio Giovannini, *based on sketches by* Federico Fellini; *Costumes:* Danilo Donati; *Special Effects:* Adriano Pischiutta; *Music:* Nino Rota, Ilhan Mimaroglu, Tod Dockstader, and Andrew Rubin; *Running Time:* 138 minutes.

CAST

Martin Potter *(Encolpio)*; Hiram Keller *(Ascylto)*; Max Born *(Gitone)*; Salvo Randone *(Eumolpus)*; Fanfulla *(Vernacchio)*; Capucine *(Tryphaena)*; Mario Romagnoli *(Trimalchio)*; Alain Cuny *(Lichas)*; Pasquale Bal-

dassare *(Hermaphrodite)*; Giuseppe Sanvitale *(Habinnas)*; Hylette Adolphe *(Oriental Slave Girl)*; Donyale Luna *(Oenothea)*; Magali Noël *(Fortunata)*; Gordon Mitchell *(Robber)*; Lucia Bosé *(Suicide Wife)*; Joseph Wheeler *(Suicide Husband)*; Eugenio "Genius" Mas-

190

tropietro *(Cinedo)*; Danica La Loggia *(Scintilla)*; Antonia Pietrosi *(Widow of Ephesus)*; Wolfgang Hillinger *(Soldier at Ephesus's Tomb)*; Elio Gigante *(Owner of Garden of Delights)*; Sibilla Sedat *(Nymphomaniac)*; Lorenzo Piani *(Nymphomaniac's Husband)*; Luigi Zerbinati *(Nymphomaniac's Slave*; Vittorio Vittori *(Notary)*; Carlo Giordana *(Captain of Eumolpus's Ship)*; Marcello Di Folco *(Proconsul)*; Luigi Montefiori *(Minotaur)*; Elisa Mainardi *(Adriadne)*; Suleiman Ali Nashnush *(Tryphaena's Attendant)*; Luigi Battaglia

FELLINI-SATYRICON Alain Cuny (seated) and Capucine.

191

historical anthology films of Pier Paolo Pasolini (*Arabian Nights*, *Decameron*, etc). And while scarcely considered a cinematic masterpiece by the filmmaker's critics, *Fellini-Satyricon is* an eye-filling *pictorial* wonder, not only of costume, lighting, and cinematography but most certainly of *mise en scène* as well. And for that one must honor the maestro. For in its very summation of cumulative bizarre effects, *Fellini-Satyricon* remains, first and last, pure Fellini—the overall creative force behind the sets and costumes of Danilo Donati, the highly stylized makeup by Rino Carboni, and master cinematographer Giuseppe Rotunno's permanent recording of it all.

There is little plot per se. Essentially, *Fellini-Satyricon* is simply a series of events that befall its central character, the beautiful young student Encolpio (Martin Potter, looking like a male Bo Derek), as he and his friends wander through the ancient Roman Empire, witnessing an eye-filling succession of pagan orgies, weird rituals, tortures, killings, and sexual couplings—occasionally involving the youths with one another,

FELLINI-SATYRICON   Martin Potter and Hiram Keller.

(Transvestite); Tani Duckworth *(Brothel Girl)*; Maria De Sisti *(Fat Woman)*; Tanya Lopert *(Caesar)*.

THE FILM

Federico Fellini's least characteristic film bears more than a passing resemblance to the near-pornographic

FELLINI-SATYRICON   Hiram Keller and Hylette Adolphe.

especially with regard to Encolpio's rivalry with his friend Ascylto (the perpetually sneering Hiram Keller) over a pretty lad named Gitone (Joan Collins look-alike Max Born). Totally a director's film (the actors are little more than his freak-show puppets), *Fellini-Satyricon* both dazzles the eye and boggles the mind with its overkilling array of visual riches. It is all underscored by the pseudoancient music devised by Nino Rota, aided and abetted by a trio of lesser-known composers.

Granted that filmmaking costs have more than skyrocketed in the decades since *Fellini/Satyricon* was produced, this 1969 epic was reportedly made for a then-relatively-modest $3 million. *New Yorker* critic Pauline Kael, for one, found it "just a hip version of *The Sign of the Cross*" but "less entertaining than DeMille's kitsch." Yet it is Fellini who is the ringmaster here, offering his public more of a dazzling show in *Fellini-Satyricon* than he has ever done before or since.

Queimada!

(BURN!)

A Coproduction of P.E.A. (Rome) and Les Productions Artistes Associés (Paris) / 1969

(U.S. release by United Artists: 1970)

QUEIMADA! Marlon Brando and Renato Salvatori.

CREDITS

Director: Gillo Pontecorvo; *Producer:* Alberto Grimaldi; *Screenwriters:* Franco Solinas and Giorgio Arlorio; *DeLuxe Color Cinematographers:* Marcello Gatti and Giuseppe Bruzzolini; *Editor:* Mario Morra; *Production Designer:* Piero Gherardi; *Art Director:* Sergio Canevari; *Set Decorator:* Francesco Bronzi; *Costumes:* Piero Gherardi; *Special Effects:* Aldo Gasparri; *Music:* Ennio Morricone; *Running Time:* 132 minutes (*U.S. Running Time:* 112 minutes).

CAST

Marlon Brando *(Sir William Walker)*; Evaristo Marquez *(José Dolores)*; Renato Salvatori *(Teddy Sanchez)*; Norman Hill *(Shelton)*; Tom Lyons *(General Prada)*; Wanani *(Guarina)*; Joseph Persuad *(Juanito)*; Gianpiero Albertini *(Henry)*; Carlo Palmucci *(Jack)*; Cecily Browne *(Lady Bella)*; Dana Ghia

(Francesca); Mauricio Rodriguez *(Ramón)*; Alejandro Obregon *(English Major)*.

THE FILM

The neo-Marxist director Gillo Pontecorvo's motion pictures have been few and far between, probably his most notable being the 1966 semidocumentary *The Battle of Algiers*, a powerful work sandwiched between the stark concentration-camp melodrama *Kapò* and *Burn!*, a colorful but equally downbeat epic of colonialism in the Caribbean of the nineteenth century. Filmed on locations in Morocco and Colombia (notably the seaport of Cartagena), Pontecorvo's 1969 drama initially attracted attention by casting the issue-committed Marlon Brando in its leading role, affording the actor an opportunity to recycle the effete British accent he had adopted in 1962 for the critically drubbed remake of *Mutiny on the Bounty*.

193

QUEIMADA! Renato Salvatori, Marlon Brando and Evaristo Marquez.

Sir William Walker (Brando) is dispatched by the British government to the Caribbean island of Queimada to covertly disrupt Portugal's sugar monopoly there. The island's name (meaning "burn") derived from the sixteeth-century European colonists who razed it by fire to put down a native rebellion. Walker's arrival coincides with the execution of the island's only known rebel chief, Santiago, who had led a slave insurrection. The Englishman determines that the way to open up trade is by fomenting a revolt of the African slaves brought there to repopulate the island. He chooses a highly motivated dockside porter named José Dolores (Evaristo Marquez) and methodically turns him into a revolutionary. Soon many of the plantation slaves join his robber band. Walker than persuades Teddy Sanchez (Renato Salvatori), the liberal, mulatto spokesman for the plantation owners, that independence for the colonists could be gained by assassinating Queimada's Portuguese governor. The insurrection is

successful, but Walker convinces José Dolores that he is lacking in economic expertise to govern his people. When the colonists gain control, the slaves resume the harvest of sugar cane. His assignment completed, Walker leaves the island.

Ten years later, Walker is a drunken derelict in London, recruited by the British Sugar Company to return to Queimada with troops to subdue José Dolores, who is still practicing the guerrilla activities long ago taught him by Walker. The island's present governor, Teddy Sanchez, protests the Englishman's ruthless tactics. Walker realizes the necessity of now eliminating José Dolores, but first he has Sanchez assassinated by a military junta and then leads the governor's soldiers in pursuit of José Dolores. History repeats itself: Much of the island is once again burned by the soldiers in the hunt for their quarry.

The guerrilla chief is captured alive but refuses Walker's offer of clemency on the condition that he

194

leave Queimada. Wary of the Englishman's methods, José Dolores prefers to serve his cause by being executed. With the insurrection stamped out, Walker prepares to leave the island, only to be stabbed to death by a dockside porter who offers to carry his luggage— just as José Dolores had done a decade earlier.

It has been thought that *Burn!* might likely have reached a larger audience had not the Spanish government brought pressure against distributor United Artists to eliminate any depiction of Spaniards in a bad light. As a result, delays caused by the needed editing seemingly made UA lose faith in the picture. The distributor gave it little more than a nervous, half-hearted promotion.

QUEIMADA! Evaristo Marquez and Marlon Brando.

Il Conformista

(THE CONFORMIST)

A Coproduction of Mars Film (Rome), Marianne Productions (Paris), and Maran Films (Munich) / 1970

(U.S. release by Paramount Pictures: 1971)

CREDITS

Director: Bernardo Bertolucci; *Executive Producer:* Giovanni Bertolucci; *Producer:* Maurizio Lodi-Fè; *Screenwriter:* Bernardo Bertolucci; *Based on the novel by* Alberto Moravia; *Technicolor Cinematographer:* Vittorio Storaro; *Editor:* Franco Arcalli; *Art Director:* Ferdinando Scarfioti; *Set Decorator:* Nedo Azzini; *Costumes:* Gitt Magrini; *Music:* Georges Delerue; *Running Time:* 115 minutes.

CAST

Jean-Louis Trintignant *(Marcello Clerici)*; Stefania Sandrelli *(Giulia)*; Dominique Sanda *(Anna Quadri)*; Pierre Clementi *(Nino Seminara)*; Gastone Moschin *(Manganiello)*; Enzo Tarascio *(Professor Quadri)*; José Qùaglio *(Italo)*; Milly *(Marcello's Mother)*; Giuseppe Addobbati *(Marcello's Father)*; Yvonne Sanson *(Giulia's Mother)*; Fosco Giachetti *(the Colonel)*; Benedetto Benedetti *(the Minister)*; Pasquale Fortunato *(Marcello as a Child)*; Marta Lado *(Marcello's Daughter)*.

THE FILM

Bernardo Bertolucci finally established himself as an important Italian director with this, his fifth feature (five and one-half if one counts his episode for the 1967 anthology film *Amore a Rabbia/Love and Anger*). With his own adaptation of Alberto Moravia's novel *The Conformist*, Bertolucci etches a rich, complex, and multitextured portrait of his nominal hero, the upper-class young Fascist gunman Marcello Clerici (Jean-Louis Trintignant).

Essentially, the story takes place in and around the Paris of 1938. En route to a deadly rendezvous,

IL CONFORMISTA Jean-Louis Trintignant.

IL CONFORMISTA   Jean-Louis Trintignant, Stefania Sandrelli, Enzo Tarascio and Dominique Sanda.

Marcello is being driven into the bleak, wintry countryside, affording him time to reflect on his past. At thirteen, he had nearly been seduced by a chauffeur named Nino Seminara (Pierre Clementi), whose gun the victimized boy had turned on his tormentor. The traumatizing incident has influenced Marcello's adult life, driving him to reject all standards not considered "normal" by society. As a result, he had left behind his unstable father and drug-addict mother to join Mussolini's Fascist party in its counterespionage division. And he had entered into a marriage of convenience with Giulia (Stefania Sandrelli), a dull but socially acceptable girl whom he didn't love. During their Paris honeymoon, Marcello spied on the activities of his former university instructor then Professor Quadri (Enzo Tarascio), now an anti-Fascist agitator in exile and an eventual assigned target for Marcello's gun. In

Paris, Marcello became smitten with Quadri's seductive young wife, Anna (Dominique Sanda), only to discover that *she* was more physically attracted to Giulia. Because of his feelings for Anna, Marcello warned her of the plot to assassinate her husband and was shocked to find she knew all about the plan, as well as *his* involvement.

Back to the present . . . Marcello's car reaches the assigned meeting place. He remains passively immobile in his seat as the Fascisti ritually stab Quadri in the snow, *Julius Caesar*-style. The shocked Anna sees it all from her car. As the killers approach, she vainly seeks refuge in Marcello's vehicle, but while he sits motionless, she is run down and murdered.

The scene shifts to Rome in July 1943, where it is announced that Mussolini has fled the city ahead of the Allies' arrival. By chance, Marcello catches sight of a

IL CONFORMISTA   Jean-Louis Trintignant and Dominique Sanda.

familiar face—an older man who is making obvious overtures to a young boy. Marcello immediately recalls his own childhood and realizes it is the same predatory chauffeur he thought he had killed. With the sudden realization that his life of restriction and conformity derived from this mistake, he lashes out at the man, chasing him off into the night. Alone in the street, Marcello notices a young male hustler in a shadowy doorway, and their eyes meet.

With its elegant period look, meticulously photographed by Vittorio Storaro, *The Conformist* overcomes its sometimes eliptical narrative with the poetic strength of Bertolucci's storytelling skills and the stunning impact of such set pieces as the lesbian-flavored tango performed by an impassioned Dominique Sanda and Stefania Sandrelli or the deadly rendezvous to eliminate the professor and his wife in the snowy woods outside Paris.

In the United States, *The Conformist* became the talk of the 1970 New York Film Festival. And although it won no awards, the picture was named by the National Board of Review as one of the five-best foreign-language films of 1971, the year of its American release.

Dramma della Gelosia—Tutti i Particolari in Cronaca

(THE PIZZA TRIANGLE / A DRAMA OF JEALOUSY / JEALOUSY, ITALIAN STYLE)

A Coproduction of Dean Film/Jupiter Generale Cinematografica (Rome) and Midega Film (Madrid) / 1970

(U.S. release by Warner Bros.: 1970)

CREDITS

Director: Ettore Scola; *Producers:* Pio Angeletti and Adriano De Micheli; *Screenwriters:* Age (Agenore Incrocci), Scarpelli (Furio Scarpelli), and Ettore Scola; *Based on a story by* Age and Scarpelli; *Technicolor-Panavision Cinematographer:* Carlo Di Palma; *Editor:*

Alberto Gallitti; *Art Director:* Luciano Ricceri; *Costumes:* Ezio Altieri; *Music:* Armando Trovajoli; *Running Time:* 106 minutes.

CAST

Marcello Mastroianni *(Oreste)*; Monica Vitti *(Adelaide)*; Giancarlo Giannini *(Nello)*; Manolo Zarzo *(Ugo)*; Marisa Merlini *(Silvana)*; Hercules Cortez *(Ambleto Di Meo)*; Ferando S. Polak *(District Head of Communist Party)*; Gioia Desideri *(Adelaide's Friend)*; Josefina Serratosa *(Antonia, Oreste's Wife)*; Juan Diego *(Antonia's Son)*; Bruno Scipioni *(a Pizza Maker)*; Corrado Galpa *(President of Tribunal)*; Giuseppe Mattioli *(a Lawyer)*.

THE FILM

A dark-textured romantic satire that manages to poke fun at Roman Marxism, social mores, and even the films of Fellini, *The Pizza Triangle* is an oddball hybrid of a movie that owes its success to its solid-gold

cast—Marcello Mastroianni, Monica Vitti (dark-haired and a long distance from Antonioni), Giancarlo Giannini—and, of course, director Ettore Scola.

In flashback form, a triangular crime of passion is reconstructed. A young flower vendor named Adelaide (pronounced, of course, "Ah-del-ah-*EE*-dah") is killed, and it appears that two rather confused men are involved: the bushy-haired, middle-aged Communist bricklayer Oreste (Mastroianni) and his young friend, the sad-eyed pizza cook Nello (Giannini). The story begins following a Communist rally, when Oreste is accosted by Adelaide (Vitti), who impulsiely identifies him as the man of her dreams. Although already married to a battle-ax, Oreste soon enters into an impassioned affair with Adelaide, leaving his wife to live with the young woman. All is bliss for the couple until Oreste makes the mistake of bringing home his friend Nello, to whom Adelaide is immediately attracted. Their ensuing affair causes her to leave Oreste when the truth is revealed. This results in a terrible public scene, after which Adelaide is hospitalized. Both men visit their beloved, who now cannot decide whom she really loves. All three try living together, but the

DRAMMA DELLA GELOSIA—TUTTI I PARTICOLARI IN CRONACA Marcello Mastroianni, Monica Vitti and Giancarlo Giannini.

199

DRAMMA DELLA
GELOSIA—TUTTI I PARTICOLARI
IN CRONACA Monica Vitti
and Giancarlo Giannini.

DRAMMA DELLA
GELOSIA—TUTTI I PARTICOLARI
IN CRONACA Marcello
Mastroianni, Monica Vitti
and Giancarlo Giannini.

ménage à trois is a disaster, and the distraught Adelaide tries suicide. At her sister's urging, she now moves in with the kind but oxlike butcher Ambleto (Hercules Cortez). But when she hears that Nello has tried to kill himself, she runs to his sickbed and consents to be his wife. Equally distraught over the loss of Adelaide, Oreste has lost his job and turned derelict. En route to her wedding to Nello, Adelaide catches sight of the miserable Oreste and is once again torn between her affection for both men. Nello threatens Oreste with flower shears, but in the ensuing fracas it is Adelaide who is accidentally stabbed to death.

As the foregoing plot description indicates, *The Pizza Triangle* is somewhat off-the-wall, even as ribald Italian comedies go. Passions frequently run amok, and Mastroianni in particular enjoys expressive outbursts that would earlier have been more closely identified with the great Anna Magnani at her most volatile. But it is his vivid but empty-headed character that holds the narrative together, and Mastroianni was consequently named Best Actor at the 1970 Cannes Film Festival. Monica Vitti provides a beautiful balance to his histrionics with a sort of dumbly poetic goofiness that comments amusingly on all the wistful waifs and lower-class heroines endemic to the Italian cinema of its neorealist past. Hers is a brilliant comedy performance, balanced equally by the woebegone countenance of Giancarlo Giannini.

Faced with a challenging script, Ettore Scola doesn't always manage to keep this episodic oddity afloat, but he fills so much of *The Pizza Triangle* with cunning parody and outrageous, inspired wit that there is more than enough to relish for those able to track it down.

Indagine su un Cittadino al di Sopra di Ogni Sospetto

(INVESTIGATION OF A CITIZEN ABOVE SUSPICION)

A Vera Film Production / 1970

(U.S. release by Columbia Pictures: 1970)

CREDITS

Director: Elio Petri; *Producer:* Daniele Senatore; *Screenwriters:* Ugo Pirro and Elio Petri; *Technicolor* *Cinematographer:* Luigi Kuveiller; *Editor:* Ruggero Mastroianni; *Art Director:* Carlo Egidi; *Music:* Ennio Morricone; *Running Time:* 115 minutes.

CAST

Gian Maria Volonté *(the Police Inspector)*; Florinda Bolkan *(Augusta Terzi)*; Salvo Randone *(the Plumber)*; Gianni Santuccio *(the Police Commissioner)*; Arturo Dominici *(Mangani)*; Orazio Orlando *(Biglia)*; Sergio Tramonti *(Antonio Pace)*; Massimo Foschi *(Augusta's Husband)*; Aldo Rendine *(Homicide Functionary)*.

THE FILM

The Oscar-winning Best Foreign Film of 1970 (it also took that year's Special Jury Prize at Cannes) is quite likely the most celebrated work of the Commmunist writer-director Elio Petri. In the sixties, American audiences had sampled his effective flair for melodrama in such imports as the sci-fi oddity *La Decima Vittima/The Tenth Victim* (1965) and the Mafia-oriented *A Ciascuno il Suo/We Still Kill the Old Way* (1967). In 1970, Petri's *Investigation of a Citizen*

INDAGINE SU UN CITTADINO AL DI SOPRA DI OGNI SOSPETTO   Florinda Bolkan and Gian Maria Volonté.

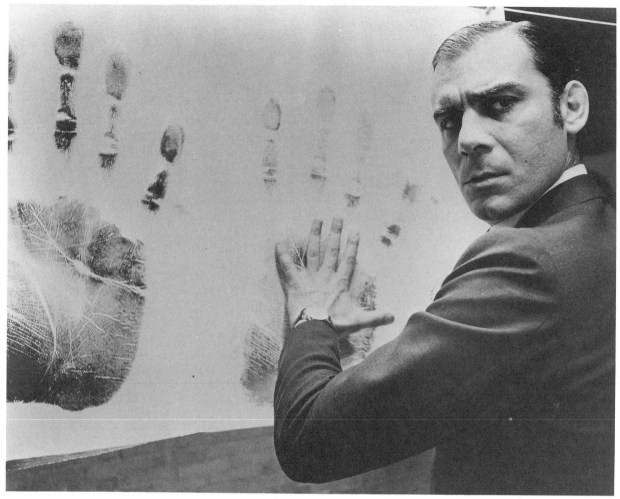

INDAGINE SU UN CITTADINO AL DI SOPRA DI OGNI SOSPETTO Gian Maria Volonté.

Above Suspicion caused quite a stir in Italy, because its repellent antihero reflected Fascist ideals that harked back to Il Duce and because of its contemporary relevance. A few of the film's critics considered filmmaker Petri's polemics too heavy-handed to be effective. Others lauded the picture's ingenious construction and tense atmosphere.

Gian Maria Volonté portrays a power-driven Rome police inspector who controls a network of subordinates, spies, and informants. So rigid is their collective devotion to the sociopolitical Establishment that it is always open season on such "subversive" elements as Maoists, homosexuals, and student radicals. The inspector's beautiful, masochistic mistress Augusta (Florinda Bolkan) enjoys involving him in perverse sexual games that include photographing her as a series of pseudomurder victims. But she pushes him to the limit by not only questioning his manhood but also flaunting her young student-lover Antonio (Sergio Tramonti). In a jealous fury, the inspector cuts her throat.

Promoted to chief of political intelligence, the inspector now considers himself above the law, and he deliberately establishes a trail of clues that implicate him in the crime—purely to goad his former colleagues, to whom he is beyond suspicion. The inspector then gives way to his prejudices by first directing an investigation of Augusta's gay husband (Massimo Foschi) and finally the young activist Antonio, who turns out to be the one witness who saw the inspector leave Augusta's house. Realizing he's trapped, the inspector files a full confession. Subsequently, he dreams that the police commissioner's staff, unable to believe his guilt, toast him instead. As the film ends, he awaits their arrival—and his own punishment.

Unnervingly underscored by the jangling background music of Ennio Morricone, Petri's unusual motion picture is at its best as a fascinating political parable. Dominating its every scene is the energized acting of Gian Maria Volonté, whose chameleon-like characterization veers between the extroverted and the

202

introverted, the blustery and the obsequious. It is a performance of high style and finite, studied detail—a vital force in making *Investigation of a Citizen Above Suspicion* an international box-office success.

Il Giardino dei Finzi-Contini

(THE GARDEN OF THE FINZI-CONTINIS)

A Coproduction of Documento Films (Rome) and CCC Filmkunst (Berlin) / 1970

(U.S. release by Cinema V: 1971)

CREDITS

Director: Vittorio De Sica; *Executive Producer:* Fausto Saraceni; *Producers:* Gianni Hecht Lucari and Arthur Cohn; *Screenwriters:* Ugo Pirro, Vittorio Bonicelli, Vittorio De Sica, and Giorgio Bassani; *Based on the semi-autobiographical novel by* Giorgio Bassani; *Eastmancolor Cinematographer:* Ennio Guarnieri; *Editor:* Adriana Novelli; *Art Director:* Giancarlo Bartolini Salimbeni; *Set Decorator:* Franco D'Andria; *Costumes:* Antonio Randaccio; *Music:* Manuel De Sica; *Song "Vivere" performed by* Tito Schipa; *Running Time:* 103 minutes (*U.S. Running Time:* 95 minutes).

CAST

Dominique Sanda *(Micol)*; Lino Capolicchio *(Giorgio)*; Helmut Berger *(Alberto)*; Fabio Testi *(Malnate)*; Romolo Valli *(Giorgio's Father)*; Raffaele Curi *(Ernesto)*; Camillo Angelini-Rota *(Micol's Father)*; Katina Viglietti *(Micol's Mother)*; Inna Alexeieff *(Micol's Grandmother)*.

THE FILM

Despite critical concurrence that this was an eloquent and admirable adaptation of Giorgio Bassani's autobiographical 1962 novel, screenplay collaborator Bas-

IL GIARDINO DEI FINZI-CONTINI   Fabio Testi and Helmut Berger.

IL GIARDINO DEI FINZI-CONTINI   Dominique Sanda and Lino Capolicchio.

Mussolini's "racial laws," denying them the right to marry outside their religion, serve in the military, attend public school, possess telephone listings, or have their obituaries published. But the justified apprehensions that spread through northern Italy's Jewish communities seem not to affect the aristocratic Finzi-Continis, who isolate themselves behind the protective walls of their palatial home, oblivious to the ominous spread of anti-Semitism. When another Fascistic order bans Jews from Ferrara's public tennis

sani later repudiated both the movie and his contribution to it. According to the picture's director Vittorio De Sica, this was "because of the character of the father, which has been minimized in the film. Always the author is against me."

With the exception of the Sophia Loren vehicle *Two Women*, many of De Sica's sixties films *(Woman Times Seven, A Place for Lovers, Sunflower)* had been critically roasted disappointments, far removed from his black-and-white period as perhaps Italy's most respected *auteur*. In fact, De Sica has said that his experience working with the interfering producer Carlo Ponti on *Sunflower* (1970) "was so terrible that I decided to rebel. And my rebellion is *The Garden of the Finzi-Continis*." As he further admitted to an interviewer: "After the disaster of *Sunflower*, I wanted to make a true De Sica film, made just as I wanted it. I accepted this subject because I intimately feel the Jewish problem. I myself feel shame, because we are all guilty of the death of millions of Jews. I wasn't a Fascist, but I belong to the country that collaborated with Hitler."

Set in the town of Ferrara (where it was filmed), the movie centers on the elegant estate of the Jewish Finzi-Contini family during the years 1938–43. In 1938, organized persecution of the Jews begins with

IL GIARDINO DEI FINZI-CONTINI   Helmut Berger and Dominique Sanda.

204

clubs, the Finzi-Continis open their gardens to all of the town's persecuted youth. On those spacious grounds, Micol (Dominique Sanda) and her sickly, devoted brother Alberto (Helmut Berger) cling to their sheltered past, sharing the sunny summer afternoons with friends, with whom they bicycle and play tennis. Their regular companions include the sensitive student Giorgio (Lino Capolicchio); a Jewish merchant's middle-class son, who adores Micol; and the young Communist engineer Malnate (Fabio Testi).

IL GIARDINO DEL FINZI-CONTINI   Dominique Sanda and Fabio Testi.

Fellow college students Micol and Giorgio have been pals since childhood. But when she realizes that Giorgio is in love with her, Micol suddenly departs for Venice "to complete her thesis," later returning to inform him that they can never be more than just friends.

When Giorgio takes money to his brother Ernesto (Raffaele Curi) who is studying at a French university, he meets a youth who has escaped from Dachau and relates shocking stories of German Jews being liquidated in Nazi concentration camps. Back in Ferrara, Giorgio is thrown out of a cinema for shouting "stupid bastards" at a newsreel showing goose-stepping troops.

News that Alberto is seriously ill takes Giorgio back to visit the Finzi-Continis, where he once again declares his affection for Micol, who persists in rejecting him. He leaves in anger, vowing never to return. As Jewish persecution increases, Italy declares war. On the eve of Malnate's departure for service, Giorgio sees his friend in bed with Micol at the latter's summer-house. Noticing Giorgio spying on them, she coolly returns his saddened gaze.

As the war goes on, Malnate is killed on the Russian front, and Alberto succumbs to his illness. Giorgio hears that all Jews are being arrested by the Italian authorities, and on a wintry day in 1943, the police lead Micol and her family away. She and her elderly grandmother (Inna Alexeieff) are herded, along with the other Jews of the town, into the local schoolhouse. There they encounter Giorgio's father (Romolo Valli), who informs them that he has arranged for the escape of Giorgio and the remainder of his family. But in answer to Micol's question of where they'll be sent, he can only reply: "Who knows? Pray God, they at least let us stay together—those of us from Ferrara."

Originally, the movie ended with Micol, en route to a concentration camp, having flashbacks to the tennis-playing summer of 1938. For the U.S. version, however, De Sica cut out those visual recollections and substituted evocative footage of Ferrara's deserted streets and of the now-neglected Finzi-Contini gardens.

The Garden of the Finzi-Continis earned widespread critical acclaim, taking the Golden Bear (first prize) at the Berlin Film Festival and Italy's David di Donatello Award for Best Italian Film of its year. It also won a 1971 Academy Award for Best Foreign Film.

Morte a Venezia

(DEATH IN VENICE)

A Coproduction of Alfa Cinematografica (Rome) and P.E.C.F. Film (Paris) / 1971

(U.S. release by Warner Bros.: 1971)

CREDITS

Producer-Director: Luchino Visconti; *Executive Producer:* Mario Gallo; *Screenwriters:* Luchino Visconti and Nicola Badalucco; *Based on the novel by* Thomas Mann; *Technicolor-Panavision Cinematographer:* Pasquale De Santis; *Editor:* Ruggero Mastroianni; *Art Director:* Ferdinando Scarfiotti; *Set Decorator:* Nedo Azzini; *Costumes:* Piero Tosi; *Music:* Gustav Mahler (from the Third and Fifth symphonies); *Running Time:* 130 minutes.

CAST

Dirk Bogarde *(Gustav von Aschenbach)*; Bjorn Andresen *(Tadzio)*; Silvana Mangano *(Tadzio's Mother)*; Marisa Berenson *(Frau von Aschenbach)*; Mark Burns *(Alfred, Aschenbach's Pupil)*; Romolo Valli *(Hotel Manager)*; Masha Predit *(Street Singer)*; Nora Ricci *(Governess)*; Carol Andre *(Esmeralda)*; Leslie French *(Travel Agent)*; Franco Fabrizi *(Barber)*; Luigi Battaglia *(Scapegrace)*; Sergio Garafanolo *(Tadzio's Friend)*; Ciro Cristofoletti *(Hotel Clerk)*.

THE FILM

Regarding Luchino Visconti's somewhat altered adaptation of the Thomas Mann novella, there was much critical disagreement, especially among homophobes, who were outraged at witnessing the novelist's central character of Gustav von Aschenbach change from idealist heterosexual writer to idealist homosexual composer. That Aschenbach (especially in the guise and makeup of Dirk Bogarde) is made to resemble composer Gustav Mahler—and that *Death in Venice* was written in the year of Mahler's death—may have seemed too obvious a device, especially accompanied, as it is, by Mahler's sweepingly romantic music on the movie's sound track.

Visconti always denied that *Death in Venice* was any kind of a gay love story, but, rather, an aging artist's intense appreciation of the beauty of youth—personified here by the Polish boy Tadzio (pronounced "Todd-joo"). And yet one scene alone is sufficient to make the situation wordlessly clear. On the lido adjoining their hotel, the strolling, dandified Aschenbach spies the lad walking toward him, clad only in a one-piece striped bathing suit that leaves little to the imagination. Their eyes meet, and Tadzio's mouth forms the faintest suggestion of a Mona Lisa smile. Aschenbach responds with a raised eyebrow and a secretive, revealing smirk. That scene is fleeting, but its effect lingers, coloring all that subsequently transpires. And despite flashbacks that show us a younger Aschenbach in the happy company of his wife (Marisa Berenson) and child, we have little recourse but to accept the composer as an aging closet case who discreetly entertains his private fantasies.

Despite its length, *Death in Venice* contains little plot. In leisurely, strikingly visual fashion, it tells its story with rich detail, both in setting and character. In

MORTE A VENEZIA   Luchino Visconti directing
Dirk Bogarde.

1911, the ailing composer Aschenbach visits Venice during a period of personal creative inertia. There, at the lido's elegant Hotel des Bains, he is struck by the androgenous blond beauty of fellow guest Tadzio (Bjorn Andresen), a fourteen-year-old in the company of his mother (a largely silent Silvana Mangano), three younger sisters, and their French governess. The fastidious, waspish Aschenbach proceeds to keep close tabs on Tadzio, following the Polish family's comings and goings, from dining hall to beach to the city's canal-side byways. Frequently their eyes meet, the older man and the young boy, yet they never speak. Later, after learning news of the Asiatic cholera that has secretly infested Venice, Aschenbach imagines that he confronts the Polish family, pleading with them to leave at once lest they take ill. Not long thereafter, having pathetically resorted to a barber's cosmetic "makeover," the composer begins to perspire with a

MORTE A VENEZIA   Bjorn Andresen and Dirk Bogarde.

MORTE A VENEZIA   Silvana Mangano, Bjorn Andresen and Dirk Bogarde.

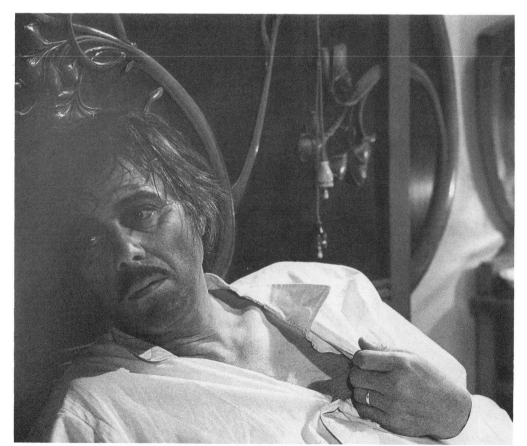

MORTE A VENEZIA   Dirk Bogarde.

choleric fever, eventually succumbing in a beach chair as he watches Tadzio frolic with his friends.

It is difficult to fathom why Visconti's detractors faulted the casting of Dirk Bogarde on the grounds of his being either too British or too young for Aschenbach. Then in his early fifties, the actor had long since proven his excellence at creating character, though perhaps none so complex as this one, whose moods and shadings are brilliantly reflected in his expressive face. In gesture, walk, and stature, his Aschenbach is a marvelous characterization. That Aschenbach remains among Bogarde's favorite roles is evident in the actor's recollection that being asked by Visconti to play him was "like being asked by Laurence Olivier to play Hamlet, only better."

Death in Venice was awarded a Special Prize at the 1971 Cannes Film Festival.

Addio, Fratello Crudele

('TIS PITY SHE'S A WHORE)

A Clesi Cinematografica Production / 1972

(U.S. release by Euro International: 1973)

CREDITS

Director: Giuseppe Patroni Griffi; *Producer:* Silvio Clementelli; *Screenwriters:* Giuseppe Patroni Griffi,

ADDIO, FRATELLO CRUDELE   Charlotte Rampling.

ADDIO, FRATELLO
CRUDELE Charlotte Rampling
and Fabio Testi.

Alfio Valdarnini, and Carlo Carunchio; *Based on the play* 'Tis Pity She's a Whore *by* John Ford; *Technicolor Cinematographer:* Vittorio Storaro; *Editor:* Kim Arcalli; *Art Director:* Mario Ceroli; *Set Decorator:* Massimo Tarazzi; *Costumes:* Gabriella Pescucci; *Music:* Ennio Morricone; *Running Time:* 109 minutes (*U.S. Running Time:* 102 minutes).

CAST

Charlotte Rampling *(Annabella)*; Oliver Tobias *(Giovanni)*; Fabio Testi *(Soranzo)*; Antonio Falsi *(Bon-*

ADDIO, FRATELLO
CRUDELE Oliver Tobias and
Charlotte Rampling.

aventura); Rik Battaglia *(Father)*; Angela Luce *(Father's Woman)*; Rino Imperio *(Soranzo's Manservant)*.

THE FILM

Admittedly, *Addio, Fratello Crudele* (Farewell, Cruel Brother) is a liberal adaptation of the 1633 Renaissance tragedy by Britain's John Ford (not to be confused with the renowned twentieth-century Irish-American film director), a reworking of the original play to focus on its four central characters. As such, it emerges as a strikingly effective period piece, a tri-umph of production design, cinematography, and impassioned performances by its well-cast leading players. That *'Tis Pity She's a Whore* is still little known in America is undoubtedly due to its limited release by a small independent distributor that never even secured a New York opening for the picture. And yet its availability on videocassette, while perhaps equally elusive, at least assures a somewhat wider American audience, for those who can manage to locate it.

In medieval Italy, the young Giovanni (Oliver Tobias) returns home from the university to find his younger sister Annabella (Charlotte Rampling) grown to ripe and fascinating womanhood. At first reunion,

each is irrevocably attracted to the other, to the exclusion of any and all possible suitors for the young beauty. Giovanni confides his incestuous passion to his monastic friend Bonaventura (Antonio Falsi), but the latter has little sympathy with Giovanni's romantic obsession. What begins as innocent passion soon leads to a sexual relationship that results in Annabella's becoming pregnant. And when Giovanni again confides in Bonaventura, the shocked monk can only consult the head of his order, who decrees Annabella's immediate marriage and directs that Giovanni should never again see her. So upset is he by his friend's revelation that Bonaventura takes leave of the monastery, his religious faith shaken. Unaware of his daughter's precarious condition, Annabella's father arranges for her marriage to the handsome aristocrat Soranzo (Fabio Testi), her most ardent suitor. After their wedding, Giovanni disappears, although he soon finds it impossible to stay away from his sister. But the union isn't consummated, and the mystified Soranzo takes his bride away to Venice, where the atmosphere turns out to be more conducive to their lovemaking—an event that also reveals Annabella's pregnancy. In a vengeful rage, Soranzo plans a family banquet at which he will murder all of her kin. But Giovanni reappears on the scene, reuniting briefly with Annabella in a love pact that results in his killing her, cutting the heart from her warm body to flaunt it—and their forbidden love—before the banqueting Soranzo and his family, to whom he reveals the scandalous truth. Ordering his servants to kill all of the guests, Soranzo completes his vengeance by ritually slashing Giovanni to death.

Giuseppe Patroni Griffi's initial feature *Il Mare/The Sea* anticipated this, his third film, in its concentration on a triangular relationship, told against a wintry background. In *'Tis Pity She's a Whore*, the desolation of the season is as certain as the visible breath of its performers amid the Parmesan and Venetian locations. Most imposing of all are the unusual, unpainted wooden sets (with their carved sculptures) by Mario Ceroli, whose eerie stands of forestlike flagpoles and well-chosen landscapes are so artfully photographed by Vittorio Storaro. Ennio Morricone, famed for his scores for the spaghetti westerns of Sergio Leone, here reveals a sensitive knowledge of ancient instruments and Renaissance sounds that evoke a haunting background score for this near–Grand Guignol melodrama.

'Tis Pity She's a Whore is more than worthy of rediscovery.

Una Breve Vacanza

(A BRIEF VACATION)

Verona Produzione (Rome)/Azor Films (Madrid) / 1973

(U.S. release by Allied Artists: 1975)

CREDITS

Director: Vittorio De Sica; *Producers:* Marina Cicogna and Arthur Cohn; *Screenwriter:* Cesare Zavattini; *Based on a story by* Rodolfo Sonego; *Technicolor Cinematographer:* Ennio Guarnieri; *Editor:* Franco Arcalli; *Music:* Christian De Sica; *Song "Stay" by* Michael De Sica and Gene Lees *performed by* Christian De Sica; *Running Time:* 112 minutes.

CAST

Florinda Bolkan *(Clara Martaro)*; Renato Salvatori *(Franco Martaro)*; Daniel Quenaud *(Luigi)*; José Maria Prada *(Dr. Ciranni)*; Teresa Gimpera *(Gina)*; Hugo Blanco *(Franco's Brother)*; Adriana Asti *(La Scanziani)*; Julia Peña *(Edvige)*; Miranda Campa *(Nurse Guidotti)*; Angela Cardile *(La Rossa)*; Anna Carena *(Franco's Mother)*; Monica Guerritore *(Maria)*; Maria Mizar *(Nurse Garin)*; Alessandro Romanazzi *(Maria's Son)*; Christian De Sica *(Young Man on Train)*.

THE FILM

Partly a throwback to neorealism (in its opening scenes) and partly a glossy romantic drama, *A Brief Vacation* recalls both the Barbara Stanwyck–David Niven melodrama *The Other Love* (1947) and Elizabeth Taylor's face-lift drama *Ash Wednesday* (1973). But Vittorio De Sica's final collaboration with longtime writing colleague Cesare Zavattini has its base slightly more grounded in contemporary reality and mid-seventies pessimism.

In a role ideally suited for De Sica's favorite Sophia Loren, the striking Brazilian actress Florinda Bolkan (in what remains her finest and warmest performance) was chosen instead to play Clara Martaro, the Milan factory-employee wife of a working-class Sicilian (Renato Salvatori), who is temporarily incapacitated with a leg injury. Housed uncomfortably with her three children, complaining mother-in-law, and husband's

UNA BREVE VACANZA   Anna Carena, Hugo Blanco, Florinda Bolkan and Renato Salvatori.

UNA BREVE
VACANZA   Adriana Asti and
Florinda Bolkan.

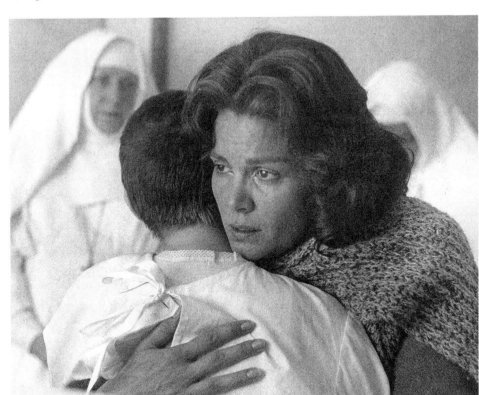

layabout brother, Calabrian-born Clara is nearing the end of her emotional tether when it is discovered that she has tuberculosis. Since her medical insurance will cover her expenses, Clara ignores the selfish protests of her family and goes to seek recovery in a mountain clinic in northern Italy. There this shy, unsophisticated woman fairly blossoms in a friendly environment where many of her fellow patients are generously affluent matrons. Among her closest friends there is a flamboyant music-hall star named La Scanziani (Adriana Asti), whose mood swings drive her to attempt suicide before eventually succumbing to disease. For Clara, romance blooms in the unwanted form of her fellow-Calabrian physician Dr. Ciranni (José Maria Prada) and, more temptingly, in Luigi (Daniel Quenaud), a handsome young mechanic and fellow patient with whom she shares unfulfilled affection. But Clara is brought back to a certain reality by an awkward visit from her family, and shortly thereafter, when she is confirmed cured, Clara elects to return home to face the same dreary existence from which she escaped to enjoy that necessary "brief vacation."

De Sica's last memorable film (there remained the misconceived Sophia Loren–Richard Burton period piece *Il Viaggio/The Voyage*), *A Brief Vacation*'s strength lies in Bolkan's quietly persuasive portrayal of an unhappy, overburdened woman, temporarily awakened to the possibilities of an independence she had not previously envisioned. With her consciousness

raised and her previously undeveloped cultural needs considerably nourished, Clara not only finds herself faced with moral decisions that could change her previously drab and claustrophobic existence but also realizes new confidence as a woman.

As La Scanziani, the doomed fellow patient whose desperate gaiety masks her fear of mortality, Adriana Asti offers an unforgettable cameo in a blend of extravagant behavior and pathetic vulnerability. And although this is clearly what would once have been termed "a woman's picture," Renato Salvatori delineates Clara's boorish husband vividly enough to make understandable her frustrations and Alpine temptations, with the gentlemanly, personable Daniel Quenaud entirely convincing as a viable, well-contrasted alternative to Salvatori.

Ever compassionate with Clara's dilemma, De Sica films his early scenes without minimizing Clara's grubby home life or her factory job in industrially polluted Milan. Nor does he make the comfortable Alpine sanitorium quite as glamorous a setting as have his Hollywood predecessors. Despite its current obscurity, *A Brief Vacation* stands as a final De Sica milestone.

Amarcord

A Coproduction of F. C. Produzioni (Rome) and P.E.C.P. Films (Paris) / 1974

(U.S. release by New World Pictures: 1974)

CREDITS

Director: Federico Fellini; *Producer:* Franco Cristaldi; *Screenwriters:* Federico Fellini and Tonino Guerra; *Technicolor Cinematographer:* Giuseppe Rotunno; *Editor:* Ruggero Mastroianni; *Art Director and Costumes:* Danilo Donati; *Music:* Nino Rota; *Running Time:* 127 minutes.

CAST

Magali Noël *(Gradisca)*; Bruno Zanin *(Titta Biondi)*; Pupella Maggio *(Miranda Biondi)*; Armando Brancia *(Aurelio Biondi)*; Giuseppe Lanigro *(Titta's Grandfather)*; Nando Orfei *(Pataca)*; Ciccio Ingrassia *(Uncle Teo)*; Luigi Rossi *(the Lawyer)*; Gennaro Ombra *(Bisein)*; Josiane Tanzilli *(Volpina)*; Maria Antonietta Beluzzi *(Tobacconist)*; Gianfilippo Carcano *(Don*

UNA BREVE VACANZA   Florinda Bolkan and Daniel Quenaud.

AMARCORD   Maria Antonietta Beluzzi and Bruno Zanin.

Baravelli); Ferrucio Brembilla *(Fascist Leader)*; Dina Adorni *(Math Teacher)*.

THE FILM

Its unusual title (untranslated for its U.S. release) means "I remember" in the provincial Romagna dialect of this movie's seaside village—very similar to the one in which its *auteur*, Federico Fellini, grew up in the thirties. The filmmaker disclaims *Amarcord* as autobiographical, but it is his childhood memories that color this episodic, anecdotal account of the passing scene in one Italian town during 1935—the year, according to Fellini, "representing a whole life span."

The plotless film's chief structural device lies in the changing of the four seasons, during which some of the villagers grow up, while others become old and die. *Amarcord* opens as it closes—in a sky-filling cloudburst of *manine* thistledown, the first harbinger of spring. It precipitates the lighting of a huge bonfire that night in the town square, and a native recalls some of the history of the village. The local nymphomaniac Volpina (Josiane Tanzilli) sashays down the beach, flirting with Aurelio Biondi (Armando Brancia) and his fellow construction workers. Later, during an argumentative family meal, Aurelio upbraids his son Titta (Bruno Zanin) for not working. The boy's mother Miranda (Pupella Maggio) sends him to confession with the local priest. The youth recalls, and proceeds to embellish upon, encounters with townswomen.

A visiting dignitary is greeted with a Fascist rally, and all the town lights go out, the only sound heard that of a solo violin playing a Socialist hymn from the church belfry. Troops fire on the belfry, halting the music, only to find that they have killed a phonograph. Prevented from attending the rally by his wife, Aurelio is subjected to brutal interrogation by the authorities.

At the luxurious Grand Hotel, Gradisca (Magali

215

Nöel), the glamorous local hairdresser, trysts with Don Baravelli (Gianfilippo Carcano), a visiting nobleman; a pushcart peddler is invited into the suite of an Arabian potentate. Titta's family brings back his crazy Uncle Teo (Ciccio Ingrassia) from an asylum. En route, Teo climbs a tree, shouting that he wants a woman; a dwarf nun from the institution coaxes him down.

The villagers go out to sea in boats for a glimpse of the *Rex*, a luxurious ocean liner on its maiden voyage. Titta is titillated by a startlingly robust tobacconist (Maria Antonietta Beluzzi) who invites familiarities; we next glimpse him ill in bed.

In the first snowfall of winter, villagers leave the movie theater to wage a snowball fight. Aurelio and Titta visit the ailing Miranda in the hospital, where she dies. A funeral is held. And as the thistledown returns to herald spring, Gradisca appears as the bride of the local military policeman at a festive outdoor wedding reception.

Despite the cast of mostly unknowns, *Amarcord* cost a then-pricey $3.5 million having been in production for nearly a year. Many critics were initially at a loss as to how to take this film after the Fellini masterpieces of the past. In the *Village Voice*, Andrew Sarris questioned: "Where does Fellini go from here? Is he marking time, or is *Amarcord* an experiment in social, as

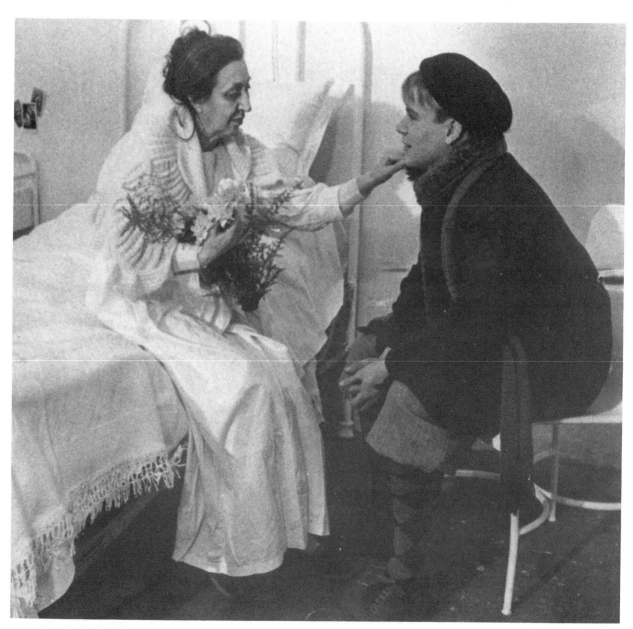

AMARCORD Pupella Maggio and Bruno Zanin.

AMARCORD   Maria Antonietta Beluzzi, Magali Noël, Marina Trovalusci, Bruno Bartucci and Fiorella Magalotti.

opposed to personal, memory?" More puzzling was the seesaw critical perspective of the *New York Times*'s Vincent Canby. From the 1974 Cannes Film Festival he wrote: "*Amarcord* looks as if Fellini were spending his time extravagantly doodling while awaiting an idea for his next real movie." But four months later, by the time of its New York opening, Canby had moved over to the cheering section: "*Amarcord* may possibly be Federico Fellini's most marvelous film." Perhaps he had listened to his colleagues, most of whom championed the movie. Whatever the case, *Amarcord* went on to win the Academy Award for the Best Foreign Film of 1974.

Pane e Cioccolata

(BREAD AND CHOCOLATE)

A Verona Cinematografica Production / 1974

(U.S. release by World Northal Corp.: 1978)

CREDITS

Director: Franco Brusati; *Producer:* Maurizio Lodi-Fé; *Associate Producer:* Turi Vasile; *Screenwriters:* Franco Brusati, Iaia Fiastri, and Nino Manfredi; *Based on a story by* Franco Brusati; *Eastmancolor Cinematographer:* Luciano Tovoli; *Editor:* Mario Morra; *Art*

Director: Luigi Scaccianoce; *Set Decorator:* Bruno Cesari; *Costumes:* Costumi 2000; *Music:* "Serenade" *by* Joseph Haydn, "Sonata in D" *by* Wolfgang Amadeus Mozart (*arranged by* Daniele Petrucchi), and "Symphony No. 1 in D Major" *by* Georges Bizet; *Songs:* "Sekt mit Sugar" *by* G. Patrizio and D. Patrucchi *performed by* Guido Patrizio, "Odor di Nebbia" *by* F. Brusati and D. Patrucchi; "Simmo e Napule Paisa" *by* G. Fiorelli and N. Valente; "Torna a Surriento" *by* G. B. De Curtis and Ed. De Curtis, and "Buongiorno a Te" and "L'Uomo Non e' di Legno" *by* I. Fiastri and U. Calise. *Running Time:* 112 minutes.

CAST

Nino Manfredi *(Nino Garofoli)*; Anna Karina *(Elena)*; Johnny Dorelli *(Industrialist)*; Paolo Turco *(Gianni)*; Ugo D'Alessio *(Old Man)*; Federico Scrobogna *(Grigory)*; Gianfranco Barra *(Turk)*; Giorgio Cerioni *(Police Inspector)*; Max Delys *(Renzo)*; Francesco D'Adda *(Rudiger)*; Geoffrey Copplestone *(Boegli)*; Umberto Raho

PANE E CIOCCOLATA   Nino Manfredi and Anna Karina.

PANE E CIOCCOLATA   Ugo D'Alessio and Nino Manfredi.

218

(Head Waiter); Nelide Giammarco *(Blonde)*; Manfred Freyberger *(Sporting Swiss)*.

THE FILM

The picaresque, *Candide*-like misadventures of a klutzy but ambitious working-class Italian attempting to move upward in a disapproving milieu of German-speaking Swiss society provides the basis of this bitter-sweet comedy-drama. It is a satire of class prejudice and cultural barriers devised by its star, the antic and hilariously inventive Nino Manfredi, in collaboration with director Franco Brusati and Iaia Fiastri.

In Switzerland, southern Italian Nino Garofoli (Manfredi) typifies thousands of foreigners struggling to support their families back home by working as a temporary waiter at a Swiss resort. But he loses that job to a Turk (Gianfranco Barra) after being questioned by the police about a murder of which he is completely innocent. Jobless and lacking a work permit, Nino manages to avoid deportation by finding refuge with Elena (Anna Karina), a Greek refugee. They enjoy a brief love affair, but she soon turns to Rudiger (Francesco D'Adda), a Swiss policeman, to whom marriage could ensure that she and her young son would not be sent back to politically dangerous Greece. Relief comes for Nino when he is hired as butler to a shady Italian industrialist (Johnny Dorelli), who takes an overdose of drugs because of suffocating personal problems. Again jobless and now penniless as well, Nino finds employment among his countrymen slaughtering chickens on a remote poultry farm, where the workers inhabit a converted chicken coop. Watching their employers' Teutonic offspring disport themselves naked in the forest inspires Nino to attempt passing himself off as German by dying his hair blond. But his Italian national pride surfaces, and he is expelled from the country, only to meet Elena again at the railroad station. About to marry Rudiger, she helps Nino by offering him a six-month work permit secured by her fiancé. Nino decides to return to Italy, then changes his mind. As the film ends, Nino jumps off the slow-moving train to try again to succeed in Switzerland.

Alternately shifting back and forth between humor and pathos, *Bread and Chocolate* won both critical and commercial success—and an array of international awards—before a popular U.S. engagement more than four years after its Italian premiere. The New York Film Critics named it Best Foreign Film of 1978, and the National Board of Review voted *Bread and Chocolate* one of the year's five-best foreign-language pictures.

C'Eravamo Tanto Amati

(WE ALL LOVED EACH OTHER SO MUCH)

A Dean Cinematografica–Delta Production / 1975

(U.S. release by Cinema V: 1977)

CREDITS

Director: Ettore Scola; *Producers:* Pio Angeletti and Adriano De Micheli; *Screenwriters:* Ettore Scola, Age (Agenore Incrocci), and Scarpelli (Furio Scarpelli); *Technicolor Cinematographer:* Claudio Cirillo; *Editor:* Raimondo Crociani; *Art Director:* Luciano Ricceri; *Music:* Armando Trovaioli; *Running Time:* 136 minutes (*U.S. Running Time:* 124 minutes).

CAST

Nino Manfredi *(Antonio)*; Vittorio Gassman *(Gianni)*; Stefania Sandrelli *(Luciana)*; Stefano Satta Flores *(Nicola)*; Giovanna Ralli *(Elide)*; Aldo Fabrizi *(Elide's Father)*; Isa Barzizza *(Landlady)*; Marcella Michelangeli *(Nicola's Wife)*; and, as themselves: Vittorio De Sica, Federico Fellini, Marcello Mastroianni, and Mike Bongiorno.

THE FILM

This often-melancholy comedy of human errors covers thirty-odd years in the lives of three men who first came together as partisan fighters in World War II. In fragmented fashion, mixing black-and-white flashbacks with more contemporary color footage, director-coauthor Ettore Scola tells their story of hopes, longings, qualified successes, and failures over the decades. Much of their interconnecting dreams have hinged on Luciana (Stefania Sandrelli), the dark-haired beauty all have desired at one time or another. Antonio (Nino Manfredi), the proletarian hospital orderly, met her first and was establishing a solid friendship with her—until his old wartime buddy Gianni (Vittorio Gassman) meets her. Suddenly, she and the bourgeois opportunist Gianni have eyes only for one another. The third and last of the trio to meet and be smitten with

C'ERAVAMO TANTO AMATI   Nino Manfredi and Vittorio Gassman.

C'ERAVAMO TANTO AMATI   Stefania Sandrelli and Nino Manfredi.

C'ERAVAMO TANTO AMATI   Stefano Satta Flores, Vittorio Gassman and Nino Manfredi.

220

Luciana (albeit from afar) is their partisan comrade Nicola (Stefano Satta Flores), whose career as a professor of film clashes with his radical intellectualism. As the years pass, each makes compromises that fail to fulfill their youthful dreams. Luciana wants only to become a glamorous movie actress but appears destined for little more than bit parts. Nicola achieves fleeting national fame as a television contestant specializing in the Italian film classics. Gianni marries the superficial Elide (Giovanna Ralli), daughter of a wealthy old builder (Aldo Fabrizi). And Antonio never rises much beyond his original hospital job, although he is the one who eventually winds up with Luciana. In the long run, perhaps his lot, while the least ambitious, will be the most satisfying.

Scola weaves a complex tapestry of these intertwined lives over the course of the two hours and sixteen minutes of the movie's original Italian version. (Cuts totaling some twelve minutes were made prior to its American release.) The film is rich in human experience, with the bittersweet foibles of one protagonist offset by the foolish antics of another. And although there is much amusement to be found in the continuity, there is also serious observation of the spiritual and social failures of Italy's postwar generations, compared with their aspirations.

We All Loved Each Other So Much (an ironic title) also pays an affectionate homage to the postwar Italian film, from screened footage of De Sica's *The Bicycle Thief* to a behind-the-scenes recreation of the Trevi Fountain filming of *La Dolce Vita,* with no less than Marcello Mastroianni and director Federico Fellini performing bit roles in support of Manfredi and Sandrelli. One of this film's humorous highlights occurs here when an admirer compliments Fellini, addressing him as "Mr. Rossellini." Fellini's amused reaction in itself is priceless.

Pasqualino Settebellezze

(SEVEN BEAUTIES)

A Medusa Produzione Presentation / 1975

(U.S. release by Cinema V: 1976)

CREDITS

Director-Producer-Screenwriter: Lina Wertmuller; *Associate Producers:* Giancarlo Giannini and Arrigo Colombo; *Technicolor Cinematographer:* Tonino Delli Colli; *Editor:* Franco Fraticelli; *Art Director:* Enrico

PASQUALINO SETTEBELLEZZE   Giancarlo Giannini.

Job; *Music:* Enzo Iannacci; *Running Time:* 115 minutes.

CAST

Giancarlo Giannini *(Pasqualino Frafuso)*; Fernando Rey *(Pedro)*; Shirley Stoler *(Commandant Hilde)*; Elena Fiore *(Concetta)*; Piero Di Iorio *(Francesco)*; Enzo Vitale *(Don Raffaele)*; Ermelinda De Felice *(Pasqualino's Mother)*; Francesca Marciano *(Carolina)*; Lucio Amelio *(Lawyer)*; Roberto Herlitzka *(Elderly Socialist)*; Doriglia Palmi *(Lady Doctor at Asylum)*.

THE FILM

Of Italy's two female directors of the seventies, Liliana Cavani is best known for the controversial sex-oriented melodrama *Il Portiere di Notte/The Night Porter*; Lina Wertmuller, for a far richer body of work, including *Mimi Metallurgico Ferito nell' Onore/The Seduction of Mimi* and *Travolti da un Insolito Destino nell' Azzurro Mare d'Agosto/Swept Away . . . .* But the picture still considered her masterpiece is *Pasqualino Settebellezze/Seven Beauties,* coproduced by—and tailored as a vehicle for—Wertmuller's favorite actor, the often-Chaplinesque Giancarlo Giannini.

The film is set in World War II Germany, where Pasqualino (played by Giannini) and Francesco (Piero Di Iorio) are a pair of Italian deserters on the run. Recoiling in horror from the sight of civilians massacred by German soldiers in a forest, Francesco suffers the guilt of nonintervention, while Pasqualino recalls that he once killed a pimp over a woman in prewar Naples. Then known as "Pasqualino Seven Beauties" because of his prowess with the opposite sex, he had

PASQUALINO SETTEBELLEZZE   Fernando Rey (in white suit) and Giancarlo Giannini.

lived off the proceeds of a sweatshop where his mother and sister stuffed mattresses. There followed an unlikely series of events that saw him caught trying to dispose of the pimp's body in three suitcases (under the direction of the local Mafia don), sent to an insane asylum, becoming the rapist of a fellow inmate, and enjoying a chance at rehabilitation via the army.

When Pasqualino and Francesco are captured by the Germans, they are thrown into a concentration camp, where the former characteristically sets forth to improve his lot by charming the large and sadistic female camp commandant Hilde (Shirley Stoler, who replaced the originally cast Shelley Winters). Consequently, he submits to her gross humiliations, becoming work leader. To survive, he even obeys Hilde's command to kill Francesco, who has sided with an old anarchist named Pedro (Fernando Rey). When the war ends, Pasqualino returns home to Naples—and a big

surprise: In the midst of the Yank "invasion," his mother, sisters, and girlfriend Carolina (Francesca Marciano) have all turned happily to prostitution. Pasqualino determines to wed Carolina and father many offspring.

Mixing the harrowing with the hilarious, Lina Wertmuller's outrageous comedy-drama shocked and dismayed some but pleased many others. In the *New York Times*, Vincent Canby called it "the work of a filmmaker at the peak of her energies, so full of ideas and images that she can afford to throw away moments that other, less talented directors would tediously emphasize." The hard-to-please John Simon, writing for *New York* magazine, deemed *Seven Beauties* "a masterpiece," praising Wertmuller for having "succeeded where Brecht had failed." And in *The Film Encyclopedia*, Ephraim Katz summed the movie up as "a terrifying vision of life and death, pride and degradation, honor and survival in a Nazi concentration camp, intensified by Wertmuller's sense of the comic and the absurd and deepened by her humanity and taste for paradox."

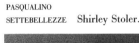

PASQUALINO
SETTEBELLEZZE   Shirley Stoler.

In 1976, Giancarlo Giannini's inspired acting won him one of the few Academy Award nominations for a foreign-language performance.

Seven Beauties made Lina Wertmuller a virtual cult figure of the cinema in the United States and elsewhere, a reputation that she has been hard put to live up to in her sporadic, subsequent motion pictures.

L'Innocente

(THE INNOCENT)

A Coproduction of Rizzoli Film (Rome), Société Imp. Ex. Ci (Nice), and Les Films Jacques Leitienne / Francoriz Production (Paris) / 1976

(U.S. release by Analysis Film Releasing Corporation: 1979)

CREDITS

Director: Luchino Visconti; *Producer:* Giovanni Bertolucci; *Screenwriters:* Suso Cecchi D'Amico, Enrico Medioli, and Luchino Visconti; *Based on the novel by* Gabriele D'Annunzio; *Technicolor-Technovision Cinematographer:* Pasqualino De Santis; *Special Photographic Effects:* Goffredo Rocchetti, Gilberto Provenghi, and Luigi Esposito; *Editor:* Ruggero Mastroianni; *Art Director:* Mario Garbuglia; *Costumes:* Piero Tosi; *Music:* Franco Mannino, *incorporating selections by* Chopin, Mozart, Liszt, and Gluck. *Running Time:* 128 minutes (U.S. Running Time: 115 minutes).

CAST

Giancarlo Giannini *(Tullio Hermil)*; Laura Antonelli *(Giuliana Hermil)*; Jennifer O'Neill *(Countess Teresa Raffo)*; Rina Morelli *(Tullio's Mother)*; Massimo Girotti *(Count Stefano Egano)*; Didier Haudepin *(Federico Hermil)*; Marie Dubois *(Princess di Fundi)*; Roberta Paladini *(Elviretta)*; Claude Mann *(the Prince)*; Marc Porel *(Filippo D'Arborio)*.

THE FILM

In failing health following a massive stroke after the

L'INNOCENTE   Jennifer O'Neill and Giancarlo Giannini.

224

L'INNOCENTE   Laura Antonelli and director Luchino Visconti.

L'INNOCENTE   Giancarlo Giannini and Laura Antonelli.

completion of *Ludwig* in 1972, Luchino Visconti struggled to continue with the only thing that mattered to him—his work as a creative artist. First he filmed the disappointing *Conversation Piece* (1975); then he settled on what would be his final work, the generally acclaimed *L'Innocente/The Innocent.*

For this adaptation of Gabriele D'Annunzio's 1892 novel, Visconti wanted two of his favorite stars of past films, Alain Delon and Romy Schneider. But Delon was tied to a five-picture contract in France, and Schneider was pregnant. And so the director settled on actors new to his circle: Giancarlo Giannini, celebrated for his comic heroes in the works of Lina Wertmuller and, more surprisingly, Laura Antonelli, a beauty best known until then for taking off her clothes in sexploitation pictures. Under Visconti's direction, both would emerge with new critical respect for their acting talents—as would *The Innocent*'s third lead, Jennifer O'Neill.

The film's setting is turn-of-the-century Rome, where a musicale takes place in the salon of Princess di Fundi (Marie Dubois). In attendance are the aristocratic liberal Tullio Hermil (Giannini) and his stunning but neglected wife Giuliana (Antonelli), whom he leaves there so he may be with his possessive mistress, the free-living widow Countess Teresa Raffo (O'Neill). Later, he admits his infidelity to Giuliana, while insisting that they remain together for mutual support. Tullio's secret love affair becomes public knowledge after he challenges one of Teresa's admirers, Stefano Egano (Massimo Girotti) to a duel. Meanwhile, Tullio's brother Federico (Didier Haudepin) introduces the lonely Giuliana to a worldly writer named Filippo D'Arborio (Marc Porel), to whom she is immediately attracted. Tullio is later shocked to discover that she and Filippo have enjoyed a brief, secret affair. While visiting an old family villa where he formerly lived, his sexual interest in his wife is renewed, and they make love.

When Tullio's mother (Rina Morelli) soon thereafter informs him that Giuliana is with child, he realizes that it is not he but D'Arborio who is responsible. Giuliana refuses to undergo the abortion her husband insists upon, and he resumes his liaison with Teresa. Tullio is somewhat pacified when D'Arborio contracts a disease

225

and dies. Giuliana gives birth to "the innocent," and the family servants express surprise at the new parents' general lack of interest in the child. While everyone else is out attending Christmas mass, Tullio urges the baby's nurse to join the others at prayer, then deliberately exposes the infant to the wintry cold, causing its death.

Giuliana realizes what has transpired and bitterly turns on Tullio, denouncing his protestations of affection and devastating him by her confession of love for D'Arborio. With Teresa, Tullio returns to the deserted villa, where he takes his own life.

The critics were united in their praise of *The Innocent*'s rich visual qualities, an exquisite tribute to those artisans Visconti had entrusted for so many years, including art director Mario Garbuglia, costumer Piero Tosi, and cinematographer Pasqualino De Santis. The ailing Visconti directed *The Innocent* from his wheelchair and died a mere three months after filming was completed. Some criticism was evoked from those who found the film too long and leisurely. However, the strong dramatic performances of Giannini and Antonelli pleasantly surprised many. All told, *The Innocent* marked a rewarding finale to a distinguished career.

Novecento

(1900)

A Coproduction of P.E.A. (Rome), Artistes Associés (Paris), and Artemis (West Berlin) / 1976

(U.S. release by Paramount Pictures: 1977)

CREDITS

Director: Bernardo Bertolucci; *Producer:* Alberto Grimaldi; *Screenwriters:* Bernardo Bertolucci, Franco Arcalli, and Giuseppe Bertolucci; *Technicolor Cinematographer:* Vittorio Storaro; *Editor:* Franco Arcalli; *Art Director:* Ezio Frigerio; *Set Decorator:* Maria Paola Maino; *Costumes:* Gitt Magrini; *Special Effects:* Luciano Byrd; *Music:* Ennio Morricone. *Running time:* 311 minutes (*U.S. Running Time:* 245 minutes).

NOVECENTO   Robert De Niro and Gérard Depardieu.

NOVECENTO Pippo Campanini and Alida Valli.

CAST

Robert De Niro *(Alfredo Berlinghieri)*; Gérard Depardieu *(Olmo Dalco)*; Burt Lancaster *(Alfredo Berlinghieri Sr.)*; Dominique Sanda *(Ada Fiastri Baulhan)*; Donald Sutherland *(Attila)*; Sterling Hayden *(Leo Dalco)*; Stefania Sandrelli *(Anita Foschi)*; Francesca Bertini *(Desolata, Alfredo's Sister)*; Werner Bruhns *(Ottavio)*; Romolo Valli *(Giovanni)*; Anna-Maria Gherardi *(Eleonora, Giovanni's Wife)*; Ellen Schwiers *(Amelia, Eleonora's Sister)*; Laura Betti *(Regina, Amelia's Daughter)*; Tiziana Senatore *(Regina as a Child)*; Paolo Pavesi *(Alfredo as a Child)*; Pippo Campanini *(Don Tarcisio)*; Alida Valli *(Signora Pioppi)*; José Quaglio *(Aranzini)*; Paolo Branco *(Orso, Leo's Elder Son)*; Giacomo Rizzo *(Rigoletto)*; Antonio Piovanelli *(Turo Dalco)*; Liu Bosizio *(Nella Dalco)*; Maria Monti *(Rosina Dalco, Leo's Daughter-in-Law)*; Roberto Maccanti *(Olmo as a Child)*; Edoardo Dallagio *(Oreste Dalco)*; Anna Henkel *(Anita, Olmo's Daughter)*; Stefania Cassini *(Nevi, the Laundrywoman)*; Salvator Mureddu *(Leader of the Gardes Royaux)*; Allen Midgette *(Vagabond)*.

THE FILM

Bernardo Bertolucci's sprawling, five-hour-plus Marxist epic of forty-five years of social and personal turmoil in twentieth-century Italy was completed in May 1975, following ten months of filming in the Po Valley. Cut to just over four hours at the insistence of Paramount, its original American-release version failed to garner much critical praise. Nor did it attract the public despite an impressive cast and the promise of more sex and violence than the average foreign import of 1977. However, *1900* gradually managed to build a cult following in its eventual revival engagements, and finally there was a "restoration" that allowed U.S. audiences to view the original, uncut 311-minute version, as approved by director Bertolucci.

Beginning in the north Italian province of Emilia-Romagna on Italy's Liberation Day of World War II, the narrative flashes back to the beginning of the

NOVECENTO   Robert De Niro and Dominique Sanda.

NOVECENTO   Robert De Niro and Gérard Depardieu.

century, when, on the same day—January 1, 1900—two boys were born. Alfredo Berlinghieri (played as an adult by Robert De Niro) is the son of a wealthy landowner, while Olmo Dalco (Gérard Depardieu) is born into the large family of their peasant overseer Leo Dalco (Sterling Hayden). As boys, little Alfredo (Paolo Pavesi) and Olmo (Roberto Maccanti) are the best of pals. But as they grow to manhood and approach middle age, they turn bitterly antagonistic as a result of the class struggles that coincide with Mussolini's rise to power. Olmo turns activist, while the wealthy Alfredo retreats into passive isolation. His implicit backing of the rising Fascist political climate later costs him the affections of his wife Ada (Dominique Sanda). Olmo, meanwhile, has become involved not only with Anita (Stefania Sandrelli), a free-loving Socialist and the town's schoolteacher, but also in the local political battle against fascism. An interwoven subplot involves Alfredo's lovelorn cousin Regina (Laura Betti), who assuages her disappointment by an alliance with the vicious estate manager Attila (Donald Sutherland), who ruthlessly encourages the peasants to rise up against the landowners during World War II. Eventually, Olmo and the peasants manage to overthrow this power-hungry couple. Alfredo's feuding relationship with Olmo accompanies them into old age.

Of the leading performers, the impressively sensitive Depardieu fares better than De Niro, who is not at his best in a role of such passivity. Stars like Burt Lancaster, Sterling Hayden, Dominique Sanda, Stefania Sandrelli, and Alida Valli make the most of what little this actor-swallowing saga allows them. As the film's "heavies," Donald Sutherland and Laura Betti are encouraged to lay on the villainy a bit heavily. Technically, there is faultless camera work by Vittorio Storaro and the usual exemplary score from Ennio Morricone. However, in the final analysis, this film belongs to Bernardo Bertolucci, whose exhausting blend of dynastic sex, psychology, and politics makes *1900* a flawed, vibrant masterwork.

Una Giornata Particolare

(A SPECIAL DAY)

A Coproduction of Compagnia Cinematografica Champion (Rome) and Canafox Films (Montreal) / 1977

(U.S. release by Cinema V: 1977)

CREDITS

Director: Ettore Scola; *Executive Producer:* Carlo Ponti; *Production Supervisor:* Maurizio Anticoli; *Screenwriters:* Ruggero Maccari, Ettore Scola, and Maurizio Costanzo; *Technicolor Cinematographer:* Pasqualino De Santis; *Editor:* Raimondo Crociani; *Art Director:* Luciano Ricceri; *Costumes:* Enrico Sabbatini; *Music:* Armando Trovaioli; *Running Time:* 105 minutes.

CAST

Sophia Loren *(Antonietta)*; Marcello Mastroianni *(Gabriele)*; John Vernon *(Emanuele)*; Françoise Berd *(Concierge)*; Nicole Magny *(Officer's Daughter)*; Patrizia Basso *(Romana)*; Tiziano De Persio *(Arnaldo)*; Maurizio De Paolantonio *(Fabio)*; Antonio Garibaldi *(Littorio)*; Vittorio Guerrieri *(Umberto)*; Alessandra Mussolini *(Maria Luisa)*.

THE FILM

Most of the box-office hits of Sophia Loren and Marcello Mastroianni as a team have occurred under the guidance of master director Vittorio De Sica, often with top-notch results *(Yesterday, Today and Tomorrow; Marriage Italian Style)*—but not always *(Sunflower)*. With the passing of Loren's mentor De Sica, it fell to Ettore Scola to reunite the popular team in a vehicle worthy of their talents. As a screenwriter, Scola had had a hand in one of Loren's early exploitation

UNA GIORNATA PARTICOLARE   Marcello Mastroianni and Sophia Loren.

229

pictures, *Two Nights With Cleopatra* (1954), and had much later directed Mastroianni in a lesser effort called *Permette? Rocco Papaleo* (1971). For *A Special Day*, each was offered the opportunity of a totally unglamorous change of pace, casting them against type. The result: awards and nominations.

The setting is a large apartment complex in Rome. It is May 6, 1938, the very day that Hitler has come to meet with Il Duce to announce the unity of the two Fascist parties, and most of the city has taken to the streets to participate in the parade and festivities. Two who remain at home are unacquainted apartment neighbors Antonietta (Loren), a tired housewife with six children, wed to a Fascist party official (John Vernon), and Gabriele (Mastroianni), a closeted gay who has recently lost his job as a radio announcer because of his sexual preference. Both are lonely and unhappy: she, because she is the neglected wife of a man who now prefers the company of whores; he, because he is a friendless anti-Fascist with little hope of future employment.

With the flats nearly deserted except for the concierge (Françoise Berd), whose radio broadcasts a running commentary on the unseen rally, Gabriele plans to commit suicide. But Antonietta's myna bird escapes from its cage, flies out the window, and lands on Gabriele's sill—which leads to a meeting of the strangers, who proceed to spend a few hours together, assuaging their loneliness over coffee as they share their secrets and insecurities. A virtual slave to boring routine, Antonietta has hopes of conceiving a seventh child that would bring the family a financial reward from the government, while Gabriele questions the ethics of a regime that would deny him employment for a circumstance he cannot help. Despite Gabriele's displays of temper and bitterness, Antonietta is attracted to him, and while the radio transmits Mussolini's tributes to *der Führer*, these two lonely people make tentative love, then part. Later, after welcoming her excited husband and children back from the parade, Antonietta sees Gabriele being taken away by the authorities. Emotionally refreshed by her meeting and lovemaking, she is now better able to return to the endless needs of her family.

While praising the performances of the two stars, some critics thought *A Special Day* too undernourished in content to support nearly two hours of screen time. Others found much to admire, including cinematogra-

230

UNA GIORNATA PARTICOLARE Sophia Loren and Marcello Mastroianni.

pher Pasqualino De Santis's use of desaturated color to simulate black and white, save for an occasional blush of color here and there. And if Loren possessed far too much natural beauty to be completely convincing as a household drudge, she was nevertheless actress enough to enable most of us to suspend our disbelief. Chameleon that he is, the customarily macho Mastroianni remained secure enough in his masculinity to make the bold acting choice of portraying a gay character. Consequently, *A Special Day* received Academy Award nominations as Best Foreign Film and, for Mastroianni, Best Actor. Director Scola was awarded the Special Jury Prize at Cannes in 1977, and in Italy he and Sophia Loren each received a David di Donatello Award for the film.

Padre Padrone

(MY FATHER, MY MASTER)

An RAI–Radiotelevisione Italiana Production / 1977

(U.S. release by Cinema V: 1977)

CREDITS

Directors-Screenwriters: Paolo and Vittorio Taviani; *Executive Producer:* Tonio Paoletti; *Producer:* Giuliano G. De Negri; *Based on the autobiographical novel* Padre Padrone: L'educazione di un pastore *by* Gavino Ledda; *Eastmancolor Cinematographer:*

231

Mario Masini; *Editor:* Roberto Perpignani; *Art Director:* Giovanni Sbarra; *Costumes:* Lina Nerli Taviani; *Music:* Egisto Macchi and excerpts from the Concerto for Clarinet and Orchestra *by* Mozart, the operetta "Die Fledermaus" *by* Johann Strauss, Jr., the Sardinian songs "Misere" and "Duru Duru," and the German popular song "Trink, Trink"; *Running Time:* 114 minutes.

CAST

Omero Antonutti *(Efisio Ledda)*; Saverio Marconi *(Gavino Ledda)*; Marcella Michelangeli *(Gavino's Mother)*; Fabrizio Forte *(Gavino as a Child)*; Marino Cenna *(Shepherd)*; Stanko Molnar *(Sebastiano)*; Gavino Ledda *(Himself)*.

THE FILM

Since the twin filmmaking team of Paolo and Vittorio Taviani are among the younger writer-directors whose works are featured in this volume, it is difficult to realize that they are now all of sixty years old. In the eighties, the brothers enjoyed both critical success (the acclaimed *The Night of the Shooting Stars*) and failure (the English-language *Good Morning, Babylon*, about young Italian artisans emigrating to work in Griffith's Hollywood of the teens).

To some, the twins' most memorable work is their 1977 breakthrough movie *Padre Padrone*, a rarity in that it won both the Grand Prix and the International

PADRE PADRONE   Saverio Marconi.

PADRE PADRONE   Saverio Marconi and unidentified actress.

Critics Prize at the Cannes Film Festival, something no film had previously achieved. Significant, in an increasing trend, was that the picture had originally been shot in 16-millimeter for Italian television.

Padre Padrone derives from Gavino Ledda's 1974 autobiographical book about his triumph over a Sardinian peasant background that threatened to keep him an ignorant, unschooled rustic. The eldest of six children, little Gavino (portrayed as a child by Fabrizio Forte and as a young man by Saverio Marconi) is pulled out of his elementary school classroom by his severe father Efisio (Omero Antonutti), who makes him tend the family sheep. And so he is forced to spend his boyhood confined to the sheepfold, away from human contact, unable to read or write or even speak Italian. Like his father, the boy can only speak the local Sardinian dialect.

Gavino makes an unsuccessful attempt to emigrate to Germany with other young men of the area. Upon his return, his father informs him he is selling their land and sending Gavino into the army to learn a trade. For Gavino, this is the turning point in his life. He is befriended, learns the Italian language, is trained in building radios, and earns a high school diploma. Leaving the army to get an advanced education, Gavino returns home against the wishes of his father, who works him so hard that the young man fails his college examinations.

An angry confrontation ensues between them, and Gavino leaves to concentrate on getting his degree. The young man eventually returns to the village to write his life story. Gavino the writer is last seen among the olive groves, a solitary figure amidst the sheep.

Filmed chiefly in the Sardinian countryside, *Padre Padrone* was shot on a low budget. The camera work in particular (Mario Masini is the credited cinematographer) displays considerable ingenuity, alternating close-ups of the leading characters with mobile long shots of the Sardinian mountain terrain, often filmed from high above. Heightened realism is the filmmaking style here, obviously a seventies counterpart to the neorealism of thirty years earlier. And it is worth noting the Tavianis' inventive use of sound, especially in the deployment of folk music and unaccompanied peasant song. The result is a moving, sometimes fascinating narrative about a youth's fierce determination to succeed despite the tyranny of a formidable father.

The real-life Gavino Ledda, who became a self-taught linguistics expert, introduces the film of his story.

Dementicare Venezia

(TO FORGET VENICE)

A Coproduction of Rizzoli Film (Rome) and Action Film (Paris) / 1979

(U.S. release by Quartet Films: 1980)

CREDITS

Director: Franco Brusati; *Producer:* Claudio Grassetti; *Screenwriters:* Franco Brusati and Iaia Fiastri; *Based on a story by* Franco Brusati; *Technicolor Cinematographer:* Romano Albani; *Editor:* Ruggero Mastroianni; *Art Director:* Luigi Scaccianoce; *Costumes:* Luca Sabatelli; *Music:* Benedetto Ghiglia and the songs "Dementicare Venezia" *performed by* Dik Dik, "Rondo alla Russe" *by* Saverio Mercadante *performed by* Severino Gazzelloni, and "Oh del mio dolce ardor" *by* C. W. Gluck *sung by* Adriana Martino; *Running Time:* 110 minutes.

CAST

Erland Josephson *(Nicky)*; Mariangela Melato *(Anna)*;

DEMENTICARE VENEZIA   Erland Josephson and David Pontremoli.

233

DEMENTICARE VENEZIA   Erland Josephson, Mariangela Melato, Eleonora Giorgi, Hella Petri and David Pontremoli.

Eleonora Giorgi *(Claudia)*; David Pontremoli *(Picchio)*; Hella Petri *(Marta)*; Fred Personne *(Rossino)*.

THE FILM

With the popular *Bread and Chocolate*, writer-director Franco Brusati displayed his earthy insights into the human condition in broad, basic strokes. *To Forget Venice*, his subsequent excursion into time, memory, and human complexities, revealed intellectual depths previously unsuspected by those who admired his earlier work. Poles apart from one another, the films bear scant resemblance. *To Forget Venice* deals with varying levels of mood and character as it explores the interrelationships of its four central personalities—all identified simply by their Christian names.

Despite its promising title, this movie is no treat for armchair travelers, for we never see that most picturesque of Italian cities. Instead, it centers on the country estate of a once-famed but now-retired diva named Marta (Hella Petri), who lives near Venice with Anna (Mariangela Melato), her adopted "niece," who looks after the adjoining farm, and Anna's schoolteacher-inamorata Claudia (Eleonora Giorgi). Arriving by car

to spend a holiday with Marta are her middle-aged brother Nicky (Erland Josephson) and his much younger lover—and partner in a vintage car business—Picchio (David Pontremoli). Back once again in his childhood home, Nicky reflects on an idyllic youth, and he recalls his long-ago chum Rossino. At the same time, Anna ponders her own, less happy younger years. Refusing to take on the full responsibilities of adulthood, Both have accepted Marta as a mother figure, ignorant of the fact that the former opera star now requires medication to sustain her. The hours this unusual quintet spend together are filled with pleasant reminiscences of the past, made sober by hatreds, fears, and recriminations. To celebrate their togetherness, Nicky arranges an evening out at a neighboring restaurant where a wedding party is led by the bride's old and balding father—none other than Nicky's former pal Rossino (Fred Personne). The following day, they are set to visit Venice, but the excitement proves too much for Marta, who suffers a fatal heart attack. And with her goes the maternal shield that had sustained the two couples' false illusions of time standing still. Marta's sudden demise brings to a head the meaning of ongoing changes in both gay relationships.

DEMENTICARE VENEZIA Eleonora Giorgi and Mariangela Melato.

L'ALBERO DEGLI ZOCCOLI Luigi Ornaghi and Omar Brignoli.

Brusati approaches homosexuality in this film with a European matter-of-factness that precludes exploitation, although the picture doesn't shy away from frontal nudity. And yet nothing is sensationalized for its own sake. Much deeper than a superficial display of skin is what the movie has to say about adult human feelings and the cruel and evasive games that otherwise mature individuals sometimes play with each other, whether intentional or not. Brusati frequently colors the narrative with symbols and suggestions, leaving the story open-ended and his central characters far too deeply realized for facile analysis. And his cast is beyond criticism in their complex approach to a richly textured, multilayered story of five adults coming to terms with their past, their present, and mortality.

To Forget Venice was awarded Italy's David di Donatello prize for Best Picture of 1979, but Germany's *The Tin Drum* surpassed it to win that year's Best Foreign Film Oscar.

L'Albero degli Zoccoli

(THE TREE OF WOODEN CLOGS)

A Coproduction of RAI-Radiotelevisione Italiana and Italnoleggio Cinematografico for G.P.C. (Gruppo Produzione Cinema) / 1978

(U.S. release by New Yorker Films: 1979)

CREDITS

Director-Screenwriter-Gevacolor Cinematographer-Editor: Ermanno Olmi; *Art Director:* Enrico Tova-glieri; *Set Decorator:* Franco Gambarana; *Costumes:* Francesca Zucchelli; *Music:* Johann Sebastian Bach *performed by* organist Fernando Germani, "Turkish March," and excerpt from "Don Giovanni" *by* Wolfgang Amadeus Mozart; *Running Time:* 186 minutes (*U.S. Running Time:* 185 minutes).

CAST

Luigi Ornaghi *(Batisti)*; Francesca Moriggi *(Batistina, His Wife)*; Omar Brignoli *(Minek)*; Antonio Ferrari *(Tuni)*; Teresa Brescianini *(Widow Runk)*; Giuseppe Brignoli *(Grandpa Anselmo)*; Carlo Rota *(Peppino)*; Pasqualina Brolis *(Teresina)*; Massimo Fratus *(Pierino)*; Francesca Villa *(Annetta)*; Maria Grazia Caroli *(Bettina)*; Battista Trevaini *(Finard)*; Giuseppina Sangaletti *(Finarda, His Wife)*; Lorenzo Pedroni *(Grandpa Finard)*; Felice Cervi *(Usti)*; Lucia Pezzoli *(Maddalena)*; Franco Pilenga *(Stefano)*.

THE FILM

Filmmaker Ermanno Olmi's reputation lies in making "personal," offbeat films about ordinary people, utilizing amateur actors. Most celebrated for *Il Posto/The Sound of Trumpets* (1961) and *I Fidanzati/The Fiances* (1963), he wasn't much heard from in the next fifteen years—until *The Tree of Wooden Clogs*. In Europe, it won the Golden Palm at the 1978 Cannes Film Festival, followed by a British Academy Award

L'ALBERO DEGLI ZOCCOLI.

and, in the United States, placement on the *New York Times*' ten-best list and a citation by the National Board of Review as one of 1979's five-best foreign-language films.

Olmi's focus here is on peasant sharecropper life in the Lombardy region of northern Italy, near Bergamo, during the year of 1896, especially as it affects the members of several different families who live communally in a sprawling farmhouse on one landlord's estate. Their collective stories are plotless and episodic: The priest Don Carlo persuades Batisti (Luigi Ornaghi) to send his son Minek (Omar Brignoli) to school; the oldest of Widow Runk's (Teresa Brescianini) six children, Peppino (Carlo Rota) gets a job with the local miller; the Brenas worry about their young Maddalena (Lucia Pezzoli), who's seen spending time with Stefano (Franco Pilenga), a neighboring farmer's son; Finard (Battista Trevaini) constantly argues with his boys; Anselmo (Giuseppe Brignoli), the widow's father-in-law, grows his prized tomatoes in secret; Peppino discards the priest's suggestion that some of the troubled widow's younger offspring be put in an orphanage and her ailing cow gets better after drinking "consecrated" river water.

It is the spring feast of the Madonna of St. Augustine: The peasants carry on with carefree enjoyment; Finard finds a gold coin but eventually loses it; a Socialist speaker addresses the suspicious farmers. Batisti's wife gives birth to a third son, and that very day, the new father solves Minek's problem of a broken wooden shoe by secretly cutting down one of the revered poplar trees to make the boy a new pair of clogs. Maddalena and Stefano are wed and travel by boat to Milan, where they are surprised to encounter incidents of civil unrest; lodging with Maddalena's aunt, who is the mother superior of a convent orphanage, they are offered the gift of a year-old boy.

Anselmo and his granddaughter Bettina are the first to bring their ripened tomatoes to market. The landlord discovers that one of his trees has been cut down and learns that Batisti is at fault. As punishment, Batisti's possessions are confiscated, and he and his family are evicted from the farm.

Serving in the multitalented capacities of director, writer, photographer, and editor, Ermanno Olmi enjoys a unique place in the annals of Italian filmmaking, where most movies seem to require anywhere from three to eight screenwriters just to fashion a script. Nor is he likely to employ professional actors, preferring instead to mold naturalistic performances from ordinary folk. Having come from Bergamo himself, Olmi employs here incidents from his own family's past to

236

weave a lengthy but fascinating tapestry of nineteenth-century peasant life.

Most of the film's acting—performed with a minimum of dialogue—is marvelous, as is Olmi's evocative Gevacolor photography. Lacking in melodramatic incidents to heighten the story content, Olmi's screenplay also avoids scenes of sexploitation. Instead, *The Tree of Wooden Clogs* remains what New York's *Village Voice* aptly called ". . . a towering testament of Christian love, devotion and humility in the midst of heartrending injustice." In summation, The *New York Times*'s Vincent Canby wrote: "The awkwardly titled The Tree of Wooden Clogs . . . has almost nothing going for it except that it may well be a masterpiece."

La Notte di San Lorenzo

(THE NIGHT OF THE SHOOTING STARS)

A Coproduction of RAI (Radiotelevisione Italiana) and Ager Cinematografica/1982

(U.S. release by United Artists Classics: 1983)

CREDITS

Directors: Paolo and Vittorio Taviani; *Producer:* Giuliani G. De Negri; *Screenwriters:* Paolo and Vittorio Taviani, Giuliani G. De Negri, and Tonino Guerra; *Agfa Color Cinematographer:* Franco di Giacomo; *Editor:* Roberto Perpignani; *Art Director:* Gianni Sbarra; *Music:* Nicola Piovani, including excerpts from the music of Verdi, Wagner, and Bizet; *Running Time:* 106 minutes.

CAST

Omero Antonutti *(Galvano);* Margarita Lozano *(Concetta);* Claudio Bigagli *(Corrado);* Massimo Bonetti *(Nicola);* Norma Martelli *(Ivana);* Enrica Maria Modugno *(Mara);* Sabina Vannucchi *(Rosanna);* Dario Cantarelli *(the Priest);* Sergio Dagilana *(Olinto);* Giuseppe Furia *(Requiem);* Paolo Hendel *(Dilvo);* Micol Guidelli *(Cecilia, aged six).*

THE FILM

Italy's filmmaking Taviani brothers, Vittorio and Pa-

LA NOTTE DI SAN LORENZO.

olo, enjoy an unusual working partnership as writer-directors. Their most notable critical success has been *Padre Padrone* (1977), which won awards but not widespread popularity. That came belatedly with *La Notte di San Lorenzo/The Night of the Shooting Stars* in 1982.

The movie begins on August 10, the year's most prevalent night for shooting stars, as a woman relates to her child the events of another such night long ago—August 10, 1944. The setting is Tuscany, where "it is said that every shooting star fulfills a wish." And although the majority of the narrative takes place during a long flashback to wartime in the rural town of San Martino, the romantic colorations of remembrance diffuse the story's harsher, realistic aspects.

San Martino's villagers have been warned by the enemy that their houses have all been mined and will be destroyed prior to the German withdrawal. They have been further advised to seek the refuge of their

cathedral. But it is common knowledge that the Americans are approaching, and some decide to sneak off and make contact—a defiant move that could result in execution were they to be caught by the Nazis. As it develops, death is in the cards regardless; the Germans blow up the cathedral. The surviving village priest emerges with a dead child in his arms to face a scene of destruction in the town square. In anguish, he collapses, overwhelmed by the thought that the death and maiming of those he was supposed to protect was not only an act of betrayal by the Germans but by his God as well.

Meanwhile, the search for the Americans proves daunting to some of the less hardy villagers, who can only return to their doomed homes. Some, reacting to the distant thunder of explosions, throw away their house keys in despair; a few others choose to retain them as souvenirs of the past. Still more are killed by local Fascists, while friends find themselves on opposing sides. When the young son of a brutal Fascist gets cornered in a tree, his father commits suicide after pleading in vain for the life of the boy, who is slain.

But the film's best sequence occurs when the townsfolk join forces with the Resistance fighters in hand-to-hand combat with the local Fascists—all of which takes place in a wheat field rampant with confusion. And Franco di Giacomo's artful photography manages to give these peasants and their naturally beautiful surroundings the look of early Cézanne paintings.

An unusual and unexpected choice of classical music can sometimes add immeasurably to a motion picture,
and such is the case with the excerpts from Wagner, Verdi, and Bizet with which Nicola Piovani supplements his own original background score. Considering the subject matter of this film, it may seem difficult for the uninitiated to imagine how it can be at once both a joyous salute to the heroism of the Italian people and a testament to the human spirit. But that is the strength and the talent of Paolo and Vittorio Taviani.

The Night of the Shooting Stars was awarded the Special Jury Prize at the 1982 Cannes Film Festival.

Ginger e Fred

(GINGER AND FRED)

A Coproduction of P.E.A. (Produzioni Europée Associate; Rome), Revcom Films in association with Les Films Ariane, FR3 Films (Paris), and Stella Films in association with Anthea (Munich), in cooperation with RAI-1 / 1986

(U.S. release by M-G-M / UA: 1986)

CREDITS

Director: Federico Fellini; *Producer:* Alberto Grimaldi; *Associate Producers:* Walter Massi, Gianfranco

238

Coduti, Roberto Mannoni, and Raymond Leplont; *Screenwriters:* Federico Fellini, Tonina Guerra, and Tullio Pinelli; *Color Cinematographers:* Tonino Delli Colli and Ennio Guarnieri; *Editors:* Nino Baragli, Ugo De Rossi, and Ruggero Mastroianni; *Art Director:* Dante Ferretti; *Set Designer:* Nazzareno Plana; *Set Dressers:* Italo Tomassi and Luigi Sergianni; *Costumes:* Danilo Donati; *Special Effects:* Adriano Pischiutta; *Choreographer:* Tony Ventura; *Music:* Nicola Piovani; *Running Time:* 127 minutes.

CAST

Giulietta Masina *(Amelia Bonetti, "Ginger")*; Marcello Mastroianni *(Pippo Botticella, "Fred")*; Franco Fabrizi *(Show Host)*; Frederick von Ledenburg *(Admiral)*; Augusto Poderosi *(Transvestite)*; Martin Maria Blau *(Assistant Producer)*; Jacques Henri Lartigue *(Flying Priest)*; Toto Mignone *(Toto)*; Ezio Marano *(Intellectual)*.

GINGER E FRED   Marcello Mastroianni.

GINGER E FRED   Giulietta Masina.

THE FILM

Few great artists manage to sustain a consistent level of creativity throughout the decades of a lengthy career. Not even Federico Fellini was able to equal the excellence of the award-winning *Amarcord* (1973), for the movies that emerged in the following thirteen years proved minor Fellini—until *Ginger and Fred*. Its title immediately conjures up terpsichorean images of Rogers and Astaire, and, indeed, Ginger Rogers was sufficiently outraged by the very notion that Italy's foremost filmmaker might be ridiculing Hollywood's best-loved dance team that she took legal action (to no avail). The veteran American star, of course, had no substantial grounds for complaint; although appropriately named, *Ginger and Fred* really has nothing to do with those cinema giants other than to offer homage of the gentlest sort. The main thrust of this devastating satire is television.

"Ginger and Fred" is the professional moniker of a dance team of yesteryear that specialized in the popular tunes and choreography associated with the thirties' RKO films of Rogers and Astaire. To portray these

239

over-the-hill cabaret artists, actually named Amelia Bonetti and Pippo Botticella, Fellini scored a brilliant casting coup by uniting for the first time on screen his wife Giulietta Masina and his favorite leading man and on-screen alter ego, Marcello Mastroianni.

The fictional pretext for their union (actually a *re*union for Amelia and Pippo) is a special Christmas edition of a television variety show called "We Are Proud to Present," on which Ginger and Fred are scheduled to fill the nostalgia segment of a bizarre and otherwise tasteless array of "talent" that puts the viewer in mind of a sort of Roman mightmare version of "The Ed Sullivan Show." Among their bill-sharing colleagues: flamenco dancing midgets, celebrity look-alikes, senile wind musicians, a psychic, an edible-panties huckster, famed kidnap victims, a levitating monk, a handcuffed mafioso, and a cow with twenty udders.

Some thirty years earlier, Ginger and Fred performed their dance routines and were, for a time, lovers before breaking up the act to lead separate lives. Now a widowed grandmother who runs a small business in the north, Amelia accepts the television offer solely to see Pippo again, hopeful of recapturing their old magic. He, in turn, has become a seedy, boozy, anarchistic womanizer who has apparently accepted this gig only for the money. Ever the professional, Amelia worries about adequate rehearsals, her makeup, and dressing quarters. Pippo, when he belatedly arrives, is more concerned about telling his television audience his low opinion of them. Finding a quiet hallway, the team practices their old steps; Amelia is still able to

GINGER E FRED Marcello Mastroianni and Giulietta Masina.

240

carry it off, but Pippo is soon out of breath. Endless commercials and a power blackout that nearly cancels the performance make them consider, only briefly, running out on the show. Gamely, if apprehensively, they perform their "Cheek to Cheek" routine in the requisite marabou-decorated evening dress and white tie and tails. And the studio audience responds with ecstatic applause. Fred and Ginger have had their big moment in the spotlight, and later, at the train station, they're badgered by autograph seekers who recognize them from the television show. Amelia's relieved to say good-bye when her train comes, but Pippo stays behind to savor the acclaim of his renewed celebrity status.

Masina and Mastroianni remain, in their autumnal years, masters of comedy and drama, subtle clowning, and unsentimentalized pathos. And *Ginger and Fred* offers them a marvelous showcase for their talents. But it is also very much Fellini's picture as he mercilessly skewers a television-crazed, valueless society with its endless appetite for the vulgar, the tawdry, and the loud.

Otello

A Coproduction of Cannon Italia and RAI (Radiotelevisione Italiana) / 1986

(U.S. release by the Cannon Group, Inc.: 1986)

CREDITS

Director: Franco Zeffirelli; *Executive Producer:* John Thompson; *Producers:* Menahem Golan and Yoran Globus; *Associate Producer:* Fulvio Lucisano; *Screenwriter:* Franco Zeffirelli; *Based on* the Arrigo Boito libretto for the opera by Giuseppe Verdi; *Eastmancolor Cinematographer:* Ennnio Guarnieri; *Special Photography:* Deborah Imogen Beer; *Editors:* Peter Taylor and Franca Silvi; *Art Director:* Gianni Quaranta; *Set Decorators:* Bruno Carlino and Stefano Paltrinieri; *Costumes:* Anna Anni and Maurizio Millenotti; *Special Effects:* Giovanni Corridori and Samiotis Grigoris; *Verdi's score conducted by* Lorin Maazel, with the orchestra and chorus of Milan's Teatro alla Scala; *Running Time:* 123 minutes.

CAST

Plácido Domingo *(Otello);* Katia Ricciarelli *(Desde-*

OTELLO Plácido Domingo.

OTELLO Katia Ricciarelli.

mona); Justino Diaz (Iago); Petra Malakova (Emilia); Urbano Barberini (Cassio); Massimo Foschi (Lodovico); Edwin Francis (Montano); Sergio Nicolai (Roderigo); Remo Remotti (Brabanzio); Antonio Pierfederici (Doge). Voices for nonsinging actors: Ezio Di Cesare (Cassio); John Macurdy (Lodovico); Constantin Zaharia (Roderigo); Edward Toumajin (Montano).

THE FILM

Franco Zeffirelli's wealth of stage experience as a designer-director of live opera in Milan, London, and New York had given him a solid preparation for filmed opera, as first evidenced by his 1965 *La Boheme*, a straightforward movie production seen chiefly in limited, reserved-seat bookings. Seventeen years later, Zeffirelli filmed a *La Traviata* that evoked ecstatic reactions from critics and audiences alike, utilizing—in Teresa Stratas and Plácido Domingo—opera singers who could act and creating a work that, while faithful to Verdi, stood on its own as a movie. Four years later, his creative talent offered us yet another Verdi masterpiece in *Otello*. Although dismaying purists with its textual and musical excisions—especially the soprano "Willow Song"/*Salce, Salce*—and juxtapositions of the order of the music, one of New York's more astute music critics nevertheless termed it "prob-

ably the finest cinematic treatment of an opera yet to reach the screen."

On behalf of the fifteenth-century Venetian republic, the Moor Otello (Plácido Domingo) has been named military governor of Cyprus. Amid a virtual hurricane, his ship arrives on the island and is met by his relieved bride Desdemona (Katia Ricciarelli) and her lady-in-waiting Emilia (Petra Malakova). But their happiness is not shared by Otello's ensign, Emilia's husband Iago (Justino Diaz), who resents the appointment of Cassio (Urbano Barberini) as Otello's captain, a position the rejected Iago jealously believes should have been *his*. The latter is equally angry over the black Otello's marriage to blond and pale-skinned Desdemona. At the feast celebrating the Moor's safe arrival, Iago successfully plots to get Cassio drunk; as a result, Cassio engages in an embarrassing brawl that culminates in his demotion. While slyly appealing to a sympathetic Desdemona to plead with her husband for Cassio's reinstatement, Iago also plants seeds of doubt in Otello's mind as to the intensity of Cassio's interest in Desdemona. Eventually, it is her lace handkerchief that becomes Iago's evil weapon of proof that the two are lovers. In a vengeful rage, Otello strangles his innocent wife, while Emilia is slain by Iago, but not before she reveals that he is the instigator responsible for Desdemona's cruel death. Upon realizing the de-

OTELLO   Justino Diaz and Plácido Domingo.

242

ception, Otello murders his ensign and then takes his own life.

Shakespeare's classic stage play is, of course, the basis for Arrigo Boito's suitably operatic libretto for this, Verdi's penultimate grand opera. And so Zeffirelli can hardly be faulted for making the most of his original material. Utilizing such atmospheric locations as a magnificent castle on Crete, brilliantly photographed by Ennio Guarnieri, he not only realizes every visual possibility inherent in the stage work, but he goads his trio of opera stars into intensely committed acting suitable to the probing eye of the camera. *Otello*'s thrilling sound track is due in no small part to the orchestra and chorus of Milan's justly celebrated La Scala opera house and its renowned conductor Lorin Maazel.

It has been widely reported that, upon reviewing this film, one of this century's greatest Shakespearean stars, Laurence Olivier, complained: "Domingo not only acts the part as well as I ever did—he can *sing*, too!"

The National Board of Review in the United States voted *Otello* Best Foreign Film of 1986.

L'Ultimo Imperatore

(THE LAST EMPEROR)

A Coproduction of TAO Film (Rome) and Yanco Films (Hong Kong) / 1987

(U.S. release by Columbia Pictures: 1987)

CREDITS

Director: Bernardo Bertolucci; *Producer:* Jeremy Thomas; *Associate Producers:* Franco Giovale and Joyce Herlihy; *Screenwriters:* Mark Peploe, Bernardo Bertolucci, and Enzo Ungari; *Eastmancolor-Technovision Cinematographer:* Vittorio Storaro; *Editor:* Gabriella Cristiani; *Production Designer:* Ferdinando Scarfiotti; *Art Directors:* Gianni Giovagnoni, Gianni Silvestri, Maria Teresa Barbasso, and Wang Jixian; *Set Decorators:* Wang Chunpu, Bruno Cesari, Osvaldo Desideri, and Dario Micheli; *Special Effects:* Gino De Rossi, Fabrizio Martinelli, and Yang Jingguo; *Costumes:* James Acheson and Ugo Pericoli; *Music:* Ryuichi Sakamoto, David Byrne, and Cong Su *and* "Kaiser Waltz" *by* Johann Strauss *and* "Am I Blue?" *by* Harry Akst and Grant Clarke; *Running Time:* 163 minutes.

L'ULTIMO IMPERATORE   On the set with Peter O'Toole, director Bernardo Bertolucci and Cary Hiroyuki Tagawa.

CAST

John Lone *(Pu Yi)*; Joan Chen *(Wan Rong)*; Peter O'Toole *(Reginald Johnston, "R.J.")*; Ying Ruocheng *(the Governor)*; Victor Wong *(Chen Pao Shen)*; Dennis Dun *(Big Li)*; Ryuichi Sakamoto *(Amakasu)*; Maggie Han *(Eastern Jewel)*; Ric Young *(Interrogator)*; Wu Jun Mei *(Wen Hsiu)*; Cary Hiroyuki Tagawa *(Chang)*; Jade Go *(Ar Mo)*; Fumihiko Ikeda *(Yoshioka)*; Richard Vuu *(Pu Yi, aged three)*; Tijger Tsou *(Pu Yi, aged eight)*; Fan Guang *(Pu Chieh, adult)*; Henry Kyi *(Pu Chieh, aged seven)*; Alvin Riley III *(Pu Chieh, aged fourteen)*; Lisa Lu *(Empress Dowager Tzu Hsui)*.

THE FILM

Prior to this enthusiastically received, award-winning hit about China's last emperor, Bernardo Bertolucci had not had a major success since *Last Tango in Paris* in 1972. After *La Tragedia di un Uomo Ridicolo/Tragedy of a Ridiculous Man* (1981), Bertolucci took six years to come back with *The Last Emperor*, an ambitious $25-million epic chronicling the fascinating life of Pu Yi, the final ruler to sit on the Dragon Throne.

The film begins in 1950 Manchuria. Pu Yi (portrayed as an adult by John Lone) is among a train shipment of war criminals arriving from Russia. Prevented from committing suicide, he is sent to a correction camp, where he recalls his unusual past.

At the age of three in 1908, Pu Yi becomes heir to the world's largest empire, with the death of China's empress dowager. For the next sixteen years, he is confined to the Forbidden City.

In 1919, with China in turmoil under the warlords, Pu Yi is given a patrician Scottish tutor Reginald Johnston (Peter O'Toole), who influences the teenager's thoughts with his liberal-reformist ideas.

A bride named Wang Rong (Joan Chen) is selected for him, but Pu Yi insists on adding a "secondary consort," Wen Hsiu (Wu Jun Mei). He dreams of studying abroad, but when he finally leaves the palace, it is 1924, and Pu Yi and his wives and household are escorted into exile by armed soldiers of the new republic. By now, the emperor has become Westernized in appearance and manners. Johnston tells him that the

British embassy will afford him asylum, but instead he finds only the Japanese embassy willing to help. In Japanese-occupied Tientsin, he becomes a Westernized "playboy," influenced by American music and dancing. News comes that Gen. Chiang Kai-shek has taken Shanghai. Pu Yi's "number-two wife" demands a divorce, insisting that "you can only have *one* wife in the *West*," and so Wen Hsiu leaves the household, to be replaced by the aggressive Eastern Jewel (Maggie Han), who works for the Japanese.

The year 1931 brings Japanese troops to Manchuria and the departure of Mr. Johnston for Britain. Pu Yi is appointed Menchu, emperor of Manchukuo. His wife's addiction to opium has put an end to their marital

L'ULTIMO IMPERATORE   Richard Vuu.

L'ULTIMO IMPERATORE   John Lone (seated).

L'ULTIMO IMPERATORE   John Lone and Joan Chen.

relationship, and a confused Wan Rong now falls completely under the predatory influence of Eastern Jewel.

In 1935, Pu Yi dares to speak out against Manchukuo, losing the support of his satellites. His wife announces she'll bear Pu Yi a child by their chauffeur Chang (Cary Hiroyuki Tagawa), a humiliating revelation soon known to everyone. The child is born dead, and Wan Rong is taken away to a clinic against Pu Yi's will.

Now a "puppet emperor," he witnesses newsreels of World War II Japanese atrocities against his people and the terrible results of Hiroshima. His wife returns, ill and in a nurse's care. She fails to recognize her husband.

Imprisoned by the Russians, Pu Yi confesses to crimes of which he could have had no knowledge—involving the Japanese use of POWs for experiments in biological warfare. By 1959, Pu Yi is free again and employed in Peking's Botanical Gardens. As an old man, he revisits his childhood home, the palace, where he encounters a little boy who can't believe that this elderly gardener was once emperor of China. American tourists crowd into the palace throne room as a guide explains that the last emperor, Pu Yi, died in 1967.

Filming for the first time inside the Forbidden City reflected China's then-recent policy of opening up to the possibilities of foreign coproductions. *The Last Emperor* took home nine Oscars, including Best Picture, Director, Screenplay, Cinematography, Editing, Score, Art Direction, Sound, and Costume Design. However, the Academy overlooked John Lone's masterful performance, taking the adult Pu Yi through a long and demanding role that has him on-screen for most of the lengthy footage. As his primary wife, Joan Chen has far less to do, but the expertise with which she moves from enthusiastic young bride to jaded dope addict to premature senility is truly astonishing.

The Last Emperor may seem an odd entry in a book called *The Great Italian Films,* but its inclusion helps illustrate the changes undergone in the eighties by the Italian movie industry.

INTERVISTA Marcello Mastroianni and Federico Fellini.

Intervista

(INTERVIEW)

A Coproduction of Aljosha Production, RAI-TV Channel 1, and Cinecittá / 1987

(U.S. release by Castle Hill Productions: 1992)

CREDITS

Director: Federico Fellini; *Producers:* Ibrahim Moussa and Michel Vieyte; *Screenwriters:* Federico Fellini and Gianfranco Angelucci; *Eastmancolor Cinematographer:* Tonino Delli Colli; *Editor:* Nino Baragli; *Production Designer:* Danilo Donati; *Music:* Nicola Piovani *with a tribute to* Nino Rota; *Running Time:* 108 minutes.

CAST

Federico Fellini *(Himself)*; Sergio Rubini *(the Reporter)*; Marcello Mastroianni *(Himself)*; Anita Ekberg *(Herself)*; Maurizio Mein *(the Assistant Director)*; Lara Wendel *(the Bride)*; Paola Liguori *(the Star)*; Nadia Ottaviani *(the Vestal Virgin)*; Antonella Ponziani *(the Young Girl)*.

THE FILM

It took Fellini's 1987 *Intervista* all of five years to achieve commercial release in the United States, having been previously seen here only in isolated one-day showings at film festivals and retrospectives. Made to commemorate the fiftieth anniversary of Cinecittá Studios (the heart of Italian filmmaking since 1937, when it was built by Mussolini), this delightful feature began as a television special before switching to theatrical release. Fellini's homage to Italian filmmaking and the production center of all his own films is a thoroughly absorbing, episodic sort of fantasy-documentary that keeps its audience guessing as to where truth stops and illusion takes over. In one part, it is Fellini recalling his own beginnings in cinema; in another, it is also Fellini engaged in the production of his own adaptation of Kafka's *Amerika* (apparently a genuine Fellini project that has yet to be realized on the big screen). Framing the continuity is the device of

INTERVISTA   Marcello Mastroianni and Anita Ekberg in a revisited moment from *La Dolce Vita* (1960).

247

<small>INTERVISTA</small> Marcello Mastroianni, Anita Ekberg and Federico Fellini.

having a Japanese television team arrive to interview the great director for a television documentary. In essence, then, this is the raw material from which that contingent will put together their Fellini special. It is a free-form format that allows Fellini to recycle all of the themes and ideas that have put his stamp so indelibly on thirty-five-odd years of Italian filmmaking. All that's missing is a guest appearance by his wife and frequent star, Giulietta Masina.

Instead of Masina, however, we have Marcello Mastroianni and Anita Ekberg, who turn up in *Intervista*'s later part to remind us how many years have passed since they appeared at their glamorous prime in *La Dolce Vita*. In fact, harsh present and beautiful past are cruelly contrasted in a sequence in which Fellini and company descend on Ekberg at her country villa, forcing her to play unexpected hostess to the entourage. Attired as Mandrake the Magician for a television commercial, Mastroianni performs further prestidigitation by not only conjuring up an instant screen in the star's living room but also projecting a sequence from their 1960 teaming. And as they romp nocturnally in the waters of Rome's Fontana di Trevi to Nino Rota's catchy musical theme, *Intervista* cuts relentlessly back and forth between those youthful black-and-white images and the colorful present, providing a probing look at what time and their own private indulgences have wrought with the middle-aged faces and forms of Mastroianni and Ekberg (now considerably more full figured, in all respects).

In an era when the glory of the Italian cinema is more a past memory than a current event, Fellini's slight but richly detailed and charmingly wrought valentine to the art of making films not only gives a lift to the now-intermittent pleasures of moviegoing but also reminds us of the treasures of the past that remain to be enjoyed in revival theaters or on videocassette.

Nuovo Cinema Paradiso

(CINEMA PARADISO)

A Coproduction of Cristaldi Film (Rome) and Films Ariane (Paris), in association with RAI, TRE, and TFI Film Production, and Forum Pictures / 1988

(U.S. release by Miramax Films: 1990)

CREDITS

Director: Giuseppe Tornatore; *Executive Producer (RAI):* Gabriel Carosio; *Producer:* Franco Cristaldi; *Screenwriters:* Giuseppe Tornatore and Vanna Paoli; *Eastmancolor Cinematographer:* Blasco Giurato; *Editor:* Mario Morra; *Production Designer:* Andrea Crisanti; *Costumes:* Beatrice Bordone; *Music:* Ennio Morricone and Andrea Morricone; *Running Time:* 155 minutes *(U.S. and U.K. Running Time:* 123 minutes).

CAST

Philippe Noiret *(Alfredo);* Jacques Perrin *(Salvatore Di Vitta);* Salvatore Cascio *(Salvatore as a Boy);* Mario Leonardi *(Salvatore as an Adolescent);* Agnese Nano *(Young Elena);* Brigitte Fossey* *(Elena);* Pupella Maggio *(Old Maria);* Antonella Attili *(Young Maria);* Isa Danieli *(Anna);* Leopoldo Trieste *(Father Adelfio);* Enzo Cannavale *(Spaccafico);* Nicola Di Pinto *(Madman).*

THE FILM

Writer-director Giuseppe Tornatore's charming salute to the magic of the cinema lacked superstar names and exploitable subject matter, but it impressed the critics and attracted so-called discriminating audiences to such a degree that *Cinema Paradiso* became a top-grossing import and the first picture from Italy to make such a mark in years.

*Cut from U.S. and U.K. release prints.

The bittersweet story is a simple one: filmmaker Salvatore Di Vitta (Jacques Perrin) is summoned back from Rome to Giancaldo, the small Sicilian town of his birth, for the first time in thirty years. A phone call from his aged mother (Pupella Maggio), informs him that "Alfredo is dead." As memories carry him back to his childhood, Salvatore journeys there for the funeral, and the movie begins a lengthy flashback concerning the unusual relationship between his ten-year-old self (Salvatore Cascio)—then nicknamed "Toto"—and the gruff but kindly movie projectionist at Giancaldo's only movie theater, the Cinema Paradiso. A boy who adores movies, Toto badgers Alfredo (Philippe Noiret) into giving him the footage excised from local showings—mostly kissing scenes rejected by the town's self-appointed censor-priest, Father Adelfio (Leopoldo Trieste). Toto also manages to learn "the secrets of the projection room" by blackmailing Alfredo into instructing him. When Alfredo is tragically blinded in a nitrate fire that guts the cinema, Toto becomes his eyes. Later, a local lottery winner spends his winnings restoring the theater, now renamed the Nuovo Cinema Paradiso, and kissing scenes are screened intact. Upon Alfredo's retirement, the now-adolescent Toto (Mario Leonardi) takes over as projectionist, at the same time preparing to film his own documentary. But he is distracted by love in the form of a pretty new resident Elena (Agnese Nano). While Toto serves in the military, Elena goes to university, and their affair fizzles. Upon his return, Toto takes Alfredo's advice, leaving Sicily to capitalize on his love of the movies.

When he comes back to Giancaldo for Alfredo's funeral, the now-middle-aged Salvatore is dismayed to

NUOVO CINEMA PARADISO   Mario Leonardi and Agnese Nano.

see the new Cinema Paradiso being demolished, having fallen victim to a television-oriented society. He is presented with a package left him by Alfredo—a special reel of film made up of all those previously censored love scenes.

At thirty-two, having directed only one previous 1986 feature *(Il Camorrista)*, Giuseppe Tornatore has credited Buster Keaton's silent classic *The Cameraman* and Woody Allen's *The Purple Rose of Cairo* for having inspired *Cinema Paradiso*. In addition, his own

Sicilian boyhood had been spent in admiration of the movies. And although there was apparently no "Alfredo" in Tornatore's youth, he, too, left for Rome to study film when he reached adulthood.

With its wealth of old film clips, *Cinema Paradiso* leans heavily on charm and nostalgia, too much so for some of its critics. But, theorizes Tornatore, "although it seems like a contradiction, the best way to cut the bridges with our past is to go back over them."

Especially pleasing to the director was the collective response of his fellow villagers when he screened *Cinema Paradiso* for them: "They were very happy that all these beautiful things could be said to the world about Sicily. And it was not about the Mafia!"

With all its charm, *Nuovo Cinema Paradiso* ran three hours in its original prerelease version. Cut to 155 minutes for Italian audiences, the film lost thirty-two additional minutes before its distribution in Britain and the United States, eliminating entirely the scenes showing Salvatore with a middle-aged Elena (Brigitte Fossey).

Among this film's various international accolades have been the Special Jury Prize at Cannes and, in the United States, a Golden Globe as Best Foreign Film, which was matched by an Academy Award.

Stanno Tutti Bene

(EVERYBODY'S FINE)

A Coproduction of Erre Produzioni (Rome) and Les Films Ariane / TFI Films Production (Paris), in collaboration with Silvio Berlusconi Communications / 1990

(U.S. release by Miramax Films: 1991)

CREDITS

Director: Giuseppe Tornatore; *Executive Producer:* Mario Cotone; *Producer:* Angelo Rizzoli; *Screenwriters:* Giuseppe Tornatore, Tonino Guerra, and Massimo De Rita; *Color Cinematographer:* Blasco Giurato; *Editor:* Mario Morra; *Art Director:* Andrea Crosanti; *Set Designer:* Nello Giorgetti; *Costumes:* Beatrice Bordone; *Music:* Ennio Morricone; *Song:* "Dream Theme" *by* Andrea Morricone; *Running Time:* 126 minutes (*U.S. Running Time:* 112 minutes).

CAST

Marcello Mastroianni *(Matteo Scuro)*; Michele Morgan *(Woman on Train)*; Marino Cenna *(Canio)*; Roberto Nobile *(Guglielmo)*; Valeria Cavalli *(Tosca)*; Norma Martelli *(Norma)*; Antonella Attili *(Matteo's Mother)*; Giorgio Libassi *(Lo Piparo)*; Gioacchino Civiletti *(Stationmaster)*; Nicola Di Pinto *(Hotel Porter)*; Suzanna Schemmari *(Angela Scuro)*; Salvatore Cascio *(Little Alvaro)*; Fabio Iellini *(Antonello)*.

THE FILM

In a world in which sentiment seems almost to have become a four-letter word, the films of Giuseppe Tornatore have been both criticized and praised for that emotion. While human feelings and behavior are what interest this contemporary Italian filmmaker most, accusations of his *sentimentalizing* his material are simply incorrect. The return of the middle-aged, unmarried filmmaker to his childhood roots for the old projectionist's funeral in *Cinema Paradiso* is hardly overplayed for sentiment. Is there not every reason to believe that the grown man would feel some emotion

NUOVO CINEMA PARADISO   Philippe Noiret and Salvatore Cascio.

for the death of the one who had first instilled in him a love of motion pictures? Similarly, the viewer cannot help but be moved by the elderly protagonist of *Everybody's Fine* who, in seeking out his five grown offspring to confirm his pride in their various career achievements, discovers only failures instead. Fortunately, with *Everybody's Fine*, in Marcello Mastroianni (barely recognizable behind age makeup and Coke-bottle eyeglasses), Tornatore chose a remarkable actor who never overplays for sympathy. Tornatore doesn't manipulate his audience; he leaves that to the low-keyed exposition of his material.

Matteo Scuro (Mastroianni), a widower living in rural Sicily, tires of never seeing his five adult children. He sets out to surprise each of them in their widespread Italian homes. Provincial in manner and boringly loquacious with others (he often insists that newly met strangers ask him questions so that he can tell them

about himself), Matteo first visits Naples, where he fails to connect with his son Alvaro, who never seems to be home. Reluctantly, the father must talk to Alvaro's phone-answering unit. In Rome, son Canio (Marino Cenna) isn't the politician his father thinks he has become; only a lowly speechwriter. In Florence, Matteo enjoys a reunion with his daughter Tosca (Valeria Cavalli), an unmarried actress-model who disguises the fact that her luxurious apartment isn't really hers—and that the infant she is minding *is*. En route to his next destination, Matteo meets a beautiful older woman (Michele Morgan) on the train and spends a few days with her retirees' group as they tour the sights of Rimini; Matteo leads her to believe that he has a wife waiting for him back home. (Indeed, Tornatore keeps her death a secret from us until the film's last scene.) Next, while he visits his son Guglielmo (Roberto Nobile) in Milan, an orchestra rehearsal reveals that the man's job isn't that of a lead violinist but merely a bass drummer. Moving on to Turin, Matteo visits his other daughter Norma (Norma Martelli), whom he thinks is a high-powered executive. (She is only a phone operator.) Fooled by some of his children and openly disappointed by others, the old man absorbs the hardest blow of all when he forces them to tell him the truth about Alvaro, who has committed suicide (a fact none had wanted to reveal to their father).

On the journey home, Matteo collapses, with his diminished family only reunited when they gather at his bedside. Upon his eventual return to Sicily, Matteo is asked by the stationmaster how his trip went. His response reflects the façade he continues to retain, even at his wife's graveside; he ironically tells them both, "Everybody's fine." Unable to face the profound disappointment in the offspring he had so proudly idealized, the old man now seems to have convinced himself of the truth of that statement.

Tosca

A Rada Film Production in association with ARD-ZDF, BBC, Thirteen/WNET, CAMI Video, ABC/Australia, Doordarshan, TBS/MAX JAPAN, and CFI/1992

(U.S. premiere presentation on PBS-TV stations: 1993)

CREDITS

Director: Giuseppe Patroni Griffi; *Producer:* Andrea Andermann; *Screen adaptation of the opera, with music by* Giacomo Puccini, *libretto by* Luigi Illica and Giuseppe Giacosa; *Based on the stage play* La Tosca *by* Victorien Sardou; *Color Cinematographer:* Vittorio Storaro; *Television Director:* Brian Large; *Art Director:* Aldo Terlizzi; *Editor:* Gary Bradley; *Puccini's score conducted by* Zubin Mehta with the RAI Symphony Orchestra and Chorus; *Running Time:* 120 minutes.

CAST

Catherine Malfitano *(Floria Tosca);* Plácido Domingo *(Mario Cavaradossi);* Ruggero Raimondi *(Baron Scarpia);* Giacomo Prestia *(Cesare Angelotti);* Giorgio Gatti *(Sacristan);* Mauro Buffoli *(Spoletta);* Silvestro Sammaritono *(Sciaronne);* Franco Federici *(Jailer);* Simone Scatarzi *(Voice of Young Shepherd).*

THE FILM

Puccini's *Tosca,* first performed in 1900, remains as popular in the world's operatic repertoire as it once was for such great actresses of the theater as Sarah Bernhardt, for whom Victorien Sardou originally wrote it. Its many film adaptations range from the silent 1918 Pauline Frederick vehicle *La Tosca* to a 1973 Italian version that starred Monica Vitti, emoting to background music by Armando Trovaioli. As a filmed *opera,* it was last seen in U.S. cinemas in director

TOSCA   Catherine Malfitano.

TOSCA Ruggero Raimondi.

Carmine Gallone's lavish 1956 motion picture that starred soprano Franca Duval (albeit with her singing dubbed by the more celebrated Maria Caniglia), along with tenor Franco Corelli and baritone Afro Poli.

However, the version under discussion here is unique: It was shot on the three actual Roman locations designated in the opera's libretto: the church of Sant'Andrea della Valle, the grand Farnese Palace, and the Castel Sant'Angelo. As seen by its European audiences, this ambitious production was originally a television presentation, telecast *live* from each of those three locations—and at the respective times of day specified in the opera: midday for Act I, evening for Act II, and dawn for the final act. It would be an understatement to say this provided considerable logistic problems for cast and crew, with many forgoing sleep altogether throughout the noon-to-daybreak "shoot." This *Tosca* was filmed with a multitude of cameras, under the photographic guidance of Oscar winner Vittorio Storaro and with veteran movie director Giuseppe Patroni Griffi up to the challenges posed by the locations.

Musical problems were solved by stationing conductor Zubin Mehta and the RAI Orchestra in studios two miles away, with wig-hidden microphones connecting singers with musicians.

Set in 1800, *Tosca* centers on the prima donna Floria Tosca (portrayed by Catherine Malfitano), whose love for painter Mario Cavaradossi (Plácido Domingo) involves them fatefully with the ruthless Roman police chief Baron Scarpia (Ruggero Raimondi), who is also strongly attracted to the beautiful Tosca. For sheltering the escaped political prisoner Angelotti (Giacomo Prestia), Mario is tortured by Scarpia's men into revealing Angelotti's whereabouts. Tosca, intimidated by the lustful Scarpia and desperate in her love for Mario, reveals the secret hiding place with the understanding that doing so will free her lover and secure their safe escape to freedom out of the country. Knowing the price she must pay for this safe passage is nothing less than her honor, she convinces Scarpia to sign the paper for their freedom, and when he approaches her to claim his "victory," she stabs him to death rather than submit to him. Tosca then runs to Mario to tell him of their imminent freedom and explain that the "execution" will be a ruse that Scarpia had ordered before she killed him. But as the guns fire and Mario falls dead on the ground, Tosca realizes that Scarpia has, in fact, arranged an execution that is all too real. Damning Scarpia, Tosca hurls herself to her death from atop the Castel Sant'Angelo.

TOSCA Catherine Malfitano and Plácido Domingo.

Musically speaking, this isn't a *Tosca* to end all *Tosca*s. But with handsome singing actors of the caliber of Malfitano, Domingo, and Raimondi, Puccini remains in very good hands—and throats. In the case of Raimondi, seldom has Baron Scarpia been portrayed in so many facets of mesmerizing evil without overacting. Malfitano, on the other hand, borders on silent-screen emoting amid the melodramatics of that last act—which may work well onstage at the opera house but requires a less-is-more approach for films and television, where camera close-ups magnify each nuance.

Utilizing actual locations also has its drawbacks, as illustrated by Scarpia's entrance into the church amid Act I. In the opera house, accompanied by ominous orchestral chords, Puccini creates a chilling moment. But here it is lost in the vastness of the actual church. However, the loss of effect is negligible and hardly spoils a fine performance of one of this century's enduring works of musical art.

ORDER NOW!
More Citadel Film Books

If you like this book, you'll love the other titles in the award-winning Citadel Film Series. From James Stewart to Moe Howard and The Three Stooges, Woody Allen to John Wayne, The Citadel Film Series is America's largest and oldest film book library.

With more than 150 titles--and more on the way!--Citadel Film Books make perfect gifts for a loved one, a friend, or best of all, yourself!

A complete listing of the Citadel Film Series appears below.
If you know what books you want, why not order now!
It's easy! Just call 1-800-447-BOOK and have your MasterCard or Visa ready.

STARS
Alan Ladd
Arnold Schwarzenegger
Barbra Streisand: First Decade
Barbra Streisand: Second
   Decade
The Barbra Streisand Scrapbook
Bela Lugosi
Bette Davis
Boris Karloff
The Bowery Boys
Brigitte Bardot
Buster Keaton
Carole Lombard
Cary Grant
Charlie Chaplin
Clark Gable
Clint Eastwood
Curly
Dustin Hoffman
Edward G. Robinson
Elizabeth Taylor
Elvis Presley
Errol Flynn
Frank Sinatra
Gary Cooper
Gene Kelly
Gina Lollobrigida
Gloria Swanson
Gregory Peck
Greta Garbo
Henry Fonda
Humphrey Bogart
Ingrid Bergman
Jack Lemmon
Jack Nicholson
James Cagney
James Dean: Behind the Scene
Jane Fonda
Jeanette MacDonald & Nelson
   Eddy
Joan Crawford
John Wayne Films
John Wayne Reference Book

John Wayne Scrapbook
Judy Garland
Katharine Hepburn
Kirk Douglas
Laurel & Hardy
Lauren Bacall
Laurence Olivier
Mae West
Marilyn Monroe
Marlene Dietrich
Marlon Brando
Marx Brothers
Moe Howard & the Three
   Stooges
Norma Shearer
Olivia de Havilland
Orson Welles
Paul Newman
Peter Lorre
Rita Hayworth
Robert De Niro
Robert Redford
Sean Connery
Sexbomb: Jayne Mansfield
Shirley MacLaine
Shirley Temple
The Sinatra Scrapbook
Spencer Tracy
Steve McQueen
Three Stooges Scrapbook
Warren Beatty
W.C. Fields
William Holden
William Powell
A Wonderful Life: James Stewart
DIRECTORS
Alfred Hitchcock
Cecil B. DeMille
Federico Fellini
Frank Capra
John Huston
Woody Allen
GENRE
Black Hollywood

Black Hollywood: From 1970 to
   Today
Classic Foreign Films: From
   1960 to Today
Classic Gangster Films
Classic Science Fiction Films
Classics of the Horror Film
Classic TV Westerns
Cult Horror Films
Divine Images: Jesus on Screen
Early Classics of Foreign Film
Films of Merchant Ivory
Great Baseball Films
Great French Films
Great German Films
Great Italian Films
Great Science Fiction Films
Harry Warren & the Hollywood
   Musical
Hispanic Hollywood: The Latins
   in Motion Pictures
The Hollywood Western
The Incredible World of 007
The Jewish Image in American
   Film
The Lavender Screen: The Gay
   and Lesbian Films
Martial Arts Movies
The Modern Horror Film
More Classics of the Horror Film
Movie Psychos & Madmen
Our Huckleberry Friend: Johnny
   Mercer
Second Feature: "B" Films
They Sang! They Danced! They
   Romanced!: Hollywood
   Musicals
Thrillers
The West That Never Was
Words and Shadows: Literature
   on the Screen
DECADE
Classics of the Silent Screen
Films of the Twenties

Films of the Thirties
More Films of the 30's
Films of the Forties
Films of the Fifties
Lost Films of the 50's
Films of the Sixties
Films of the Seventies
Films of the Eighties
SPECIAL INTEREST
America on the Rerun
Bugsy (Illustrated screenplay)
The "Cheers" Trivia Book
Comic Support
Cutting Room Floor: Scenes
   Which Never Made It
Favorite Families of TV
Film Flubs
Film Flubs: The Sequel
First Films
"Frankly, My Dear": Great
   Movie Lines About Women
The Greatest Stories Ever
   Filmed
Hollywood Cheesecake
Howard Hughes in Hollywood
More Character People
The Nightmare Never Ends:
   Freddy Krueger & "A Night-
   mare on Elm Street"
The "Northern Exposure" Book
The Official Andy Griffith Show
   Scrapbook
The 100 Best Films of the
   Century
The 1001 Toughest TV Trivia
   Questions of All Time
The "Quantum Leap" Book
Rodgers & Hammerstein
Sex in Films
Sex In the Movies
Sherlock Holmes
Son of Film Flubs
Who Is That?: Familiar Faces and
   Forgotten Names
"You Ain't Heard Nothin' Yet!"

For a free full-color Entertainment Books brochure including the Citadel Film Series in depth and more, call 1-800-447-BOOK; or send your name and address to Citadel Film Books, Dept. 1480, 120 Enterprise Ave., Secaucus, NJ 07094.